THE IMF HANDBOOK 2000

A GUIDE TO PROFESSIONAL BAND MANAGEMENT

INTERNATIONAL MANAGERS FORUM

An organisation representing the interests of artists/management worldwide. For details contact the General Secretary, James Fisher, at:

1 Glenthorne Mews
115a Glenthorne Road
London
W6 LLJ

Telephone: 020 7741 2555
Fax: 020 7741 4856

Website: www.imf-uk.org

Design: David Houghton

Printed by: Thanet Press, Margate

Published by: Sanctuary Publishing Limited, Sanctuary House, 45-53 Sinclair Road, London W14 0NS, United Kingdom

www.sanctuarypublishing.com

Copyright: International Managers Forum, 1999

All rights reserved. No part of this book may be reproduced in any form or by any electronic or mechanical means, including information storage or retrieval systems, without permission in writing from the publisher, except by a reviewer who may quote brief passages

While the publishers have made every reasonable effort to trace the copyright owners for any or all of the photographs in this book, there may be some omissions of credits for which we apologise

ISBN: 1-86074-257-2

THE IMF HANDBOOK 2000

A GUIDE TO PROFESSIONAL BAND MANAGEMENT

contents

INTRODUCTION	**11**		commissionable income	25
			calculation of commission	26
1 • MANAGEMENT CONTRACTS		post-term commission	29
			post-term activities	29
THE MANAGER	**14**		future commission	29
finding a manager	14		post-term reductions	29
when?	14	expenses	30
how?	14		out-of-pocket expenses	30
presentations	14		approvals	30
what to look for in a manager	15		reimbursement	30
the decision	16	accounting	31
making a commitment	16		usual method	31
the danger of delay	16		alternative method	31
procedure	16		pitfalls	31
		termination	32
THE LEGAL FRAMEWORK	**17**		termination for breach	32
the nature of the contract	17		key-man clauses	32
the difficulty of enforcement	17			
alternative arrangements	18	**2 • IMF GUIDELINES FOR ARTIST MANAGEMENT AGREEMENTS**		
undue influence	19			
THE CONTRACT	**19**	the contract	35
duration	19	the schedule	38
contracts terminable upon notice	19	touring income	40
fixed-term contracts	20			
typical duration	20	**3 • RECORDING CONTRACTS**		
trial period	20			
exclusivity	21	**THE DEAL**	**50**
the scope of the agreement	22	finding the deal	50
territory	22	the team	50
non-music activities	22	the manager	50
areas of responsibility	23	agents	50
the manager's remuneration	24	lawyers	50
commission	24	the pitch	51
commission rates	24			
variable rates	25			

publishers	51
which company?	51
individual executives	52
indie or major?	52
the conventional deal	52
independents	53
flexibility	53
creative control	53
short or long term	54
territory	54
royalty rates	55
share of profit	55
financial insecurity	55
international deals	55
advances	56
strength in depth	56
the final choice	56
the proposal	57
false hopes	57
who makes the first move	57
high or low?	58
the legal framework	58
practicalities	58
legal advice	59
lessons	60
THE CONTRACT	**60**
the term	60
long-term contracts	60
development deals	61
extension periods	61
delays	62
how many options?	63
product commitment	63
artistic standards	63
additional material	64
two albums firm	64
greatest hits and live albums	65
exclusions	65
territory	66
worldwide deals	66
restricted territory deals	66
interaction	66
creative issues	67
approval rights	67
control	67
the record company's obligations	68
one sided?	68
release commitments	68
reversion	69
overseas releases	69
territorial reversions	69
is a release commitment worth having?	70
marketing and promotion	70
ownership	70
copyright	70
you pay, we own	71
reversion of copyright	71
restrictions	71
artwork	71
marketing restrictions	72
group provisions	73
leaving members	73
cross recoupment	73
leaving member's commitment	73
solo work	74
controlled compositions	74
back to basics	74
mechanical licences	75
availability of licence	75
the USA and Canada	75
the publisher	76
MONEY	**77**
overview	77
the basic royalty system	77
recoupable expenditure	77
what is recoupable?	77
profit shares	79
a practical example: profit share versus royalty	80
who takes what?	82
advances	83
how do they work?	83
costs inclusive?	84

how much?	84
cross-recoupment	85
associated agreements	86
royalties	86
retail or dealer price?	86
packaging deductions	87
returns and net sales	88
royalty base price	89
free goods	89
what rates?	90
real royalty rate	91
further reductions	91
performance income	94
other uses	99
new formats	100
the digital revolution	101
the watershed	101
accounting	102
accounting periods	102
reserves	103
withholding taxes	104
audit rights	104
AFTER THE DEAL	**106**
contract administration	106
filing	106
dates	106
re-negotiations	107
when?	107
how?	107

4 • ENFORCEABILITY OF AGREEMENTS

RESTRAINT OF TRADE	**110**
how the courts approach restraint of trade	110
the policy behind the restraint of trade doctrine	110
the Nordenfelt test	111
when should the test be applied?	111
reasonableness between parties	112
considerations	112

providing protection for the restricting party	112
justification of restrictions	113
public policy	117
severance	118
the doctrine of severance	118
use of severance clauses	119
effects of unreasonable restrictions	119
different terminology	119
unperformed obligations	119
UNDUE INFLUENCE	**120**
general approach	120
the court's approach	121
finding undue influence	123
equitable defences	123
laches	123
acquiescence	123
THE TREATY OF ROME	**124**
Article 85 (1)	124
music industry agreements	124
effect of Article 85	126
clearing an agreement with the EC	126
English courts	127
practical aspects of enforceability	128
schedule	129
the Frankie Goes To Hollywood case	129
the George Michael case	129

5 • PRODUCER CONTRACTS

PRODUCERS	**132**
the problem of delay	132
confusion	132
inertia	132
the role of the producer	133
the scapegoat	133
pre-production	133
budgetary control	134
samples	134

songwriting	134
mixers	135
delivery standard	135
the producer's rights	136
financial entitlement	136
the 'maker' of the recordings	136
the Re-Pro argument	137
credit	138

THE CONTRACT — **138**

the parties to the contract	138
UK and US approaches	138
direct accounting	138
standard forms	139
the deal memorandum	139
driving the deal	139
paying the lawyer	140
distribution of the deal memorandum	140
contents of the deal memorandum	141
urgency	141

MONEY — **142**

what is the producer worth?	142
basic concepts	142
artist versus producer	143
the artist pays	143
the European approach	144
royalties	144
royalty rates	144
method of calculation	145
a-side protection	145
secondary exploitation	145
performance income	146
advances	146
successful producers	146
mixers	147
per-track advances	148
advance or fee?	148
bonus advances	148
payment schedule	148
expenses	148
recoupment and deferment	149

UK and US approaches	149
example	149
pitfalls	150
accountings	150
method	150
audit rights	150

INDEPENDENT PRODUCTIONS — **151**

independent record companies	151
royalty or profit share?	151
what percentage of profit?	151
speculative work	152
basic protection	152
studio deals	152

6 • PUBLISHING CONTRACTS

WHO NEEDS A PUBLISHER? — **154**

the nature of a publishing contract	154
copyright	154
the publisher's services	154
when should the deal be done?	155
the significance of the record deal	155
funding	155
the publisher	155
choice of publisher	155
efficiency of administration	156
professional management	156

PUBLISHING INCOME — **156**

types of income	156
performance income	156
mechanical royalties	157
synchronisation fees	157
print income	158
the value of publishing income	158
past income	158
future income	158
the piggy-back approach	159
the scientific approach	159
the maverick approach	160

THE CONTRACT	**160**
the term	160
contract periods	160
extensions	161
exclusivity	161
the minimum commitment	161
delivery or release?	161
extent of the commitment	162
failure to comply	162
territory	162
overseas exploitation	162
limited territory	163
pros and cons	163
advances	163
relevant factors	163
payment schedule	164
deferred advances	164
option advances	164
royalties	165
rates of royalty	165
reduced royalties for cover recordings	166
method of calculation	167
accountings	168
statements	168
delays	168
audits	169
retention period	169
rights	170
exploitation	171
warranties	171
group provisions	171
other arrangements	172
reliance on the PRS/MCPS	172
self-administration	173
appointing an administrator	174
AFTER THE DEAL	**174**
lead sheets/demos	174
single-song assignment	175
releases	175
collaborations	175
samples	175
group changes	175
likenesses and biographies	176
the PRS	176
consents	176
exploitation	176
accountings	176
concert appearances	177
advances	177
covers	177
termination dates	178
extra funding	178
professional advice	178

7 • AGENTS

the role of the agent	180
types of agent	180
the skills required	180
the agent's reputation	182
commission	182
agency agreements	183
choosing an agent	183
large agencies	184
codes of operation	185

8 • LIVE PERFORMANCES

key personnel	188
the promoter	188
the tour manager	188
the sound engineer	189
the production manager	190
the backline technicians	190
the musicians	191
the lighting director	191
the accountant	192
other resources	192
the rider	192
ground transportation	193
flights	193
trucking	193
the stage set	194

essentials	194
costumes and props	194
special effects	195
video	195
catering	195
security	196
passes	196
signage	196
itinerary	196
insurance	200
paperwork	200
carnet	200
post-production	201

9 • PRESS AND PR

THE PUBLICIST'S ROLE	**204**
the working day	204
where to start	204
who employs publicists?	205
what skills are needed?	206
a dedicated profession	206
areas of responsibility	206
acting as a source of information	206
putting out the news	207
image building	207
promotion and protection	207
stimulating media interest	208
setting up interviews	208
arranging photography	208
travelling	208
receptions and conferences	209
ways into the business	209
academic tuition	209
journalistic experience	209
experience in the music industry	210

10 • MANAGING MERCHANDISING

tour merchandise	212
supply-only deal	212
royalty-rate deal	212
split-profit deal	213
retail	213
advances	214
APPENDIX 1 • SOCIETIES	**215**
APPENDIX 2 • INTERNATIONAL DIRECTORY OF IMF MANAGERS	**229**

introduction

by James Fisher, General Secretary of the IMF

There are a number of books purporting to tell you all about the music business. This book, however, is designed to deal primarily with one of the most important aspects in this multi-million-pound business: artist management. Behind nearly every successful act is a manager quietly working away to make all aspects of the artist's career run smoothly, and finding the right manager is one of the most important decisions an artist will make. Not only is it an important decision but it is also a very difficult one.

Most artists are self-centred, and indeed they need to be in order to stand out from the crowd. They need their manager to be a part-time psychiatrist, accountant, doctor, car mechanic, cook and general bottle washer. For his part, the manager will need to keep abreast of new technology, the Internet, digital transmission, MP3 files, studio equipment, instruments and also whatever else record and publishing companies have tried to crowbar into their contracts to maximise their earnings at the expense of those of the artist!

Managing an artist through the various minefields of the music business is not easy, but help exists in the shape of the International Managers Forum. With members including the managers of some of the biggest acts in the world, plus music business figures such as lawyers and accountants, the IMF was founded in 1992 to focus the profession of the artist manager. As well as championing the managers' and artists' cause to governments, the organisation shares its considerable knowledge and experience with its members. And now, through *The IMF Handbook*, non-members can benefit too.

(Throughout the *Handbook* the masculine pronoun 'he' is used. This is purely an expedient to the flow of the text, and is in no way meant to imply that the role of a manager is a purely male preserve.)

the IMF handbook a guide to professional band management

the contributors

STEVE BRICKLE was founding MD of Giant Merchandising, whose clients included Paul McCartney, Michael Jackson and Prince. He now runs a web management company.

BERNARD DOHERTY has managed publicity campaigns for David Bowie, Rod Stewart, Paul McCartney, The Rolling Stones and The Brit Awards. He co-ordinated the publicity for Live Aid, and has run PR campaigns for Stevie Wonder and Janet Jackson. He is chief executive officer of PR company LD.

ANDREW FORBES is a partner in the media litigation department at Statham Gill Davies. He is an expert in music industry disputes, including those involving management contracts, recording, publishing and copyright.

JEF HANLON has been lead guitarist, roadie, tour manager and agent, and has promoted tours with Gary Glitter, Bob Hope, The Village People and BB King. In 1998 he produced *Bugs Bunny* on Broadway. For two years he was president of the Agents' Association of Great Britain. He is chairman of the IMF and founder member of the Concert Promoters' Association.

RUSTY HANNON is an artists manager who has also distinguished himself as an outstanding production and tour manager.

TERRY O'BRIEN is chairperson of the National Acoustic Music Association, founder of the Playpen Acoustic Club in London's Earls Court and owner of the Playpen record label. She has been Jef Hanlon's PA for the last six years.

NIGEL PARKER is a prominent music business lawyer who practises on his own for selected clients.

DAVID STOPPS began his career as promoter of the Friars Club in Aylesbury, which played a part in the development of Genesis, David Bowie, U2, The Jam and The Clash. He has also managed a number of artists, including Marillion, Howard Jones and Miriam Stockley. He is a member of the IMF Council and the British Copyright Council.

ANDREW THOMPSON has been a commercial lawyer since qualifying as a solicitor in 1977, and since 1978 has specialised in music. In 1983 he co-founded Lee & Thompson Solicitors. In 1993 he helped form the IMF and is still its company secretary. He lectures frequently on music industry topics.

MARTIN HOPEWELL, of Primary Talent and founder of the International Live Music Conference, was recently inducted onto the IMF British Music Roll of Honour for outstanding services to the music industry.

ANDY ALLEN, through his company, Backstreet International Merchandise, has been involved with merchandising for the past ten years, working with bands such as Blur, Pulp, Skunk Anansie and Supergrass, and has also managed bands such as Swervedriver and Reef.

chapter 1

management contracts

by Andrew Thompson

The music business is just that: a business. For all the artistic aspirations of a particular musician, if he wishes to succeed as a professional recording artist then his art must be pursued within a competitive business environment. Occasionally, an artist will manage his own business affairs (or in the case of a band one or two members may assume responsibility for this task). This sometimes works quite well if the person is businesslike and if the act is focused in its area of activity, although the artist will usually need to rely heavily upon professional help from solicitors and accountants. However, most artists are not particularly businesslike. Moreover, the logistics of organising a successful recording career are normally so complex that the artist would never have time to deal with the business side of things on his own. Also, an important part of the management function involves 'selling' the artist and it is difficult for an artist to sell himself. For most artists, therefore, perhaps the single most important decision of their careers is the choice of a manager.

This chapter will cover the nature of management and look at how to find the right manager. The legal framework of the arrangement will also be reviewed, along with the component parts of a typical management contract.

the IMF handbook a guide to professional band management

THE MANAGER

finding a manager

when?

Generally, the sooner the appointment is made the better. The manager prefers to have a clean slate with which to work. For example, it would not usually be a good idea for an artist to negotiate a record deal and then ask a manager to take over. That said, this situation does not often arise – the artist would typically look for a manager as the first stage towards securing a record deal. In any event, many A&R executives prefer to deal with managers rather than artists (at least when it comes to negotiating deals), and often the artist will benefit from the additional validity brought to his project by the involvement of a respected manager. Nevertheless, artists should not rush into management arrangements. There are many different types of manager, and it is better for the artist to wait until he finds the right manager rather than be panicked into hiring the wrong one. Moreover, the artist/manager relationship is a personal one, so as with all personal relationships the parties involved should initially proceed with some caution.

how?

Sometimes the manager will find the artist. It is corny but it does often happen that, after a gig, somebody (not always smoking a cigar) will come backstage and insist that he is the man to make the artist rich and famous. Generally, however, the artist will need to adopt a more pro-active approach. He should first set about compiling a shortlist of potential candidates, and he should also talk to all of his contacts in the industry. One possible approach is to identify other admired artists and find out about their management arrangements (although it is not necessarily sensible for an artist to be with a manager who already looks after a similar, and therefore competing, artist). An artist might approach the IMF with a description of the his music and his requirements; the IMF should be able to provide a number of suggestions.

presentations

It is rarely worthwhile sending out circulars in bulk in the hope of attracting a manager. The artist will need to approach the targeted manager personally or find somebody who is prepared to do so on his behalf. The artist should put together a presentation package of some kind, like a tape of a few of his best songs (even if they are in rudimentary demo form). One or two photographs and a short biography together with any press cuttings would also be useful. Successful managers are generally very busy people, and it usually proves counter-productive for artists to be too pushy. Most managers will have the courtesy to respond to approaches, but they need to be given a little time.

what to look for in a manager

When there is a shortlist of managers demonstrating a positive interest in them, artists should consider the following points:

- How experienced is the manager?

- How successful has he been (and has that success been in a similar field)?

- How long has he worked in the music industry, and in what different capacities?

- Does he have a good reputation and what are his reputed strengths?

- Is he primarily a business manager or a creative manager?

- How long has he managed any other artists with whom he is involved (the artist should try and talk to those other artists)?

- Does the manager have the type of personality that the artist is looking for? (Is he the aggressive type or perhaps more diplomatic?)

- Where is the manager based? What back-up is available? What kind of office facilities does he have?

- How much time will he be able to spend on the artist's affairs?

- How convinced does he seem of the artist's talent?

- How extensive are his contacts in the industry?

- Does he have experience of the industry outside the UK? For example, does he have contacts in America?

- Does he have good negotiating skills?

- Will he or his staff be able to deal with the details efficiently (ie returning phone calls, dealing with correspondence, maintaining proper financial records etc)?

- If the artist already has a recording or publishing deal, does the manager have any history of dealings with the companies concerned? And, if so, what do the key personnel at those companies think of him?

the decision

An artist should adopt a thorough and professional approach to the selection process, but ultimately he must rely on his own judgement in determining whether or not the management relationship would be an effective and successful one.

making a commitment

the danger of delay

What should the artist do once he has found a suitable manager prepared to take him on? Most artists (certainly those at a preliminary stage in their careers) are reluctant to enter into discussions with a new manager about the formal terms which should apply. They are particularly shy about making a long term commitment. Likewise, many managers are reluctant during the early stages to ask an artist to sign a contract for fear of giving the wrong signals. This kind of approach benefits nobody. The manager is unlikely to perform to the best of his ability unless he feels confident and secure in his relationship with the artist. If the artist consistently avoids any discussion over the formal terms which are to apply then the uncertainty is likely to lead to problems; either there will be a dispute as to the basis upon which the manager has been working or ill will may develop as a result of one side feeling let down by the other. Of course, the artist (and the manager, for that matter) should exercise some caution before committing to a long-term arrangement. Nevertheless, this does not justify burying one's head in the sand; immediately the artist and manager begin working together efforts should be made to formalise the arrangements.

procedure

The management contract is usually prepared by the manager or his solicitor and presented to the artist. It is important from the artist's point of view that he receives expert independent advice from his own solicitor. Moreover, it is also important from the manager's point of view that the artist is independently advised (see the section on 'The Legal Framework' below). Many managers are reluctant to incur legal fees in relation to a management contract because during the preliminary stage there is often no income being generated by the project. Artists tend to be still less inclined to incur legal fees, usually for the simple reason that they have no money. Unlike a recording or publishing agreement, no money is payable to the artist upon signing a management agreement. Despite these constraints, it is important that both parties to a management contract are properly advised. There need not be protracted (and therefore expensive) negotiations between lawyers. Before the lawyers are instructed the parties should attempt to agree between themselves the basic principles which are to apply (although each party should accept that whatever is agreed will be subject to legal advice). The IMF has prepared a suggested form of contract, which is reproduced in the following chapter. This is a form of contract prepared on behalf of managers rather than artists, but it is intended to be both reasonable and straightforward. The Musicians' Union offers a scheme under which it makes available a specialist music business lawyer to provide advice to any members on a subsidised basis. Alternatively, there are several firms of solicitors prepared to undertake work of this nature on behalf of artists at a subsidised cost if persuaded that this is likely to lead to more profitable work in the future.

THE LEGAL FRAMEWORK

the nature of the contract

the difficulty of enforcement

Management contracts are essentially straightforward by nature. They are contracts for the supply of personal services. A management contract will describe the services to be provided by the manager and will specify how he is to be paid for those services. The main significance of this is that a management contract cannot be specifically enforced. The obvious analogy of this is an employment contract. An employer may enter into a fixed-term employment contract with an employee for, say, three years. If the employee leaves without good cause after one year then he will be in breach of the employment contract, and the employer would be able to sue the employee for breach of contract. Generally, however, the only recourse available to the employer in any such legal proceeding would be for an award in damages. The employee would be compelled to pay the employer a sum of money equal to any financial loss which the employer would be able to prove, to the satisfaction of the court, that it has actually suffered as a result of the breach of contract. However, the employer would generally not be able to obtain an order for specific performance from the court (ie the employee would not be forced to work for the employer for the remaining two years). An artist and his manager are in a similar position. The manager will be entitled to damages if the artist walks away from the management contract before its term has expired, but he will generally be unable to compel the artist to continue to allow the manager to represent him.

alternative arrangements

Partly for the reason mentioned above, some managers try to protect their position by entering into alternative contractual arrangements with the artist. It used to be quite common for a *de facto* manager not to enter into a management agreement but instead to require the artist to enter into recording and publishing agreements, the effect of which was that the 'manager' was exclusively entitled to the artist's songwriting and recording services and owned the copyright and all other rights in the artist's songs and recordings. The 'manager' would then seek recording and publishing deals for the artist but it would be the 'manager' (in his guise as a production company or publisher) who would enter into the agreements with the third parties concerned. Often, the 'manager' would also require the signing of a management contract. In this way, he could prevent the involvement of any other manager and would secure a financial interest (by means of management commission) in any of the artist's earnings from activities other than recording and songwriting. In the worst cases, the 'manager' would retain all of the recording and publishing income, pay a royalty of some kind to the artist, and then claim (under the terms of the management contract) a percentage commission on that royalty income. Arrangements of this kind are nowadays generally frowned upon so that, when an artist is presented with a contract by a manager, that contract will normally be a management contract rather than a recording or publishing contract. However, this is not to say that production contracts (ie recording contracts entered into with small record production companies) do not have a place in the music business; arrangements of this type might be perfectly justifiable in their own right, but they are not appropriate when they are used to disguise what is essentially a management arrangement.

undue influence

The courts may set aside an agreement if it has been entered into under circumstances where undue influence has been brought to bear by one party of a contract against another. In the context of a management contract, this does not mean that the artist has to show that he was taken to the pub and made to get drunk before signing the agreement or that a gun was held to his head – there is what is known as a 'presumption' of undue influence if the relationship is one of trust and confidence. Trust and confidence lie at the very heart of any relationship between a manager and an artist, and therefore the presumption of undue influence immediately arises. If the court is to be persuaded to recognise a management contract then the presumption of undue influence has to be rebutted. There is an automatic suspicion that the manager (who is usually older, more experienced and more businesslike than the artist) has in some way exerted pressure on the artist to accept the terms of the contract in question. The only effective means by which to rebut this is for the manager to show that the artist was independently advised, preferably with the help of a lawyer who has specialist knowledge of the music industry. This would normally be sufficient for the manager to demonstrate that there had been a genuine negotiation in relation to the terms of the contract and that its contents were properly understood by the artist, or at least that the artist was given an opportunity to fully understand its implications.

THE CONTRACT

duration

contracts terminable upon notice

Some management contracts do not run for a fixed term. Instead, they continue indefinitely unless and until either party serves a given period of notice. This period of notice would normally be three or perhaps six months, although in some cases there are more sophisticated provisions for the serving of notice so that, for example, the agreement may only be brought to an end once a particular album cycle has reached its conclusion.

fixed-term contracts

Most management contracts provide for a minimum fixed period, usually between three and five years, and there is an unwritten rule that management contracts should not continue for longer than five years. The general feeling is that if a manager were to insist upon a longer period then the artist may be able to challenge the validity of the agreement on the basis that it represents an unreasonable restraint of trade. However there is no black and white rule to the effect that a five-year contract is enforceable but that anything longer is not.

There is a current trend for management contracts to run for a given number of album cycles rather that for a specified period of years, ie for perhaps three cycles (with a cycle being defined for this purpose as the period of time which involves writing, rehearsing and recording an album and then until the end of any promotional or touring activity in relation to that album).

typical duration

However, most management agreements run for three, four or even five years. This would include any option period so that, for example, the agreement may run for three years but at the end of the initial period the manager has an option to extend for another year or two. Sometimes the option to extend will be available to the manager only if certain targets have been achieved during the initial period (perhaps a minimum level of earnings or a given chart position).

trial period

There may be often be a trial period of some kind. A typical trial period would be for six months, and this would usually work in one of two ways: the parties would sign a simple agreement on the basis that if, at the end of the trial period, both parties wished to proceed then both parties would negotiate the terms of a more formal longer term agreement; alternatively, a formal agreement would be negotiated from the outset. However, whilst this would run for five years, for example, there would be a provision to the effect that either party could terminate at any time during the period of, say, 30 days following the expiration of the initial six months. Managers are naturally reluctant to agree to a trial period of this kind because this may result in a great deal of preliminary work carried out for no purpose. Therefore, an approach adopted by many managers is to include a provision to the effect that the artist is able to terminate the management agreement after a given period (perhaps twelve or eighteen months) in certain defined circumstances (ie if at that point the artist has failed to enter into a recording contract).

exclusivity

The duration of the deal represents the period during which the manager is exclusively entitled to represent the artist. This exclusivity rarely works the other way round – the artist would not expect to be exclusively entitled to the manager's services (although some management contracts specify that the manager may not manage more than a given number of other artists). Typically, with a new recording career, a great deal needs to be done during the early stages for relatively small reward. A manager signing a contract with a new band will often face a lengthy period of hard work before the project is in good enough shape to present to record companies. The whole process of negotiating a record deal is usually a long and arduous one. After the record deal has been signed further work will need to be done in preparing rehearsing and recording the material. The record company may wish to release a single before committing to the release of an album.

For all of these reasons, it might easily be a year or two after signing the management contract before the first album is released. This may be followed by an extensive period of touring to promote the album. Assuming that the album is successful enough for the record company to exercise its option for the next album, there may then be another delay before suitable material is prepared and recorded. Because of this a three-year management contract will often fail to cover more than one album, and a four-year management contract will often cover no more than two albums. The artist's first album will have to be unusually successful for this to be sufficient to recoup the record company's initial expenditure and give rise to commissionable recording income, and it usually takes some time for even a successful artist to build a reasonable sales base. It is not difficult, therefore, to envisage circumstances whereby a manager may work very hard over a period of three or four years to establish an artist only to find that the artist then decides that he wishes to appoint another manager or to look after his own affairs, leaving the ex-manager with a commission entitlement in relation to perhaps only two albums just before the watershed is achieved with the third album (see the section on 'The Watershed' in chapter three). It is for this reason that managers seek the protection of long-term exclusive management contracts. The difference between a five-year contract and a four-year contract may be critical.

the scope of the agreement

territory

A typical management contract will grant the manager the exclusive rights to represent the artist in all areas of the entertainment industry throughout the world. Sometimes the agreement may be territorially restricted in some way (most typically when a separate manager is engaged for the American market). For example, if there are two managers – one for each of two territories (perhaps North America and the rest of the world) – then each manager will usually only earn commission upon earnings arising in his territory. However, UK-based managers usually object to the exclusion of America, or of any other territory. The income from the territory to be excluded may well make the difference between financial success and failure. There are also practical difficulties concerned with having two separate managers in that they may pull in different directions, and each will have a vested interest in persuading the artist to concentrate his attention in the one territory, at the expense of the other. One practical way of dealing with this is for a UK manager to insist upon worldwide rights but to agree to appoint a separate US manager. However, the appointment will be made by the UK manager so that, effectively, the US manager reports to the UK manager. The UK manager will still expect some financial reward from the US activities, so if he is entitled to 20% commission on worldwide earnings, for example, he may agree to pay perhaps 10% (ie one half) of the commissionable earnings originating in the US to the US sub-manager, so that he still receives the remaining 10%.

non-music activities

As well as territorial restrictions, the scope of the manager's appointment may be limited in other ways. Ordinarily the manager will wish to represent the artist in relation to all of his activities in the entertainment industry. The artist may wish to restrict his manager's influence to activities in the music industry. With a new artist, however, this would probably be unfair to the manager because in all likelihood any opportunity for the artist to profit from other activities will arise only as a result of the artist's success in the music industry. For example, the artist may be offered a part in a film or may decide to write a book. If an artist already has a career in another area of the entertainment industry – if he is an actor with a theatrical agent representing him in this area, for example – then the management contract would need to recognise this. A manager will sometimes agree that, if at some future stage the artist becomes involved in acting or literary endeavours, the manager will then agree to appoint a theatrical/film or literary agent of the artist's choice. To centralise the arrangement, the manager might insist that the appointment of agents of this kind must be made by the manager, so that any agent will be a sub-agent of the manager rather than employed directly by the artist. As with an overseas manager, the manager may agree that all or part of the sub-agent's commission is to be subtracted from the manager's commission.

areas of responsibility

It is impossible to be too precise about the respective duties and obligations of the parties under a management contract, apart from certain obvious matters, such as the manager's obligation to account to the artist for any money in the specified manner. Each artist has his own view of what a manager should do and how he should go about it. Likewise, each manager will have a different approach to his work and will attach different priorities to the various aspects of his remit. Some artists expect the manager to be at the artist's beck and call day and night to sort out every problem, whether that problem is professional or purely personal, and some managers accept that baby-sitting an artist is part of the job. Others, however, do not generally take kindly to being pestered outside normal business hours (whilst accepting that in the music business 'normal' does not mean 9am to 5pm). It is not really the manager's job to pay the artist's domestic bills and generally deal with any personal crises. Nevertheless, a successful (and therefore busy and often egotistical) artist will often expect this kind of service from his management company. The best answer for the manager is to provide the artist with a personal assistant, employed by the management company but available to do the artist's bidding on the basis that the cost of employing the person involved is recoverable from the artist's earnings. The personal assistant's job specification will often be complex. Some of the assistant's responsibilities will be managerial and others will be of the nannying variety, so that a sensible compromise is often that part only of the assistant's salary is recoverable.

We are a long way from achieving any recognised set of standards in terms of exactly how a manager's role is defined, and we probably never will because so much depends upon the particular requirements of the artist and the very personal nature of the arrangements worked out between the artist and his manager. Whilst a formal management contract will make some attempt to specify the respective obligations of the parties, in practice the contract is likely to be of little help in this area. In the IMF's suggested form of contract in the next chapter, an attempt is made to illustrate in some detail the respective objections of the parties.

the manager's remuneration

commission

On rare occasions (and usually only if he is well established), the artist may engage a manager on the basis that he will be paid an agreed fee or salary. However, in the vast majority of cases the manager will be paid by way of commission. This recognises that the music business is a volatile one and that success is by no means guaranteed. The manager runs the risk of working very hard but failing to achieve success with the artist, in which event he earns little or nothing. Conversely, if success is achieved the manager may be rewarded handsomely. The obvious benefit from the artist's point of view is that the manager will not have to be paid unless there is some money with which to pay him. Of course, the artist usually only has one career and thus one chance of success; if the manager represents other artists he will have more than one chance of achieving success.

commission rates

Commission rates have crept up over the years, and there are sound reasons for this. Historically, the manager was nicknamed 'Mr 10%'. By the 1970s the usual rate of commission was 15%. Nowadays managers invariably charge 20%, and sometimes a manager will charge 25%, although this is rarely thought to be justifiable. An inflated rate of this kind might arguably be reasonable in the case of a powerful and successful manager putting together a 'manufactured' band or if the manager is prepared to work exclusively for the artist involved. The principal reason for this increase in rates is that, when a lesser rate of perhaps 10% or 15% might have applied, the remaining terms of the typical management contract would have been more demanding from the artist's perspective. For example, the manager might have expected to receive his commission on the gross income arising from any contracts entered into during the currency of the management contract. The management contract might have run for five years, but if towards the end of the five years the artist were to enter into a long-term recording agreement, for example, the manager would nevertheless expect his commission on all earnings under that agreement, even though a large part of those earnings may have been attributable to recordings made after the expiration of the management contract. Today a manager would not usually expect to receive commission on recordings made or songs written after the expiration of the management contract, even though the manager may have negotiated the terms of the recording and publishing deals governing those subsequent recordings and songs. Moreover, most managers now accept that commission will be calculated on the gross income only after deduction of certain expenses. Not only that, but the manager will often have to accept that, following the end of the management contract, there will at some point be a reduction or even a cut-off in his commission entitlement. For these reasons, the rate of commission has increased to its usual rate of 20%. The rate of commission may be affected by what is agreed as to the extent of the manager's involvement. A manager may wish to limit his involvement to the business side of things – he may not wish to be available day and night to deal with creative issues and personal crises. If the manager is prepared to accept that he is offering something less than a full management service he may be prepared to accept a less substantial rate of commission. A manager of a producer, for example, may accept less than 20%, even perhaps 10% or 15%, considering that his role is restricted largely to seeking out work for the producer.

variable rates

Sometimes different rates of commission apply for different types of income. For example, an artist may argue that, since a manager has had little or no involvement in the songwriting process (as opposed to recording and touring activities), commission should be paid in relation to publishing income at a lesser rate. This is a spurious argument that is rarely accepted by managers. After all, it is in part the manager's work which helps create the circumstances in which the value of the artist's publishing rights may be enhanced.

commissionable income

Generally speaking, the manager will be entitled to commission calculated at the agreed percentage rate, but only from the artist's earnings arising from those activities which fall within the scope of the agreement during the term of the management contract. A manager would rarely expect to receive commission upon income attributable to work done by the artist (ie recordings made and songs written) after the expiry of the contract. However, the manager would usually expect to receive commission on income received during the term of the management contract from work undertaken by the artist prior to commencement of the management arrangements. This prevents, for example, a manager taking on a new band and being excluded from commission from the earnings attributable to the band's first album simply because the songs perhaps were written and the recordings made prior to the manager's involvement. If the artist is already established and there is a stream of income from past commercial activities then the artist may wish to exclude all or part of that income for commission purposes. The manager may object to this on the basis that it will be the work completed during the currency of the management contract which reactivates any back catalogue and gives rise to any current earnings from that back catalogue. The artist would usually concede this point, although he may be reluctant to do so if he is already paying commission on that income to an ex-manager.

calculation of commission

The old principle that the manager's commission is calculated by reference to the artist's gross earnings has been eroded in a number of respects.

RECORDING INCOME

The manager will usually be paid his commission on the amount of recording income actually received by the artist, ie all advances and any royalties which are actually paid. To the extent that royalties accrue but are not paid to the artist because they are used for recoupment purposes, then those royalties are not commissionable. If the record company pays an advance which is inclusive of recording costs then those costs are non-commissionable. Most recording contracts now provide for cost-inclusive advances, and this gives rise to some difficulty. If a record company pays £100,000, inclusive of recording costs, how does the manager calculate his commission when those costs are not yet known? The record company might pay, say, £25,000 initially and then pay the remaining £75,000 following completion of recording, after first deducting any recording costs (which the record company usually pays on the artist's behalf). The manager will commission the £25,000 and but will accept that he cannot commission the remaining £75,000 (unless the recording costs prove to be lower than this, in which event the manager would then commission any balance). If the £100,000 is paid up front (which would mean that it is the artist's responsibility to pay any recording costs) then the manager should either defer the calculation and payment of his commission or reach an agreement with the artist for an 'on-account' payment. Sometimes, if he fears profligacy in the studio, the manager may insist upon a 'cap' for recording costs (for the purposes only of calculating his commission).

PUBLISHING INCOME

The manager will expect to be paid his commission calculated by reference to the gross income paid to the artist. There are fewer complications involved with publishing income, as there are so few expenses. Some artists try to exclude from commission any performance income received by the writer direct from the PRS. The PRS accounts direct to the writer for the writer's $^6/_{12}$ share of any performance income, and accounts separately to the publisher for the remaining $^6/_{12}$ 'publisher's share'. The PRS rules are designed to protect the writer against over-enthusiastic publishers, but this has led to a belief on the part of some artists that they have an inalienable right to the 'writer's share' of performance income. Having received this direct into his bank account, the idea that the artist then has to pay a percentage of this by way of management commission is morally repugnant to him. There seems to be little justification for this argument, and logically there is no reason why the writer's share of performance income should not be commissionable in the same way as any other form of income. Most managers insist that they should be allowed to commission this stream of income.

TOURING INCOME

The major area of controversy in relation to calculating commission concerns earnings from live concert performances. Some managers still insist upon charging the agreed rate of commission upon the gross earnings from any tour, but the majority of managers now accept that this is unfair. A concert performance – and certainly a lengthy tour – might generate substantial gross income, but of course the costs of organising a worldwide tour are now so high that the net profits actually earned by the artist might be very small when expressed as a percentage of the gross. Touring activities may generate little or no profit during the early stages of an artist's career, but the artist is likely to continue with his efforts, perhaps with the record company underwriting any loss by way of 'tour support', as a means of promoting record sales. If a tour grosses £1,000,000, for example, and the expenses total £800,000, leaving £200,000 profit, then the artist is likely to be unimpressed with the suggestion that the entirety of that £200,000 (20% of the gross) should be paid over to his manager.

An increasing number of managers accept that commission should be calculated upon net touring income, ie only on any profits remaining after the deduction of all expenses. A prudent manager will at the very least impose some element of control over those expenses so that, if the artist is profligate and insists upon taking suites at five-star hotels and travelling everywhere by chauffeured limousine with a large entourage, this does not impact unfairly upon the management commission.

Many managers still believe that it is inappropriate for them to charge commission only upon net earnings. They take the view that the manager is heavily involved in the artist's touring activities, often having to gear-up the management operation in order to cope with the level of work involved, and that the manager therefore needs to know that he is assured of some income from his investment of time and labour. An obvious and standard compromise is that commission is calculated upon the gross income after deduction of certain specified (but not all) expenses. Another approach is for the commission to be calculated upon the net profits after deduction of all expenses, but also for a fee of some kind to be paid to the manager to defray or help defray any additional overhead expenses, with that fee then treated as an expense to be taken into account when determining the profits.

Managers sometimes make comparisons between the amount of work which has to be undertaken by the manager in relation to a particular tour and the amount of work required on the part of the booking agent. The manager may argue that it is unfair for the artist to accept that the booking agent should be paid his fee, which is usually 10% or 15% and calculated upon the gross income (the booking agent will always insist that this method of calculation applies for the payment of his commission), whilst the manager is expected to rely upon a share of the net profits. However, this argument does not take account of the fact that the booking agent does not earn from other sources – for example, from the additional record sales which a promotional tour is designed to achieve and from merchandising income.

Sometimes the manager will not only mastermind the touring arrangements but will also provide day-to-day tour management services. If the manager or a member of his staff acts as tour manager (thus avoiding the expense of engaging a specialist) then the manager may argue that he should be paid separately for those services. Alternatively, the manager may argue that the degree of involvement on his part supports his assertion that he should be paid a sum in direct relation to the gross income. Similarly, if the manager has sufficient experience to do so, it is possible for him to dispense with the booking agent altogether and book the dates himself. Again, this might justify a greater financial involvement on his part.

There is a compromise to this situation recommended by the IMF, even though the facts of each case might be different, in which the manager should receive 10% of the gross or 20% of the net, whichever is the greater, on the basis that, if 10% of the gross is payable and this gives rise to cashflow difficulties on the part of the artist, the commission entitlement is deferred so that this is only payable out of future commissionable income.

post-term commission

post-term activities

A manager is generally not entitled to any commission relating to income attributable to activities undertaken after the expiration of the contract. Some managers do not entirely accept this principle, and argue to the effect that they should earn commission (if perhaps at a reduced rate) on, say, the next album to be recorded after the end of the deal – although perhaps only if he negotiated the record deal under which that album is to be recorded.

future commission

A manager will often accept that he has no entitlement to commission relating to activities undertaken after the end of the contract, but will demand in return that he will expect to receive his full commission on all income arising from those activities undertaken during the currency of the management contract, irrespective of when that income is received. For example, if a management contract runs for five years and during that period three albums are recorded, the manager would then expect his full commission upon the relevant earnings from those three albums whenever those earnings arise, even to the extent that the albums in question still generate income in 20, 40 or 60 years time.

post-term reductions

The artist will often argue that there should be a reduction in commission at some point, that perhaps commission should continue to be payable at the full rate (perhaps 20%) for five years after the end of the management contract but that this should then be reduced to 10% in relation to income received over the next five years, and that the entitlement then ceases altogether. The artist will advance two arguments in support of an arrangement of this kind: firstly, he will point to the fact that, assuming that he continues with his career, he will need to find a new manager, who will no doubt insist upon receiving commission during the currency of the new management contract on earnings received from the exploitation of the artist's back catalogue, even if at a reduced rate; secondly, the artist will argue that, in large part, any future income from the exploitation of the artist's past work will be generated by the artist's continuing efforts to maintain his profile and the direct promotion of the earlier material through concert performances and the like. It is only in recent years that cut-off provisions of this nature have become fashionable. The issue remains controversial, and many managers do not accept that their financial interest in a particular body of work should be reduced with the passage of time. In many cases the point may be largely academic because, if full commission continues to be paid for, say, five years after the end of the management contract, this may catch 90% or perhaps 99% of the total income which is generated from the body of work in question. Again, however, the question of whether or not cut-off provisions should apply rather depends upon the circumstances of each case. A manager who provides a complete service and manages the artist to the exclusion of all other interests is more likely to object to provisions of this kind.

expenses

out-of-pocket expenses

A manager will invariably require reimbursement of his expenses. This should extend only to expenses incurred by the manager specifically on behalf of the artist. The manager's overhead costs should not be recoverable from the artist. The IMF's suggested form of contract includes a detailed list of reimbursable expenses, which are listed in the following chapter.

approvals

Some artists require the right to approve any expenses to be incurred above a particular limit. This is a prudent precaution during the early stages of the business relationship but tends to become unnecessary and cumbersome once the working relationship has been properly established.

reimbursement

There is often some controversy over how expenses are to be reimbursed. Most managers accept – partly out of practical necessity – that expenses are recoverable only from commissionable income. Others take the view that, since the expenses have been incurred specifically on the artist's behalf, those expenses should in effect be treated as loans and should be repayable on demand. This gives rise to the unedifying prospect of a project failing and the management relationship coming to an end with the manager then presenting the impecunious artist with a demand for repayment of outstanding expenses. No management contract will impose an obligation upon a manager to incur any particular expenses, and most managers will readily accept that, if they agree to incur a particular expense, this is done so at the manager's own risk, in the sense that this will only be reimbursable if there is sufficient commissionable income.

One possible compromise is that, if the commissionable income is insufficient, any outstanding expenses would be repayable out of the artist's future entertainment-related income, even if that income is not commissionable because the management agreement has come to an end. If the manager insists upon this, the artist might at least try to ensure that reimbursement is made only out of an agreed share of future income (in order to avoid the risk of a period during which he loses all of his earnings to his ex-manager).

accounting

usual method

Traditionally the manager has always controlled the artist's income. He is responsible for ensuring that earnings from the artist's activities are paid in full and on time. He regularly prepares management accounts (perhaps on a semi-annual or quarterly basis) showing all income received and all expenses incurred. Each set of accounts is accompanied by a cheque in favour of the artist for the amount due. This system often still applies, although semi-annual accounting is now frowned upon. Most managers agree to account to their artists either quarterly or perhaps even monthly.

alternative method

There is a growing trend of artists taking control of their own money. Some artists feel that, if a manager is entitled to 20%, it is nonsense for him to receive 100% and then account to the artist for 80%. Rather, it is more sensible for the artist to receive 100% and to account to the manager for his 20%. Some managers are delighted at this. Looking after the money is obviously important, but many managers see this as a time-consuming and dreary function, and if the artist is prepared to do it and still pay the manager his 20% then he may not complain. Other managers view artists as not particularly businesslike and sometimes unreliable, and think that they need to take control of the money themselves in order to ensure that they both get paid. Also, the significance of expenses should not be underestimated. It is likely, during the early stages of an artist's career, that the aggregate of the manager's commission and his expenses will represent the lion's share (or even all) of any available income.

pitfalls

Many managers will gladly relinquish this task of accounting, but only on the proviso that the artist employs a reputable firm of chartered accountants to receive all income on the artist's behalf and to pay the manager's commission and expenses upon presentation of invoices. Some artists think that, in this way, their money will be safer, although this is not necessarily true; unfortunately, in recent years, there have been a number of well-publicised cases of music business accountants acting improperly with their clients' money. Perhaps in the music business, as in any other, not all managers are trustworthy. Of course the vast majority of them are, and the plain fact is that, unless the artist has a proper degree of trust in his manager, he shouldn't enter into a management relationship with him in the first place. The problem is that it is not always efficient to have payments cleared through an accountant's office; an accountant will naturally charge for his services, and these changes will usually have to be borne by the artist rather than by the manager. All in all, there is perhaps more to be said for the traditional accounting arrangements, coupled maybe with some contractual safeguards for the artist. For example, the artist might insist that his money is paid into a separate client account held by the manager, rather than mixed in with his own money, and he might also demand suitable rights of audit.

termination

termination for breach

With a fixed long-term contract, either party will usually have a contractual right of termination in certain carefully-defined circumstances (ie if the other party is declared bankrupt, convicted of an offence involving dishonesty, or is incapacitated for an extended period due to illness or accident and is unable to fulfil his obligations). More controversially, the artist may require the right to terminate the contract in the event that the manager is in breach of the material terms of the agreement. This is a dangerous position from the manager's point of view, because it enables the artist to walk away from the contract arguing, for whatever (perhaps spurious) reason, that the manager has not been performing his obligations properly. This merely has the effect of muddying the contractual waters, which benefits the artist in the sense that the manager may be dissuaded in those circumstances from suing him for breach of contract

key-man clauses

If the management contract is with a management company rather than with an individual, the artist will usually insist that the individual with whom he will be dealing must be named in the contract on the basis that, if he ceases to be available, the artist is entitled to terminate.

chapter 2

IMF guidelines for artist management agreements

by David Stopps, for The IMF Copyright And Contracts Sub-Committee

This chapter includes the IMF's own guidelines for artist management agreements. This document, which has already been used in several legal cases, was compiled by the IMF Copyright and Contracts Sub-Committee under the chairmanship of the author. The clauses of the example contract are shown in italics.

It is best to think of artist management agreements as a kind of marriage. It is essential that both sides get on with each other. The artist management agreement should be the only time in the artist's career in which the artist and the manager sit on the opposite sides of the table. Thereafter, both the artist and the manager should work together as a team, with success being the common goal. When an agreement is reached, both sides should feel reasonably comfortable with it. If one side feels very happy and the other unhappy it will not have achieved the balance needed for a good working agreement. The artist/manager relationship has to be based on trust and regular discussion on all of the issues. It is important that the artist is told as much as possible, both good and bad news, at an appropriate time (it is generally not a good idea to deliver bad news just as the artist goes on stage!).

The agreement itself should clearly lay out the ground rules, but there will always be unusual situations which will need discussion and should be resolved within the spirit of common sense and compromise by all concerned. If there are any special arrangements made, they should always be made in writing and signed by both parties.

the IMF handbook a guide to professional band management

It is absolutely essential that the artist receives independent legal advice from a specialist music business lawyer. If not, the enforceability of the contract will be weakened considerably.

When a band is starting out there is usually very little money available, and the prospect of incurring huge legal fees is daunting. Lawyers are aware of this and are usually very happy to either charge a very low fee or postpone payment until a recording or publishing advance is secured in the hope that future work will be forthcoming. The IMF can provide a list of specialist music-business lawyers who specialise in the music business which could be passed on to the artist. If the artist is a member of the Musicians' Union it is possible to obtain legal advice through them, for a comparatively low fee.

In the Sixties and Seventies, artist management agreements were often unfairly weighted in favour of the manager. During the Eighties, however, artists' lawyers successfully gained more ground for the artist to the point at which many current agreements are now often unfairly weighted against the manager. (For example, some artist lawyers try to insist that managers do not commission PRS income, which the IMF recommend is firmly resisted.) This has the effect of reducing the incentive for managers and encourages poor-quality management. Also, if the agreement does not reward the manager adequately, the manager may have to take on extra artists simply to survive, which will mean that less time can be devoted to the artist and which is not in the artist's interest.

Both the manager and the artist should clearly understand that time is valuable. The manager's expert advice, whilst not charged by the hour as is the case with lawyers, clearly has a substantial value. If the manager is investing large amounts of time and/or money, the manager needs to be compensated for this risk in a way which is reflected in commission structures.

At the end of the day, the most contentious points are likely to be the arrangements for post-term commission and touring commission. It is therefore important for both the manager and the artist that the manager takes a strong stand on these issues and that a fair agreement is achieved.

It is very important for a manager to try and provide thorough high-quality management for artist. It is therefore a much better idea for managers to focus on one or two artists than to take on too many and spread themselves too thin, unless their businesses are structured with enough full-time staff to adequately administer a larger number of artists. The IMF is dedicated to providing education for and raising professional standards of artist managers.

The best way of explaining the way in which these agreements work is to give an example of an artist management agreement, such as can be seen in the example below.

the contract

Both the artist and the manager should use a specialist music-business lawyer. Failure of the artist to receive independent advice from a specialist music business lawyer may jeopardise the enforceability of the contract. It is also essential that the manager and the artist use different lawyers.

Every situation is different and will have its own unique set of circumstances. The following example is therefore intended to be a guide to understanding such contracts, hopefully providing help in arriving at a fair agreement for both parties. Below is an example of an artist/management contract based on the precepts of the preceding chapter, with notes of explanation and advice. It is not intended to be a standard artist management agreement.

1. *The Artist hereby appoints the Manager who agrees to carry out the Manager's Duties in relation to the Artist's Career throughout the Territory during the Term.*

2. *The Artist shall pay commission to the Manager at the Commission Rate during the Commission Term on all Commissionable Income earned by the Artist from the Artist's Career.*

3. *The Manager shall pay the Manager's Expenses as defined in the Schedule*

4. *The Artist shall pay the Artist's Expenses as defined in the Schedule.*

5. *The Artist and the Manager will each have the right to audit the other not more than once in any (_____)-month period. Such audit shall require 30 days written notice and must occur within normal office hours. If no objection is raised to an accounting statement rendered by either party within (_____) years of its date, such statement will be deemed correct and binding.*

With audit rights, it is common to agree that, if the party being audited is shown to have underpaid by more than 10%, in addition to reimbursing the shortfall (plus interest) they are also obliged to pay the cost of the audit. The right to audit is usually limited to no more than once in any six- or twelve-month period. The time limit in which to raise an objection is typically two or three years.

Then either:

6. *The Manager shall, during the Term, collect all income on behalf of the Artist and shall pay it into a bank account exclusively dedicated to the Artist. The Manager shall only use funds deposited in such account for the purposes directly connected to the Artist's Career.*

or:

6. *The Artist shall be responsible for all accounting concerning the Artist's Career, including all bookkeeping, tax returns, invoicing, receipts and payments etc. From time to time the Manager will invoice the Artist for Commission, which shall be paid within (_____) days of receipt.*

If adopting the second approach, ignore sections 8, 9.4 and 9.5 from the 'Schedule'. In some cases, in which a manager has several small-development artists, it may be appropriate to use one client account for several artists, although it is generally good practice to keep a separate account for each artist. The number of days in which the invoice should be paid could be anything from ten to 30 days.

7. *After the expiry of the Term, the Artist shall every (_____) months produce statements to the Manager showing all Income and Commission due and shall on receipt of an invoice from the Manager pay the Commission due within (_____) days of receipt of the invoice.*

It is normal for the artist to be obliged to produce statements every three months. The number of days in which the invoice should be paid could be anything from ten to 30 days.

8. *The Artist and the Manager shall each have the right to terminate the Term by written notice if the other:*

> 8.1.1 is declared bankrupt, or enters into a composition or agreement with creditors; or
>
> 8.1.2 is convicted of an offence involving dishonesty; or
>
> 8.1.3 is in material breach of this agreement and shall not have remedied that breach within 30 days of written notice of being required to do so; or
>
> 8.1.4 is incapacitated due to illness or accident for a period exceeding (_____) days.

The normal period of incapacity is three to four months, but it could be anything from six weeks to twelve months. A contract might also provide for a temporary replacement manager in such circumstances. Anyone can have an accident or become ill, and it seems unreasonable that managers, having suffered one misfortune, must then suffer further hardship by losing their artists. The IMF therefore recommends a period of at least four months.

> 8.2 If either party terminates the term this shall not affect either party's rights or obligations that are intended to continue in force beyond the term.
>
> 9. No variation of this agreement shall be binding unless made in writing and signed by both parties.
>
> 10. Any notice or consent to be given under this agreement shall be effective if sent by registered or recorded delivery post to the other party at the address given in the Schedule. Service shall be deemed to take place on the day following posting.
>
> 11. Nothing herein shall constitute a partnership between the Artist and the Manager.
>
> 12. The Artist and the Manager herein acknowledge that they are advised to seek independent specialist music business legal advice from a qualified music-business lawyer before signing this agreement.
>
> 13. The Manager has the right and authority to negotiate with third parties on the Artist's behalf.
>
> 14. This agreement shall be governed by (_____) law and both parties agree to submit to the exclusive jurisdiction of the High Court of Justices in (_____).

For UK managers we recommend that 'English' and 'England' are inserted respectively. The law in Wales and Northern Ireland is very similar to that of England, while the law in Scotland is very different. A Scottish manager with a Scottish artist could have the contract governed by Scottish law, but such a manager would nevertheless still be advised to have a contract governed by English law because there is a great deal more precedent in English law, and the vast majority of UK specialist music business lawyers are based in London.

A manager dealing with an artist who is based abroad and who insists on dealing in the law of a foreign country must be very careful to research the laws concerning contracts. For example, in California contracts for personal services are restricted to seven years.

15. *Terms used in this agreement shall have the meanings described in the Schedule, heretowhich is hereby incorporated into this agreement.*

the schedule

1. The Artist: (_____)

The artist could be an individual, a group of people, a partnership or a limited company. The artist's real name should appear here together with their stage name (if any) and their current address. If the artist is a band, each member's real name, together with their stage name (if any), their current address and the current name of the band, should also be shown. If the artist is a band there will need to be provision here for changes in the band's personnel with an obligation for new joining members to be party to this agreement. A band will also need to have a separate band agreement, which will deal with such issues as how income is to be split between each member and the provisions in the eventuality of a member leaving.

If the artist is contracted as a limited company, it will be necessary to have an inducement letter drafted wherein the artist is held personally responsible for the provisions of the agreement.

2. The Manager: (_____)

The manager could also be an individual, a group of people, a partnership or a limited company. If contracted as the latter, the artist may wish to have a key-man clause inserted in the agreement obliging the manager's personal services to be available, the failure of which would be a breach.

If either party contracts as a limited company, that company is not entitled to legal aid in the event of a dispute. A company is also more likely to be asked by the court for a security deposit before any case starts.

3. *Territory*

If managers are not managing the artist for the world, they must make sure that they are clear about the identities of other managers in other territories and of their roles in the international picture. If they are principal managers then they should have the right to appoint third-party managers in foreign territories. In this case, it is important for them to make sure that the commission arrangements are clear and that the artists are not paying double commission.

4. *Term: (_____) years/months commencing on (_____). Thereafter the term continues until either party gives (_____) months notice of termination.*

The term could be anything from six months to five years. Some managers prefer to go for a comparatively short term, perhaps one year, and to have a three-month notice of termination from either side after that period so that, for example, the term continues indefinitely after one year until one party gives notice to the other that the term will end in three months. The advantage of this is that managers have a stronger negotiating position in regard to the other terms of the contract. Artists are also reassured that, if things don't work out, they are not tied to managers for a long period of time.

On the other hand, some managers feel that they will need to invest a great deal of hard work into an artist in the early stages, probably with very little commission, and that they therefore need a longer term in order feel secure about making that investment of time and effort.

Another common arrangement is to have a term of perhaps two or three years and one- or two-year options. The options can only be taken up by the manager if the manager has achieved certain income levels for the artist.

Yet another approach is to define the term in albums rather than in years. In the Seventies and Eighties, an artist would typically release one album per year. These days, however, you may be lucky to get two albums released in the first five years. It may therefore be a much better approach to define the term as two or three albums, in the same way that it is defined in recording and publishing contracts. If this approach is adopted it is essential that a long-stop term is also included, as a contract cannot be open-ended (eg two years commencing from a certain date or until six months after the release of the third album, whichever is the longer, provided that in no circumstances will the basic term exceed five years).

Similarly it would be possible to combine the two approaches and have the termination of the term at, say, two years or at six months after the release of the second album, whichever is the longer.

In some cases the manager may reach an arrangement with the artist wherein, if the manager is unsuccessful in procuring a recording agreement or publishing agreement within perhaps nine to 18 months, that the term then has an earlier termination date.

5.   *Commission Rate: (_____)%*

Notwithstanding anything to the contrary in this agreement, the commission payable to the manager by the artist in respect of touring and live performance income shall be (_____)% of the gross fees in respect of touring and live performance or (_____)% of the net profit thereof, whichever is the greater.

The generally accepted commission rate for managers in the music industry is 20%. In practice, however, this can range from 10% to 25%. Take the example of a manager investing a lot of money into a new band and giving them a tremendous amount of time and belief. In such a situation it might be quite reasonable for the manager to take 25%. It may also be appropriate for a manager to take 25% if he or she agrees to manage the artist exclusively. In this case it is common to agree that the commission rate is reduced to 20% if the manager manages more than one or two other artists.

For a very well-established artist looking for a new manager, the manager will know that there is very little or no risk involved and that therefore there is quite a lot of money in the picture. In such a case the manager might be willing to agree a commission of 10-15%.

touring income

In practice there are many different arrangements in place for touring income, varying from a straight 20% of the gross to 20% of the net profits only. A large proportion of tours lose money or break even (with record-company tour support). If the manager only has a 20% of the net profits agreement, this means that he or she cannot taky any commission on the tour. Also, the manager has had to pay for all of the management staff, office costs and other management expenses connected with the tour. In such a case, the manager has done a tremendous amount of work (often much more than the agent) and ends up with a considerable financial loss. The IMF therefore feels that a commission of 20% of the net profits is unreasonable from the manager's perspective, unless the tour budget shows a substantial profit, and its recommendation is that management should take at least 10-15% of the gross touring income (less VAT and other taxes) or 20-30% of the net profits, whichever is the greater.

Another approach is for the manager to take a fixed fee for managing the tour, or for an arrangement to be worked out on a tour-by-tour basis with reference to the budgeted costs and income. Yet another approach is for the manager to receive at least the same as the highest-paid person on the tour (usually the booking agent). The level of an appropriate touring commission rate can be influenced by several other factors: is the manager also the tour manager or the booking agent?; is the artist a solo performer or is it a band, and if so how many people are in the band?; and who is in control of touring costs?

Another approach is to take a flexible view on touring commission and to add a clause such as:

> *From time to time, and at the request of either party, the fairness of this clause can be reviewed.*

This clause is not recommended by the IMF, as it could lead to difficulties and disputes. However, some managers favour its inclusion and have made it work successfully. If the arrangement is changed in such a review it is important to remember to get the change agreed in writing and signed by both parties. If an agreement is reached for a percentage of the gross and the artist is unable to pay the manager due to cashflow problems, the amount should then be rolled up with interest and paid when the artist is in a position to do so. (This process also applies to commission generally.)

Merchandising and sponsorship income associated with a tour or a retail agreement should be treated separately and commissioned at the normal rate, rather than included in the calculation of touring losses and profits.

When negotiating tour support with a record company it is important to insist that management commission is an acceptable tour cost. It is also important to clarify that merchandising income is not included as tour income in the tour accounts. For some reason some record companies accept agency commission as a *bona fide* expense but refuse to accept management commission; apart from being illogical this is also demeaning to managers and unfair to artists, and in the IMF's view this situation must change. It is important that this issue is raised with the record company as early as possible, and preferably when the recording agreement is negotiated.

We suggest that a tour is defined as a series of more than eight dates in any 21-day period. If several one-off dates occur in a month then these can be grouped and the commission calculated on a monthly basis.

6. *Commission Term:* (_____)

An accepted principle of artist/management agreements is that the manager should continue to receive commission after the term has expired for their achievements during the term.

Many managers believe very strongly that commission should be payable in perpetuity on income resulting from work carried out during the term, and this is a view supported by the IMF. If an album is successful it is generally so because of the combined efforts of the artist, the manager and the record company. Many recording contracts are signed for life of copyright (for sound recordings in the UK, this is currently 50 years from their release). Therefore the artist and the record company will receive income in perpetuity, or as good as, so in that case why shouldn't the manager? The manager is usually a key component in the success of an album, and that expertise and hard work deserves to be rewarded. This point is likely to be strongly challenged by lawyers representing artists, but it is the IMF's view that a manager should be firm in insisting this continuity of commission, as it is only fair and reasonable.

It may be the case that a compromise is reached by which the manager's commission is payable at its full rate for a period after the term, which is then followed by one or two periods in which the commission reduces, the last of these being in perpetuity.

If the commission does reduce, a second manager may be able to negotiate with the artist for the difference between the commission being paid to the first manager and the commission rate. If the previous works were commissionable at the full rate in perpetuity by the old manager, it may be a good idea to approach the old manager (with the approval of the artist) to negotiate a commission split on previous works. After all, if a new manager invests a tremendous amount of work on current and future works, and the work is successful, this could well stimulate back-catalogue sales, which would benefit the old manager. It may therefore be in the old manager's interest to encourage the new manager to try very hard in this respect by agreeing to a split commission, which would provide a further incentive.

In any case, except in unusual circumstances the aggregate of the commissions of the old manager and the new manager should not exceed the commission rate. It is also important to define which works will be commissionable on a post-term basis. It could be any of the following:

(a) anything created during the term, including writing; or
(b) anything recorded during the term, either demos or masters; or
(c) anything released during the term (although this would be unusual).

7. *Artist's Career.* All activities in the (_____) industry including without limitation the creation of Works as defined in 11 below.

Either 'music' or 'entertainment' should be inserted here. 'Entertainment' has broader scope and would include areas such as literary works, if appropriate.

8. Artist's Account: Bank Address: (_____)
Bank Account No.: (_____)
Signatories: (_____) (_____)
Interest if either party owe money to the other (_____)% over the (_____) base rate.

It is completely reasonable for the manager to charge interest if commission or expenses cannot be paid. If a payment of income or corporation tax is late, the Inland Revenue will automatically charge interest, and the situation should be exactly the same for management commission and expenses.

9. *Manager's Duties:*

9.1 *To use the Manager's reasonable endeavours to advance and promote the Artist's Career.*

9.2 *To advise and consult with the Artist regarding the collection of income and the incurring of expenditure and to use the Manager's reasonable endeavours to ensure that the Artist gets paid.*

It is important that the manager and the artist regularly consult and discuss the development of the artist's career, both in terms of assessing its past and present success and its direction.

> 9.3 To consult regularly with the Artist and keep the Artist informed of all substantial activity undertaken by the Manager, and to discuss the Artist's career development generally and to periodically offer constructive criticism.
>
> 9.4 To maintain records of all transactions affecting the Artist's Career and to send the Artist a statement within (_____) days of the end of each calendar quarter disclosing all Income, the source of Income, expenses, commission and other debts and liabilities arising during the preceding three months.

The period between the end of the quarter and the statement can be anything from 30 to 120 days. It can often take a considerable time to document and account the financial activity of a particular quarter, especially if the artist is on a world tour. We therefore suggest that managers should try to negotiate as long a period of time as possible. If the accounts are late, for some reason, this is a classic area in which an artist may rightly claim breach of contract. Supplying the accounts 120 days after the quarter end is not unreasonable, and for those cases in which a tour straddles two accounting periods it may be necessary to have a one-off agreement signed to the effect that the accounting will be deferred to the end of the period following the end of the tour. In a case such as this it is important to have a clear written agreement signed to this effect before the start of the tour.

> 9.5 To obtain the artist's approval for any expenditure over £(_____) for a single cheque or £(_____) over a period of one month.

This is sometimes seen in artist management contracts, and provides the artist with some protection against the manager misusing his or her money. In practice it is vital that there is trust between the artist and the manager. This limitation can also be a practical problem, for example if the manager is in England and the artist is in Australia and substantial funds are needed quickly.

> 9.6 To advise the Artist on appointing booking agents, accountants, lawyers, sponsors, merchandisers and other agents with due consideration to the Artist's moral views.

It is important that both the artist and the manager feel comfortable and are able to work with third-party professionals. It is also important that the manager is aware of the artist's political and moral views and does not commit the artist to anything inappropriate.

10. Artist's Duties:

   10.1 *To carry out to the best of their ability and in a punctual and sober fashion all reasonable agreements, engagements, performances and promotional activities obtained or approved by the Manager.*

   10.2 *To attend promptly all appointments and to keep the Manager reasonably informed of the Artist's whereabouts and availability at all times.*

   10.3 *To reveal to the Manager all income including but not limited to PRS, PPL, GVL, MU, AURA, PAMRA and touring overages paid directly to the Artist.*

   10.4 *To refer promptly all approaches and offers from third parties concerning the Artist's Career to the Manager.*

   10.5 *Not to engage any other person to act as the Artist's manager or representative in connection with any aspect of the Artist's Career.*

   10.6 *To consult regularly with the Manager concerning the development of the Artist's Career and to accept that it is part of the Manager's job to offer constructive criticism from time to time.*

   10.7 *To keep the Manager fully informed and to consult regularly concerning all anticipated expenditure to be incurred by the Artist, and to obtain the Manager's approval in regard to recording costs, video costs, equipment costs and touring costs.*

11. Works:

   11.1 *Sound recordings (including demos).*

   11.2 *Visual recordings including film and video.*

the IMF handbook a guide to professional band management

    11.3 Literary, dramatic and musical works.

    11.4 Merchandising, sponsorship of any name, logo, artwork or trade mark owned by or associated with the Artist.

    11.5 Performances and appearances by the Artist in concert, on radio, television or film.

    11.6 Recordings of other artists produced, engineered, programmed or arranged by the Artist.

In each case created or substantially created during the Term.

  12. Income (shall mean both 12.1 and 12.2):

    12.1 Commissionable Income. All gross fees and sums of money payable and accruing to the Artist in respect of exploitation of the Works or otherwise arising from activities in the Artist's Career excluding Non-Commissionable Income.

    12.2 Non-Commissionable Income:

        12.2.1 Sums paid by or on behalf of the Artist as budgeted, recoupable recording costs or budgeted recoupable video costs.

        12.2.2 Royalties, advances or fees paid or credited by or on behalf of the Artist to any third-party producers, mixers, programmers or engineers, to an agreed budget.

        12.2.3 Monies paid or credited to the Artist as tour support to an agreed budget.

The word 'budgeted' has been included in the above to allow the commissionable income to be calculated in a fair and reasonable way. The responsibility for budgeting should rest jointly between the artist and the manager, but if the recording costs for an album wildly exceed its budget, for example, it may be necessary for the artist and the manager to come to an agreement concerning the amount of commission which should be taken.

The modern trend in most forms of agreement is to have the advances for recording contracts to be inclusive of recording costs, and if this is the case the manager is faced with the problem of deciding how much of the advance should be set aside for recording (and therefore non-commissionable income) and how much should be regarded as commissionable income. It is a good idea to come to a separate written agreement with the artist every time a new album recording advance is received in order that an agreed level of the advance is deemed to be commissionable income. For instance, it could be the case that the entire advance is spent on recording costs, in which case the manager earns absolutely nothing.

It may also be possible to insert a re-assessment clause wherein both parties agree on an adjusted level of commissionable income when the recording of the album has been finished. Also, if the artist buys recording equipment with the advance, this should be regarded as commissionable income as the artist is using the advance to acquire an asset.

13. *Manager's Expenses.* Manager's general office and business costs including:

> *Office rent*
> *Local property tax on office*
> *Management staff salaries and wages*
> *Management staff National Insurance payments*
> *Manager's office equipment, including:*
> > *computers*
> > *fax machines and photocopiers*
> > *pagers and mobile phones*
> > *office telephone system*
>
> *Manager's car and associated costs*
> *Manager's legal fees*
> *Local telephone, fax and e-mail costs*
> *Miscellaneous office expenses*

14. *Artist's Expenses.* Any expenses reasonably incurred in connection with the Artist's Career, whether incurred by the Manager or the Artist, other than the Manager's Expenses, including but not limited to the following:

> *Commission payable to a booking agent or other agents*
> *Costs/wages payable to a Tour Manager*
> *Mailshots on behalf of Artist*
> *Advertising on behalf of Artist*

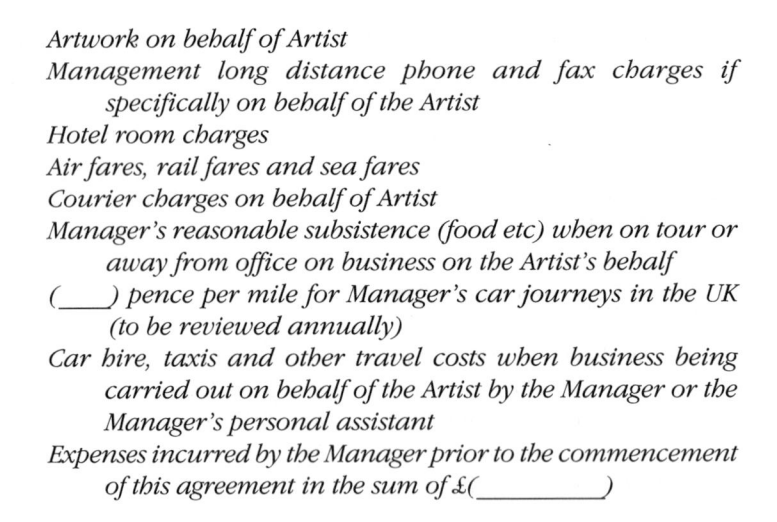

the IMF handbook a guide to professional band management

> *Artwork on behalf of Artist*
> *Management long distance phone and fax charges if specifically on behalf of the Artist*
> *Hotel room charges*
> *Air fares, rail fares and sea fares*
> *Courier charges on behalf of Artist*
> *Manager's reasonable subsistence (food etc) when on tour or away from office on business on the Artist's behalf*
> *(___) pence per mile for Manager's car journeys in the UK (to be reviewed annually)*
> *Car hire, taxis and other travel costs when business being carried out on behalf of the Artist by the Manager or the Manager's personal assistant*
> *Expenses incurred by the Manager prior to the commencement of this agreement in the sum of £(_____)*

The above to be pro rated if work for other artists is being carried out.

This is an example of a typical arrangement, although the specifics will vary. In the USA it is common practise for all phone calls concerned with an artist to be chargeable as an expense to the artist. When this convention was introduced, phone technology in the USA was ahead of that in the UK, and this independent charging was easily managed by tapping in a code dedicated to each artist for each call. The phone company then issued a monthly statement listing all calls made on each artist's behalf. Fortunately, this technology is now available in the UK. Also, the mileage rate charged for the manager's car journeys will vary according to the engine capacity of the car. The AA or the RAC will be able to supply the current rates.

It is important for the manager to write to the artist soon after their first meeting, stating clearly that expenses incurred prior to the signing of a proper agreement will be repayable. It is reasonable to reach an agreement by means of a simple letter, which should be signed by both the artist and the manager, and which should agree that clearly defined expenses connected directly with the artist should be reimbursed to the manager, whether or not an ongoing agreement is reached and whether or not the relationship continues.

The IMF Guidelines For Artist Management Agreements were created by the IMF Copyright And Contract Sub-Committee. The members of this committee, who gave a great deal of unpaid time, were as follows: David R Stopps (Chairman), Peter Jenner, Phil Nelson, Nigel Parker (Legal), David Enthoven and Tim Clark. Special thanks also to Robert Horsefall of Lee and Thompson for consultancy.

chapter 3

recording contracts

by Andrew Thompson and Nigel Parker

The recording contract is the principal means by which a recording artist earns his living. Without a record deal his ability to exploit his talent is limited. The recording contract is also the principal means by which a record company acquires its stock in trade. Record companies may also buy catalogues of recordings made by other record companies under their own recording contracts. Without recording contracts there would be very few recordings. Without recordings there would be few opportunities for songwriters and music publishers to exploit their songs. The recording agreement affects every aspect of the recording artist's career, and its importance cannot be emphasised enough.

In this chapter we will look briefly at how a recording artist might find a record deal, and at the different types of deal which might be available. We will then look more closely at a typical recording contract before examining the financial aspects of recording contracts and dealing with some of the more general considerations which apply once a recording artist has secured a record deal.

the IMF handbook a guide to professional band management

THE DEAL

finding the deal

the team

Few would-be recording artists are lucky enough to find worthwhile recording contracts. The fact is that there is no easy way to get a deal. We would all like to think that talent is the main factor, but talent alone is not enough: good luck plays a large part. Nor is there any right or wrong way to go about finding a deal, although artists can rarely secure a deal on their own, if only because it is often difficult for artists to sell themselves. It is important, therefore, that the right team of people is in place to support the artist.

the manager

In most cases an artist appoints a manager before obtaining his first record deal. Sometimes a manager (or someone else with contacts and experience) may agree to help secure a deal in return for a finder's fee, rather than enjoying any continuing involvement. This approach can be problematic because the strength of the overall team is important for the record company. In deciding whether or not to offer a deal, the company will need to feel comfortable with the organisation of the recording project, and in particular the company must have confidence in the artist's manager. The record company may therefore think twice about dealing with someone who is merely 'shopping' a deal with no intention of following through with continuing help and support. Sometimes a company will sign an artist without a manager. These cases are not common, however, and often the company then tries to ensure that a manager is appointed.

agents

If the artist is gigging regularly, his booking agent may help to find a deal. However, the major booking agencies are reluctant to sign artists until they have a good live following, and this only happens once a record deal is in place.

lawyers

A music business lawyer can sometimes help with finding a deal. Most lawyers are only of real help once a record company has shown some interest; there is only so much a lawyer is able to do to secure that interest for a new artist in the first place. A specialist lawyer, like others working in the record industry, might be in a position to put demo tapes on the appropriate desks, and he might even be able to ensure that the tape is given proper consideration. However, distributing demo tapes is rarely enough in itself to secure a deal.

the pitch

Every recording project is different, and even if it is not very different then it must be presented as if it is. Therefore, a story must be developed around the particular project before it is 'pitched' to record companies. The individual talents of the artist will always be the central feature of the story, but there will also be many other factors involved, including perhaps the songs, the intended producer, and maybe even the past history of those involved in the project. The story takes time to develop, and even then a record deal never turns up overnight.

publishers

Assuming that the artist writes some or all of his own material, he must decide whether to sign a record deal or a publishing deal first. Some years ago the conventional wisdom was that a record deal should be secured before a publishing deal, the theory being that the record deal would give extra value to the publishing rights. It is now more common for an artist to enter into a music publishing deal before a record deal (see the section on 'When Should The Deal Be Done?' in chapter six). Once a publisher has become involved, there is then one more member of the team who can provide help in securing the record deal, and the record company may be more confident in signing an artist who already has a some support.

which company?

Sometimes it never rains but it pours. When one record company finally shows interest others suddenly follow. There is nothing more likely to awaken a record company's interest in the artist than interest from another company. If the artist is lucky enough to have a choice between companies, how should he then choose which company to go with? Each company's current roster of artists should be examined: does the success of those artists (or lack thereof) suggest that the company will properly understand and work effectively with the new artist? On the other hand, an artist may wish to avoid signing with a company which already has a similar artist competing in the same field. This need not necessarily be a problem, but the new artist will then have to compete with others on the label for limited marketing and promotion budgets.

individual executives

It is important not to read to much into a company's past successes – all major companies have labels of which they are rightly proud. An artist should concentrate on the label's recent track record rather than on its previous successes. Look carefully at the current MD, head of A&R (and any other significant A&R staff) and head of marketing. Talk to them about their careers: what have they done and what do they still hope to achieve? Remember, however, that record company executives are not generally known for their loyalty. Artists may have stay with a company for six albums, but key executives change jobs frequently.

Financial considerations will affect any choice. If competing deals are roughly comparable in financial terms, the deciding factor will normally be the level of enthusiasm shown by each party. But bear in mind, in this case, that you cannot always be sure that a company is as enthusiastic as it seems. The amount of money offered is a good indication of the level of their enthusiasm, but it is only one indication. Despite the risk of key executives leaving to join another label, the most important factor is the artist's relationship with the person bringing in the deal. How experienced is that person? How much power does he have within the organisation? To what extent do you trust him to do all of the things he has promised?

indie or major?

the conventional deal

Although all record companies and publishers have standard forms of contract, no two deals are ever quite the same. The component parts of a typical record deal with a major company will be examined in detail later in this section. Under this type of deal, an artist will sign exclusively to the company on a long-term basis, and the company will then claim ownership of all of the artist's recordings made during the full length (or term) of the agreement. The artist will earn royalties on record sales, which are then used by the company to pay off (or 'recoup') any advances paid to the artist, together with recording costs and certain other expenses. Within this framework there is a great deal of flexibility, and at the end of the day every negotiation and every contract will have a distinct flavour of its own. Nonetheless, the basic ground rules remain the same for each contract.

independents

A key question for an artist is often whether he should sign with an indie or with a major. Signing to an independent label is one way to break free of the limitations imposed by some of the larger companies. At present, the majors are EMI, Warner, Sony, Universal and BMG and their various affiliates and labels, and the most well-known 'indies' are companies like Beggars Banquet, One Little Indian and Mute. For many years there was a middle category of substantial record companies (ie Island, Virgin, Chrysalis, A&M and Geffen) which did not own their own manufacturing plants and distribution networks. This middle tier has all but disappeared, as all of these companies have now been bought out by the majors.

flexibility

The main apparent advantage of signing to an indie is that the artist is able retain greater creative or artistic control. The deals offered by indies tend to be for a shorter term, and the indies are generally more flexible when these deals are drawn up.

creative control

A major will usually insist on either total or limited control over certain elements of the creative process (for example the choice of songs, producer and studio). Indies, on the other hand, are reputed to be more sympathetic to the artist's wishes. They are more likely to allow the artist to follow whatever artistic direction he wishes to pursue. One reason for this more sympathetic approach is that an indie usually invests significantly less up-front money in an artist than a major.

This is not to say that A&R managers at major companies lack artistic sympathy, but the higher level of financial investment sometimes increase the pressure to secure immediate chart success, which may deny the artist the opportunity to develop naturally and gradually. Also, the key A&R man at an indie is often the owner of the company, and is therefore more free to make decisions than his counterpart at the major. He doesn't have to justify the company's expenditure to a managing director, chairman or finance director if sales are not going that well.

Nevertheless, there is a tendency to exaggerate the level of control that a major can exert over the artistic process. It is impossible for a record company to physically force an artist to record a particular song or work with a particular producer. A good A&R manager will operate as a catalyst for all of the ideas and other artistic ingredients involved, and some of the A&R managers at major companies have substantial experience and understanding. The majors tend to shift priorities from time to time, sometimes because records by different artists may be competing for a gap in the company's release schedule, with the result that some artists may be neglected. Indies tend not to have these problems – at least, not to the same degree.

short or long term?

All majors expect a new artist to sign an agreement committing them to record probably five or six (and sometimes even seven or eight) albums. An A&R manager might sign an artist to a six-album deal only to move to another company a year or so later. Indies generally will not demand such a long-term commitment, and they may require as little as one album. Even if the indie insists on options for additional albums, this may matter less to the artist. Indies often allow an artist to develop at his own pace, thus allowing him to avoid the pressures of becoming a mainstream act too quickly, and before the artist has found his preferred artistic direction. It is not unusual for an artist to start off with an indie and move to a major later in his career. If he is successful and receives some critical acclaim with the indie he might then extract a better deal from the major than he would have as an unknown. Majors can be quick to drop new signings if there is no immediate success, and it can be difficult for an artist to recover from this.

territory

All of the majors expect to sign artists for the whole world, even if their overseas associates (often part of the same multi-national empire) have shown no particular interest in the artist in question. Indies, however, often limit their recording agreements to just a few countries (ie UK only, Europe, or the world excluding North America). This allows artists to then strike separate agreements with other record companies in those countries not covered by the initial deal, choosing companies which are genuinely enthusiastic about them or those which might be stronger in that territory.

If the artist secures separate deals overseas, he will benefit by having more than one stream of royalties. Even if the indie insists on a worldwide deal, it will have more flexibility in sub-licensing outside the UK to companies genuinely interested in the artist. Indies will sometimes agree to share with the artist any advances they receive from their overseas associates.

royalty rates

An example of a typical royalty rate on album sales for an artist signing to a major would be 16% for UK sales; 14% in major countries such as Germany, France, USA and Japan; and 12% for the rest of the world. What this means in practical terms will be examined later in this chapter. The higher rate for the home territory is sometimes referred to as the 'headline' rate of royalty. Lower rates apply outside the home territory because the company itself merely receives a royalty from its licensee and will wish to maintain a reasonable margin between the royalty received and the royalty passed to the artist. However, an artist signing to a different company in each territory will expect to obtain a headline rate in each case.

share of profit

An artist signed to an indie will often be paid a share of profit instead of a percentage of total record sales. The profit share is usually 50% of the indie's net receipts, although this might increase (or 'escalate', in record-company jargon) for later albums and perhaps for overseas income. The relationship between an artist and an indie is more like a partnership. The artist takes less money up front, and sometimes nothing at all, on the basis that, if he succeeds, he and the record company will share more or less equally in the fruits of any success.

financial insecurity

Despite the obvious advantages, there are considerable problems with following the indie route. An indie is more likely than a major to have cashflow problems or even to become bankrupt, and it may not have the sophisticated structure, financial discipline and professional management of a major. This becomes a matter of particular concern when an artist 'breaks', whether domestically or internationally, because at this stage substantial investment is needed to maintain the artist's momentum and to capitalise fully on all opportunities.

international deals

If there are separate deals for different territories, the artist or his management will become heavily involved in liaising with and co-ordinating the different distributors. Each company needs tapes, information, and promotional material, and each will expect the artist to tour in its territory, often proving quite intolerant of the artist's other commitments. If a worldwide deal is signed with a major, many of these problems are avoided. It is the responsibility of the major's international department to help with all of these conflicts.

advances

Indies do not usually pay substantial advances to their artists, unlike major companies, who usually provide a good degree of financial security. Similarly, indies are less inclined to allow the artist to spend as much on recording costs, and so the artist is therefore less likely to use the top studios and producers. Once an artist breaks, majors are more likely to have the resources to exploit the opportunities fully. They can fund more expensive videos and more substantial marketing campaigns, including TV advertising, and can usually co-ordinate international campaigns more effectively.

strength in depth

Majors employ talented, creative people in specialised departments, such as A&R, marketing, press, promotions and international, and many staff at majors have worked in the record industry for a long time. The personnel at the smaller indie companies, on the other hand, may not have such a wide or detailed experience of all aspects of the development of artists, or of maintaining success once it has been achieved. If an artist has creative flair, or an experienced and creative manager, then he will have less need to call upon a major's resources. Unfortunately, few artists have these abilities and resources, needing record companies to provide guidance, advice, support, commitment and, above all, money.

the final choice

Some of the more interesting artists have come from indies. Other artists, signed to majors, might well have made less impact had they been on indie labels. Some bands which have (or pretend to have) the indie approach feel suffocated when they move to a major. The factors to consider when deciding between the indies and majors can be reduced to perhaps five criteria:

- Current A&R relationship. How good is the artist's relationship with his A&R manager at the signing of the deal?

- Future A&R relationship. How likely is the A&R relationship to survive? Will it break down, for example, because the A&R manager is subjected to intolerable pressure from faceless executives? Or will it end with the A&R manager leaving to pursue his career elsewhere?

- Artistic ability. Might the artist's particular talents be stifled by the major's approach? The problem of the difficult second novel applies equally to musicians. Some artists clearly have enduring appeal, while others come and go. Those that fail often blame the stifling atmosphere at a major.

- The artist's management. How competent and experienced is the artist's management team? How quickly can they adapt to the artist's changing fortunes?

- The artist's style. A pop or mainstream rock artist may be better suited to a deal with a major, with its extensive marketing machinery. An alternative rock or dance artist, on the other hand, is arguably better off with an indie company – during the early stages, at least.

the proposal

false hopes

Typically, artists suffer a series of false starts. Record companies frequently offer encouragement, inspiring misplaced optimism. Too often record companies appear keen when they have no real enthusiasm. In the worst cases a company may ask for more demos, or suggest other changes, without any genuine expectation of signing a deal, and so the artist can be led down a cruel cul de sac.

who makes the first move?

Nevertheless, with luck, sooner or later a record company will decide to proceed. At this point, they will ask what kind of deal the artist is looking for. Logically, a company which has expressed an interest in signing an artist should put forward its proposals for a deal. However, the company will usually want the artist to explain his own requirements. This initial proposal is one of the most vital stages of the negotiating process, and all of the team members should be involved in its formulation. It is important, however, that the initial proposal should not be too complicated. It should deal with the suggested length of the deal, the territory, the product commitment and the basic financial requirements for the initial recordings, although it is probably better not to complicate the initial proposal with the financial arrangements for subsequent recordings. The proposal should also cover important but non-standard aspects of the deal.

the IMF handbook a guide to professional band management

high or low?

The artist should take care that the proposal is pitched sensibly in terms of what the record company is likely to agree to do and pay. The artist must avoid asking for too little, but there is also danger in asking for too much. The artist therefore needs a team member (perhaps his manager, but more probably his lawyer) with experience in striking similar deals.

the legal framework

practicalities

Much of the machinery of the music business cannot be understood without a basic knowledge of certain legal issues. In the context of recording contracts, the most important of these is the concept of restraint of trade. Put simply, the law provides that an agreement which unreasonably restricts a person's ability to carry on his trade cannot be enforced against him. This only becomes immediately important when there is a dispute between the parties to an agreement. When that happens, an artist may try to escape from his obligations under the agreement, by arguing that it is, and always has been, unreasonably in restraint of his trade. However, no record company would make a substantial investment in an artist if it felt that there was a real risk of him abrogating his obligations in this way. The issue of restraint of trade therefore has a significant impact on the obligations imposed by record companies on artists. A full breakdown of the doctrine of restrain of trade, its precedents and its legal ramifications is discussed in chapter four.

Many commercial agreements involve, to a greater or lesser degree, a restraint of trade. The courts will only enforce a particular agreement if persuaded that the restraints which it imposes are reasonable. A recording agreement is a restraint of trade because of the element of exclusivity, which gives the record company the exclusive rights to the artist's services as a recording artist. Under the terms of the agreement the artist may not carry on his trade for any other person or company, and any recordings made by the artist during the agreement automatically belong exclusively to the record company.

The extent of restraint differs from agreement to agreement and from company to company. A typical deal with a major will be worldwide, and for perhaps five or six albums. During the term of the agreement (and it may take ten years or more to record and deliver five or six albums), the artist is prevented from recording for anyone else, and there may be other restrictions. For example, for a period of time (perhaps five years) after the end of the deal, the artist may be prevented from recording any of the songs which were recorded during the term of the recording agreement for anybody else (this is known as a 're-recording restriction').

If an artist claims, in any legal proceedings against a record company, that his agreement is in unreasonable restraint of trade, the court will take into account all of the terms of the agreement. Cases concerning restraint of trade involve an exhaustive consideration of evidence supporting what is, or is not, reasonable. Such cases may run for many weeks, and are therefore expensive, which explains their scarceness. It is difficult to extract precedents from decided cases because they depend so much on their own particular facts. Except in extreme cases, lawyers find it difficult to give definitive advice as to whether or not a particular agreement might constitute an unreasonable restraint of trade and so be set aside. In 1990 the court set aside Holly Johnson's recording agreement with ZTT on the grounds that it constituted an unreasonable restraint of trade. Similarly (although the facts in this case were very different), in 1993 the court set aside the Stone Roses' recording agreement with Silvertone for similar reasons. However, more recently, George Michael failed in his bid to set aside his agreement with Sony Music. The decision against George Michael has caused some confusion, because it is difficult to reconcile it with the decisions in favour of Holly Johnson and Stone Roses (see chapter four).

legal advice

George Michael's position was prejudiced to some extent because he had re-negotiated his contract several times since first entering into a recording contract (as a member of Wham!) with Sony. On each occasion he had been properly advised by experienced music-industry lawyers. In any case of restraint of trade the court will take into account not only all of the terms of the agreement but also the circumstances under which the participants entered into the agreement. It is for this reason that the quality of any legal advice is of crucial significance. It is obviously sensible for any artist to obtain proper legal advice for his own benefit, but from the record company's perspective it is equally vital that the artist is seen to have been properly advised. A prudent record company will insist that there is clear evidence that the artist has been independently advised. For example, if the manager's lawyer deals with the matter on behalf of the artist the record company may wish to be satisfied that, whilst the lawyer concerned also acts for the manager, the lawyer has taken his instructions directly from the artist, or has at least explained the nature and content of the contract directly to the artist.

the IMF handbook a guide to professional band management

If the record company is particularly prudent then it will strive to ensure that there is genuine negotiation. This need not mean that the company has to make concessions that it is unwilling to provide but it does mean that they should avoid the approach of refusing to negotiate and of merely adopting the 'take it or leave it' approach. One particularly irritating habit adopted by some record companies is refusing even to attempt to justify a particular provision but simply insisting upon its inclusion in the contract on the basis that it is 'company policy'. The prudent record company will at least try to explain why it insists upon a particular provision.

Since it is equally important for both record company and artist that the artist is properly advised, most record companies will agree to pay the artist's legal fees, in whole or at least in part (although usually on the basis that this is to be treated as a further advance against royalties).

lessons

Record companies have learned many lessons from cases of restraint of trade. They try to safeguard their recording agreements from attack as far as possible. One major criticism often raised against recording contracts is their excessive duration. Whereas the majors used to ask for a total of seven or eight albums (sometimes as many as nine or ten), after the decisions in the cases of Holly Johnson and Stone Roses this crept down to five or six. Sony, however, held firm and continued generally to ask for eight. In the light of the decision in the George Michael case they will presumably continue to ask for this number. If a company insists on a maximum of six albums, they have probably been advised that demanding more would be too risky. If they were confident of justifying options for seven or eight albums they would no doubt insist on them.

THE CONTRACT

the term

long-term contracts

As explained earlier, most UK majors ask for up to five or, more usually, six albums when signing new artists, and Sony may call for more. When signing on their home territory, US record companies still tend to ask for seven or eight albums, although elsewhere – in Germany, France and Scandinavia, for example – there is less obsession with long-term contracts. One advantage in signing with an indie is that their contracts are usually less demanding, particularly in terms of duration. An indie may be prepared to conclude a deal for just one record, or with a very limited number of options. The artist generally needs the contract to last long enough to ensure that the record company is reasonably committed, but not as long that the record company can artistically or financially stifle his career.

development deals

In many cases, the record company will not be prepared to commit immediately to financing an album. Instead, it may ask for one or two singles, with the right to call for sufficient additional material to comprise an album. This type of agreement is often called a development deal, and they are generally unsatisfactory for artists. Whilst the company will not be obliged to continue beyond the release of the singles, it may nevertheless insist upon options for up to five or six albums, for example. Accordingly, the artist is entering into a potentially very long-term commitment, with only a limited level of commitment from the company in return. The artist signed to a development deal may also suffer from inordinate delays. In order to explain the causes of these delays, we first need to describe how the term of a typical recording agreement is structured.

extension periods

In a six-album deal, to use an example, the artist will usually be contracted to stay with the company for an initial contract period of one year. This is followed by five further successive option periods of one year each. The record company alone may decide in each case whether to exercise its option and so enter into each subsequent contract period. On the face of it, if all options are exercised the contract continues for six years. This might sometimes be referred to as a six-year deal, but would usually (and more accurately) be referred to as a six-album deal. This description is more accurate due to the 'extension' provisions. Each contract period will run for twelve months or, if longer, until a set period following delivery (or, more usually, release) of the album recorded during that contract period. In the first contract period, the recording of the album does not usually begin until the agreement has been signed. The recording process is then often lengthy, and once the completed album has been delivered to the record company there will be a further delay before it is released, often (particularly in the case of a major company) due to crowded release schedules.

As well as delays incurred by the production process, marketing and promotion campaigns have also become more sophisticated. Accordingly, lead-in times (the period between delivery and release) have become longer. It may be sensible to avoid the release of an album during August, when everybody is away on holiday, or during November and December, when there is a deluge of releases competing for the Christmas market. Generally, there is a delay of perhaps three to six months after delivery before the album is released.

The contract may provide for a further period of extension of as much as a further six months, following the album's release. This gives the record company time to evaluate the album's success before deciding whether or not to exercise the option for the next period. The problem may be worse in later option periods, when recording will not begin until after the option has been exercised. Only then will money be made available for recording. Also, the artist may still have outstanding touring commitments in relation to the promotion of the previous album, before he begins writing and recording the next album. For all of these reasons a typical album cycle might be around two years in the making, so a six-album deal might therefore take twelve years to fulfil.

delays

A development deal may be structured on the basis that, during the first contract period, only one single is to be delivered. The record company may then have an option to enter into a further contract period, during which perhaps the artist must deliver a second single. Only then might the record company be obliged to decide whether or not to commit to a third period, during which the first album would be recorded. The artist might record two singles only to find that the record company does not wish to continue. Meanwhile, as a result of the extension provisions, there might have been a delay of perhaps a year or two. This is why, for the artist, development deals are generally to be avoided if possible. A preferable alternative is to persuade the record company to finance the production of some high-quality demos without the benefit of a formal contract. If both sides are pleased with the resulting recordings then a record deal may be negotiated, with a proper level of commitment on both sides. At this point the record company is exposed to some degree, because the artist may try to use the demos to 'wind-up' the deal by fishing for interest from other companies. However, a pragmatic company may be prepared to adopt this approach if it is confident that it is far ahead of its competitors and in a better position to build a relationship with the artist.

recording contracts

how many options?

The artist should restrict the company to as few options as possible, although there may be a temptation to attach more significance to other aspects of the recording agreement, perhaps the advances and royalties. In fact, the difference between a five-album and a six-album deal may be very significant. The option for the second album is not exercised in the majority of recording contracts, and even when it is the option for the third album may not be. As a general rule, the delivery of a third album will demonstrate that the artist has achieved some real success. By then he should be a recognised talent with a secure sales base. In some cases, of course, a first album will be so successful that the artist will more or less immediately achieve significant wealth and status. Conversely, an artist about to record his fourth album may be perceived as successful, but although he may have benefited from a number of substantial advances his royalty income might not yet have begun to flow.

The artist about to deliver his third album may wish to flex his muscles at around this stage and attempt to re-negotiate his deal. At the point at which the record company wants a fourth album, the artist will find it more difficult to secure significant improvements if the company can still call for a maximum of six or more albums. The task of re-negotiation would be far easier if the deal were for only five.

In summary, then, if a record deal is not going to survive beyond the first few albums then it doesn't matter whether the maximum number of albums allowed for is five, ten or any other number. However, if a contract survives beyond three albums (at which point the stakes are higher all around), then every extra album for the company wins it perhaps two more years before it may have to give the artist improved terms.

product commitment

artistic standards

As we have seen, the artist may have to deliver up to five or six albums. Generally, the albums must be studio rather than live recordings, and the company will want to set a minimum standard. At worst, for the artist, the company will be entitled to reject any recordings which the company, in its absolute discretion, decides are *commercially* unsatisfactory – whatever that means! Ideally, for the artist, the record company's right to reject master recordings should only apply if they are *technically* unsatisfactory for records to be made from them. A suitable compromise is usually found.

additional material

The company may also acquire the right to insist upon a minimum number of additional tracks for use as B-sides. An album used to be defined as a minimum of ten tracks with a minimum playing time of around 30 minutes. With the advent of CDs, however, an artist now has to deliver a minimum of around twelve tracks (plus additional B-sides, if required) with a minimum playing time of perhaps 40 or 45 minutes. All of this is of particular significance to the artist if the advances to be paid are expressed as inclusive of any recording costs (see 'After The Deal', later in this chapter).

two albums firm

Sometimes a record company will agree to two albums firm. This means that the company does not have an option for a second album but instead commits to it from the outset. A company will only agree to this very reluctantly, and usually only in the face of fierce competition from other companies for an artist. On the face of it, two albums firm represents a victory for the artist; it shows real commitment from the record company. It shows that the company is taking a long-term view and is prepared to proceed with the second album, even if the first flops.

However, in some respects a two album firm commitment can be a double-edged sword. If the company loses interest after the first album the artist is nevertheless exclusively contracted for a significant further period. The record company may become obstructive in recording the second album or, perhaps worse, may allow it to be recorded but then put no effort into its promotion. Arguably, the artist might have been better off if the company had committed to only one album and refrained from exercising its option for the second. This would have left the artist free to pursue his career elsewhere, although this is less of an option today, when record deals are more than usually difficult to come by. That said, when a record company loses interest the usual outcome is a negotiated settlement of some kind. The artist is released from the contract and is paid a reduced sum of money in return for agreeing that the company no longer has to pay the advance and recording costs for the second album. The company might also be paid an 'override' (ie a royalty of perhaps 2% or 3% on subsequent sales of that album) by the artist's new record company. On occasions, and as part of any settlement, the artist may be given copyright in the masters for the first album.

greatest hits and live albums

On some rare occasions, a greatest hits album may qualify as a product commitment album. For example, the company may agree to restrict the deal to five studio albums rather than six, on the basis that in addition to the five studio albums the company will be entitled, after a given period, to compile and release a greatest hits album. This would represent a victory of sorts for the artist because, in reality, this means that he has to deliver only five albums rather than six. Ordinarily, the record company not only owns all of the material but it also has unrestricted rights of exploitation. In practice, a company rarely accepts any restriction on its ability to release a greatest hits album.

Similarly (but again only rarely) a company may accept that one of the albums to be delivered will be a live album. Ordinarily, if a live album is recorded the company automatically acquires exclusive rights to it, without any reduction of the minimum product commitment and without any obligation on the part of the company to pay any advance for it, or even to release it.

exclusions

Recording agreements are invariably exclusive. If the artist records additional material beyond the contracted minimum product commitment, the record company will own all of the additional material. Most recording agreements contain limitations upon this exclusivity. For example, the artist may normally undertake session work (within defined limits) and may record TV and radio broadcasts, provided that the companies concerned undertake not to exploit those recordings by any means other than broadcast. Established bands may negotiate a deal which relates solely to recordings made by the band itself, leaving the individual members to pursue solo projects outside the scope of the deal. Record companies are very nervous of this arrangement, and if they have to agree to important limitations of this kind they will always insist that any solo or other work performed outside the band must not interfere with the band's promotional activities, and that release dates must be carefully monitored.

Record contracts do not normally extend to the artist's separate activities as a record producer or engineer but, given the increasing confusion between performance and production in some areas of contemporary music, provisions are sometimes included which limit the extent to which an artist may work as a record producer for third parties.

territory

worldwide deals

When a major signs a new artist, the company's right to manufacture and sell his records will invariably extend worldwide. In special circumstances, however, particular territories may be excluded. For example, a non-UK artist launching his worldwide career from the UK may already have recording arrangements in place in his home territory, or an artist moving to a major from an indie may have granted rights in future recordings to overseas licensees. The territories in question are simply not available to the major.

restricted territory deals

Majors do not like to give up any territory, not only because they will lose profits from sales in the excluded territory but also because the company will be at risk, throughout its territory, from imports of records coming from the excluded territory. In practice, the excluded territory will often be the USA and Canada, which account for more than one third of worldwide record sales. For that reason alone, most artists aspire to success there and record companies do not want to give up their rights there. An artist may wish to exclude North America because he thinks that his company's US affiliate is either inept or is likely to dismiss the artist's talents, and believes that the UK company has little or no influence over its US affiliate. If so, the artist may prefer to achieve success elsewhere before concluding a deal directly with a US-based company which likes his work. Split-territory deals of this kind will give rise to separate streams of income. If the artist recoups in one territory he will enjoy royalty income from that territory, whereas if the deal were for the world then the accrued royalties from the recouped territory would be used to recoup generally. This practice is investigated more fully later in this chapter.

interaction

Split-territory deals are complex, for a number of reasons. Release dates have to be co-ordinated to reduce the problem of imports, and usually all distributors want to use the same artwork. There would also be no sense in each company making its promotional own video. Therefore, if the world is divided into two or more separate territories, then in addition to negotiating the two recording agreements a separate agreement is needed between the artist and both of the record companies, regulating dealings between them. The legal fees involved in setting up these arrangements can also prove to be very expensive.

A less attractive alternative for the artist is to have a right of approval over the identity of the record company's US licensee. Most majors would only give such discretion between the various US labels owned by that major.

Ultimately, an artist has to be in an exceptional negotiating position to secure a split-territory deal, and usually has to be in a strong position even to secure a right of approval over the US licensee.

creative issues

approval rights

The issues of most concern to the artist are usually the selection of songs, the choice of producer and studios, the quality of mixing and remixing, and control over artwork, photographs and videos, including the quality of the storyboard and the identity of the video's director and producer. An artist might look for other approval rights over financial matters rather than creative issues. For example, since all recording costs and at least a proportion of promotional video costs will be recouped from his royalties, it follows that the artist should ideally have a right of approval over recording and video budgets, along with any other expenditure which can be recouped.

control

There are four basic alternatives:

- The record company has complete control.

- The record company has control, subject to an obligation to consult with the artist.

- Both parties must agree upon the matters in question (perhaps on the basis that, in the event of a stalemate, the company and the artist have an alternate casting vote).

- The artist has complete control.

Most agreements contain a mixture of these four alternatives. A new artist is unlikely to achieve complete control, and would normally be happy with a mix of consultation rights and, in key areas, mutual approval.

the IMF handbook a guide to professional band management

the record company's obligations

one sided?

Recording contracts issued by majors now stretch to 60 or 70 pages. About a third of the agreement is taken up with financial provisions, most of which deal with the various means by which the artist's basic royalty is reduced, as we will discover later. The bulk of the contract is for the company's benefit. It imposes obligations on and extracts warranties (legally-binding promises) from the artist. Beyond the obligation to pay an advance and possibly some royalties, at some future time, it is difficult to find anything in the document which imposes any obligation on the company.

release commitments

That said, however, most recording agreements now include a release commitment of some kind. This would appear to favour the artist, but this can be deceptive. Record companies rarely agree to a positive commitment to release a particular record in a particular territory within a given period. A company would probably give such a commitment only for a record which has already been made, and for which there is an obvious market. In such a case, there is little benefit to the artist in securing a binding release commitment because commercial reality will ensure that the record is released in any event. The main reason for the release commitment is to satisfy the company's concern that, without it, there might be a stronger argument that the agreement constitutes an unreasonable restraint of trade. Courts do not look favourably upon an exclusive recording contract which does not contain an obligation to make the artist's work available to the public.

Most release commitments are not 'positive' commitments, and indeed are more often negative in terms of the benefits they accord to the artist. Typically, release obligations relate only to the UK, apply only to minimum-commitment albums (and not singles), and provide that the album must be released within a specified time – for example, within six months of delivery. If the company fails to release within that period, the artist may serve a 'cure' notice, which gives the company a further period, perhaps 60 days, in which to release the album. If the company has still failed to release the album by the end of the cure period, then usually the artist's only remedy is to serve a further notice on the company terminating the contract. In other words, the artist will no longer be obliged to record for the company. Since the company has persistently refused to release the album this usually would not cause the company any difficulty. Moreover, all rights in the unreleased album would still rest with the company.

reversion

In order to make release obligations more effective, the artist should try to shorten the periods involved and ensure that, if the right of termination arises, copyright in the unreleased album automatically reverts to him. This in itself is difficult to achieve, but the company may agree to it, either on repayment of all or part of the recording costs and/or in return for a small royalty (an 'override') on any subsequent sales of the album through a third party.

overseas releases

In practical terms, disputes are more likely to arise over the company's failure to release a particular record overseas, especially in North America. Even a successful artist may have difficulty in securing a release in the US. The reality is that the US is such a large market that the costs involved in breaking a new artist there are much greater than elsewhere. Artists have to compete with both American artists and other foreign artists for the limited promotion and marketing resources of the US affiliate, who may not wish to prioritise the artist. The UK company, which must grant rights to its US affiliate, may have no real influence over the extent to which the US affiliate exploits those rights, or even if it exploits them at all.

territorial reversions

It is therefore important that the artist tries to secure a positive commitment of some kind for the release of his records, not only in the US and Canada but also in all other major territories. Ideally, if the company fails to release in any overseas territory then all rights for that territory should revert to the artist, including the rights for all future recordings along with those for the unreleased album. This is very difficult to obtain and is in any event problematic because the company has usually already secured worldwide rights, on the basis that it makes and pays for all of the recordings. They have a natural reluctance to give up copies of the masters to the artist or to some other record company in another territory. This would give rise to difficulties over the appropriate level of contribution towards recording costs and other practical matters. Often, the best that can be achieved is a provision by which the artist can compel his record company to license another company to release the album in any territory in which its regular licensee is unwilling to

the IMF handbook a guide to professional band management

do so. Even this is not always possible, as the internal licensing arrangements between the affiliates of a major may not easily permit the grant of a licence to anyone outside the major's own group. Moreover, if this arrangement is accepted, the company is likely to insist upon some reduction in royalties, particularly if the royalty paid by the licensee is less than the artist's royalty for sales in that territory plus a reasonable profit margin for the company.

is a release commitment worth having?

The trend has been for release commitments to become more convoluted and of less practical relevance. The ability to force a company to release a record is of questionable value. Releasing a record is one thing, but marketing and promoting it in a positive manner is quite another. Many release provisions benefit the record company rather than the artist by limiting its exposure in the event of non-release.

marketing and promotion

It is difficult to persuade any record company to give a precise commitment on marketing and promotion. A company will sometimes agree to use 'all reasonable endeavours to exploit', but this is fairly meaningless. What the artist needs, but rarely receives, is a commitment that the company will spend a minimum sum on direct marketing and promotional expenses. A company will sometimes agree to appoint independent promoters to support a record, and may commit to spending a minimum amount on this. Beyond this, a company might commit to a minimum number of promotional videos, perhaps one or two for each album, in accordance with an agreed budget. A company might also accept a contractual commitment to provide a certain amount of 'tour support' (ie to make good the shortfall of expenditure over income from an approved promotional tour). However, even if tour support is paid the company will insist on numerous rights of approval. Tour support is normally treated as a further advance, 100% recoupable from the artist's royalties.

ownership

copyright

Almost without exception, the company owns copyright in the artist's recordings for the full period of copyright, which lasts for 50 years from first release. This feature of recording agreements reflects the perhaps outdated view that an artist's work is effectively available for outright purchase, an approach traditionally taken in music publishing. 20 years ago it was still common for writers to grant copyright in all songs to the publisher for the full life of copyright, which in the case of any song is now for the life of the composer plus a further 70 years. This is now unusual.

you pay, we own

The record company's position is difficult to justify when coupled with the practice of recouping all recording costs from the artist's royalty. Provided that sufficient records are sold, the company recoups its recording costs by deduction from the artist's royalties. The practice of insisting upon outright ownership of copyright is seen by many (and certainly by the IMF) as an abuse of power on the part of the record companies. The IMF is campaigning vigorously on behalf of its members and the recording artists which they represent to end this practice.

reversion of copyright

A very successful artist may eventually succeed in obtaining reversion of the copyright in his recordings to him. This would rarely be granted by way of concession, and would normally be conceded only reluctantly in a re-negotiation. In effect, the artist pays a price for the reversion of copyright, usually in the form of an agreement to record more material for the company.

restrictions

The artist may succeed in imposing restrictions on how the record company's rights may be exercised. The company is more likely to grant concessions to the artist over artistic matters than marketing. Artistic control was investigated earlier in this chapter (see 'Creative Issues'), while marketing control is investigated below.

artwork

The artist will often require the right of approval over any artwork. Usually the record company will pay the costs for originating all artwork on a non-recoupable basis. In the absence of any agreement to the contrary, the company will own the artwork, although the artist may nevertheless have a right of approval. In other cases, the artist will insist on the right to originate artwork, in which case he may own the artwork. Sometimes the company will pay the origination costs up to an agreed budget but nevertheless accept that the artist owns any available rights.

the IMF handbook a guide to professional band management

The artist will then grant the company a licence to use it for the promotion and sale of his recordings. This leaves the artist free to exploit the artwork for other purposes (on T-shirts and other merchandise, for example) without having to seek approval from the record company. Companies may sometimes refuse to allow an artist to make use of its artwork for merchandising unless the artist pays all or part of the origination costs. In some cases, record companies insist on a share of any merchandising profits resulting from the use of their designs, although this is now rare.

If an outside designer is commissioned or a freelance photographer is used, a clear assignment of copyright should be obtained. If this is not done, copyright in the artwork will remain with the creator. The artist and record company will have only an implied licence to use the artwork for its intended purpose on the record's packaging. Further consents may be required before it is possible to use the artwork for merchandising or other purposes.

marketing restrictions

The record company may agree to seek the artist's prior written consent to certain acts, such as the deletion of his records from the company's catalogue less than, say, two or three years after release; the release of his records on a different label; the recoupling of certain tracks with other recordings on compilation albums and the like; the use of his recordings as premiums, whereby his records are given away as an incentive to purchase another product (see the section on 'Money' later in this chapter); the granting of any synchronisation licence to use a recording in a TV advert or film; or, perhaps more importantly, before selling his albums at less than full price before, say, one or two years after initial release. Whilst some restrictions are useful, the artist should be cautious of imposing unnecessary restrictions, and in theory the record company will know best how to market his recordings. Problems often arise after an artist leaves his record company, when his new company's carefully-planned marketing campaign might be damaged by his previous company's re-release of earlier material. Accordingly, the artist may seek to impose restrictions on the release, or the frequency of release, of any greatest hits albums. However, these problems may be exaggerated – the activities of an artist's previous record company are unlikely to seriously damage the new company's efforts to release his material, and sometimes any increase in sales of an artist's back catalogue will produce additional income for him at such a time when he is likely to be unrecouped with his new company.

group provisions

leaving members

Any group recording agreement will include leaving-member provisions. These tend to be controversial because they are very restrictive, and are increasingly complex. Because of these provisions, an artist who signs a deal as a member of a group may find that, even after he has left the group, he is still tied to the record company. Despite their restrictive nature, record companies are confident that these clauses are reasonable. No sensible company, they argue, would invest substantial sums of money in a group without protection if the group splits up. No recording agreement compels a group of artists to remain together, but if the group disbands, or a member leaves, the company insists upon the right to continue with the leaving members, and retains complete flexibility. It may continue with the remaining members and drop the leaving member, it may drop the remaining members and continue only with the leaving member, it may continue with all members, or it may even drop all members entirely. If the group disbands, all members are then treated as leaving members and the company may continue with all or any of them. If a band splits acrimoniously and the company wants to continue with all members, this may give rise to a conflict of interest in that two warring factions will be competing for priority in terms of recording budgets, release schedules and promotion and marketing budgets. In practice the company will usually agree to release one side from the contract, usually in return for a payment of some kind. This is often financed by a new record company and may be coupled with an override royalty on sales of that artist's subsequent recordings.

cross recoupment

The artist should try to ensure that, if the company exercises a leaving-member option, any royalties payable to the leaving member may be used to recoup only the leaving member's share of any unrecouped balance on the group's royalty account at the time of his departure. The leaving member will probably have to concede that his share of royalties from group recordings on which he performs may be used towards recoupment of any advance (or other recoupable sums) paid under his new leaving-member contract.

leaving member's commitment

Ordinarily, a leaving-member contract will be on the same terms as the existing group contract for the balance of the commitment then outstanding. If the member leaves after four albums have been recorded under a six-album deal then the leaving-member contract should cover only two albums. The company may argue that as it now has to invest in a new project it needs the protection of a higher minimum number of albums, but the artist should resist this. The company may also try to insist that a lower royalty rate should apply for any leaving member, although again, whilst this used to be common practice it is now usually successfully resisted.

solo work

A band member may also work as a solo artist separately from his commitments as a member of the group. A recording agreement will rarely include separate provisions dealing with a solo commitment unless a particular group member has a specific project in mind when the deal is being negotiated. A group member may be required to leave the group if he is determined to pursue a particular project, a move which involves the risk of being dropped by the record company and then failing to secure a deal elsewhere.

controlled compositions

back to basics

Most recording agreements contain what are known as 'controlled compositions' clauses. These are the components of the recording agreement which interlock with the publishing arrangements of those artists who write and compose their own material. The purpose of controlled compositions clauses is to reduce the mechanical (ie publishing) royalties paid by the record company for the use of the artist's own compositions.

Before explaining controlled compositions clauses in more detail, we must first look at the differences between recording and publishing. Every recording contains at least two copyright works: firstly, copyright in the recording itself, which is normally owned by the record company; and secondly, there are separate copyrights in the music and the lyrics of the song featured on the recording, which are owned in the first place by the writers of the music and words of the song. If the writer has entered into a publishing contract then usually, under the terms of the publishing agreement, he assigns copyright in the words and music of his material to the music publisher.

mechanical licences

Each time the record company manufactures a CD or some other format it reproduces, the music and lyrics of the song. Unless that reproduction is authorised, this will amount to an infringement of copyright in the song. The record company must therefore obtain permission from the owner of the copyright in the song for it to be featured on the record. This permission is known as a mechanical licence because it allows the record company to reproduce the song by mechanical means. There is a set rate for a mechanical licence, which has been negotiated between organisations representing publishers and record companies. In most European countries the rate paid by the record company to the owner of the copyright in the song (which is usually the music publisher) is 9.306% of the dealer price of the record, although in the UK the lower rate of 8.5% applies.

availability of licence

Recording agreements always include a warranty from the artist that the publisher will grant the record company a mechanical licence on standard terms for every song used on recordings made under the agreement. The artist should take care that this warranty does not extend to songs written by other people, particularly if the record company has chosen the material.

the USA and Canada

The position is more complicated for records manufactured in the USA and Canada. Outside these territories it does not matter how many songs are used on an album because the total liability for mechanical royalty will be the same: the appropriate percentage of the dealer price of the record. On a 20-track album, each song will receive a payment equal to half of that which would be paid for a track on a ten-track album – the record company's liability remains the same. In North America, the mechanical royalty is not calculated as a percentage of the price of the record: instead record companies pay a fixed fee per song. The US Copyright Tribunal increases the per song rate from time to time, partly in response to rises in inflation, and the rate at the time of writing is 7.1c per song. This arrangement gives rise to two problems for record companies: firstly, it means that an album with an unusually large number of songs will attract too high a mechanical royalty payment; secondly, many record companies think that the US per song rate is too high. US record companies have decided that they should only have to pay 75% of the statutory per song rate. Accordingly, US record companies use controlled compositions clauses to oblige the artist to grant mechanical licences of his own works at 75% of the statutory rate. These clauses usually also limit the company's liability to a maximum of ten times the reduced per song rate for any album, no matter how many songs are used on that album. Although this problem only affects North America, record companies outside North America insist on controlled compositions clauses so that they can comply with their obligations to their North American licensees.

the publisher

The artist's publisher, if he has one, must approve the controlled compositions clauses before the record deal is signed; otherwise, if the publisher later refuses to accept them then the artist will be in breach of the recording agreement, which will normally give the record company the right to claw back any excess mechanical royalties from payments otherwise due to the artist. Understandably, publishers are very sensitive about controlled compositions clauses, because they are intended specifically to reduce their income. Of course, major publishers are affiliated to major record companies and perhaps as a result their criticisms are tempered. A ritual dance has developed whereby the artist (or his lawyer) sends the controlled compositions clauses to his publisher and asks for confirmation that the publisher will comply with them, at which point the publisher often expresses outrage at the idea of a reduced rate of mechanical royalty and seeks numerous amendments to the clauses. Depending on the flexibility of the record company, the publisher may sometimes improve the provisions. He may also insist on dealing with the record company directly, but usually any dialogue between the publisher and record company will be conducted through the artist's lawyer. After all of this huffing and puffing, the publisher will accept the controlled compositions clauses – no publisher will run the risk of being responsible for the failure of negotiations over a record deal.

Some record companies agree to pay more than 75%, even for new artists, while successful artists should expect to secure 100% at some stage, and of course some companies are more flexible than others. Sometimes a built-in escalation may be agreed upon, so that the rate improves from 75% to 85%, for example, after a given number of sales in the USA and then perhaps to 100% when a higher level is reached. Since CDs now tend to carry more than ten tracks it is sometimes possible to agree a restriction of around twelve times the per song rate for CDs rather than ten, although not for cassettes. Most controlled compositions clauses attempt to set the per song rate at that in effect when the master is first delivered, while the publisher will wish to apply the rate in force at the time of manufacture of the record.

recording contracts

MONEY

overview

the basic royalty system

Under the system used by the majors, the company pays for everything and assumes all financial risk, although certain expenses are recouped from the artist's royalties. The artist never has to pay money back to the company from his own pocket, but recoupment forms a very significant part of the calculation of the payments to be made to the artist. A common misconception is that recoupment has something to do with profit, while the truth is that the point at which recoupment occurs is different to that at which the company begins to make a profit.

recoupable expenditure

So what is recouped from the artist's royalty, and how is this calculated? The artist will be entitled to a royalty for each record sold. The calculation of the per unit royalty is complex (see the section on 'Royalties' later in this chapter). Assume that the royalty for each album sold is £1. If the company sells 100,000 albums then the artist is owed £100,000 in royalties. The company will first recoup from this any advances previously paid to the artist and any other recoupable expenditure. Recording costs are always recoupable but manufacturing and distribution expenses are not, and ordinarily neither are marketing and promotional expenses. However, a number of grey areas have been identified.

what is recoupable?

RECORDING COSTS

Recording costs are fully recoupable and the recording agreement will include a wide definition of such costs, which will extend to studio costs, musicians' fees, equipment hire, travel and accommodation expenses, producers' fees and so on, along with cutting and mastering costs. But where does the recording process end? One such grey area is the extent to which mixing costs incurred after delivery of the finished master should be treated as a recoupable recording cost. Some companies and artists like to release many different mixes of a particular single. Arguably, this is more in the nature of a marketing exercise, and so the costs involved should be borne by the company on a non-recoupable basis. An artist very rarely achieves this, however, and usually the best he can do is restrict the company's ability to recoup remix costs from royalties which accrue in relation to that particular remix.

REMIXING COSTS

As well as marketing exercises of that kind, record companies often also spend substantial sums on mixing and remixing an album, even before any of the material is released, and again these costs are recoupable. As a limited means of protection an artist should try to secure a right of approval over the budget for any remixing.

PROMOTIONAL VIDEO COSTS

Promotional costs incurred by a company are as a rule non-recoupable, although the company will argue that promotional video costs all under the umbrella of recording costs, which are recoupable. The usual compromise is that 50% of video costs are recoupable from the artist's record royalties. The company will invariably insist that any video costs which are unrecouped (including the 50% which is not recoupable from record royalties) may be recouped from video royalties. The opportunities to profit from videos are generally limited to the release of compilation videos, video jukebox payments and broadcasting. The recoupment provisions ensure that the artist is unlikely ever to receive any income from the exploitation of promotional video material.

INDEPENDENT PROMOTION COSTS

An artist may try to persuade the company to use independent promoters, although many companies will resist this because they will already have their own in-house promotion teams and will not wish to incur the extra expense of hiring outside promoters, and they will in all likelihood insist that some or all of the costs are recoupable. Independent promotion, however, is sometimes the only means of ensuring that a new release is given sufficient priority and is worked hard enough. US companies tend not to have strong in-house promotion teams, and some cynics assume that this is because it would not be seemly for a record company employee to do some of the things which promotion teams have to do in order to help break a new record. It is difficult in the US to break a new artist without liberal use of independent promoters, and US independent promoters are particularly expensive. The pressure to use independent promoters will often come from the artist or his manager, but the record company will often turn this pressure back on the artist or manager by insisting on their right to recoup all such expenditure.

recording contracts

TOUR SUPPORT

There will also often be pressure from the artist or manager for the company to provide tour support, which is again considered to be a promotional expense. The artist would not be touring at a loss (which is what gives rise to the need for tour support), except to promote record sales. At one time tour support payments tended to be 50% recoupable, but in recent years the trend has been to insist that 100% of any such payment is recoupable.

TELEVISION ADVERTISING

Most recording contracts allow the record company to decide on whether it wishes to spend money on television advertising. The usual arrangement is that such expenditure is non-recoupable, but the company will claw back all or part of the costs by reducing the royalty payable on sales promoted by the advertising campaign (see the section on 'TV Advertising' later in this chapter). A trend has recently developed in that companies will pay full royalties in the ordinary way but will instead insist on treating all or part of advertising costs (often only 50%) as recoupable.

profit shares

The alternative to the basic royalty system is the profit sharing system. Of course no major would be interested in sharing its profits, but most indies adopt this approach. Again, the indie will pay for everything and assumes all of the financial risk, but in this case the relationship between the indie and the artist is more of a joint venture. The artist supplies his talent, the indie provides its resources and they split any profits, usually 50/50. This system bears no relation to the basic royalty system, and so they are difficult to compare.

Under the profit-sharing system, an artist may be offered 50% of the net profits from an indie with no advance beyond that for actual recording costs, whereas a major company might offer a traditional royalty deal of, for example, 18% of the dealer price of each record sold and an advance of £50,000, exclusive of recording costs. Even if the artist knows exactly how many of his records the indie is likely to sell in comparison with the major, it will not be possible for him to calculate in advance which of the deals is more financially attractive, as this will depend on the amount of recoupable expenditure spent by the major and on the total expenses incurred by the indie. The equation would also have to take into account the cost-effectiveness of the indie's manufacturing and distribution arrangements.

In working out profits, the indie deducts all expenditure from its total receipts from the exploitation of the recordings, including recording costs, remixing costs, mechanical royalties, manufacturing costs, artwork origination costs, promotion, advertising, marketing costs, distribution fees and any other costs directly related to the recordings. Only the indie's own overhead costs are excluded.

a practical example: profit share versus royalty

Using the example in the paragraph above, and giving ourselves the benefit of hindsight, let us investigate which deal is financially better for the artist, in relation to a particular album. We will make the following assumptions:

- Recording costs are £50,000. Indies are normally more sparing about recording costs, but for this example assume that the costs would have been the same amount either way.

- The album sells 100,000 copies. The major might argue that, given its resources and more efficient distribution arrangements, it would expect to sell more than the indie, but for the sake of simplicity we will ignore this.

- The dealer price is £7 (excluding VAT). Based on early 1999 prices, the dealer price of a full-price cassette album would be around £6.99 and the dealer price of a full-price CD would be around £8.89, but for this exercise we will assume an average of £7.

- After taking into account packaging allowances and other provisions for royalty mitigation, and after deducting any share of the royalty payable to the producer, the royalty offered by the major averages out between the different formats at, let us say, £1 per unit. (For the sake of simplicity we will ignore the fact that singles will probably also have been released from the album, which would also affect the royalty position.)

- The indie receives only £4 of the £7 dealer price after the deduction of a £2 distribution fee and £1 for manufacturing and printing costs.

- The indie spends £20,000 on marketing and other allowable expenses.

- The total mechanical royalties on 100,000 album sales amounts to, let us say, £50,000.

- Video costs are £20,000 (ignoring the fact that the major would normally make a bigger budget available for this than the indie would).

Based on these assumptions, the indie would receive the £7 dealer price less the manufacturing and distribution costs of £3, making £4 per album. On sales of 100,000, its total income would be £400,000, but out of this it would have to recover £140,000 of expenditure (recording costs, copyright royalties, marketing and video costs), leaving £260,000. On a 50/50 split, the artist would receive £130,000.

How would the artist fare with the major? At £1 per unit the artist would earn £100,000 royalties on 100,000 sales, which would be set against £110,000 of total recoupable expenditure (comprising the £50,000 advance, 50% of the £20,000 video costs and £50,000 recording costs). The artist's royalty account would therefore still be unrecouped by the value of £10,000. Accordingly, in this example, the artist would eventually receive £130,000 from the indie but from the major he would receive only the £50,000 up-front advance.

This example serves to illustrate the differences between the two systems. However, you should not read too much into the result. The first point a major would make in response to this example is that, for a new artist seeking mainstream success, the marketing and promotion costs will often be enormous. Under the traditional royalty system most of those costs would be classed as non-recoupable, and so borne entirely by the record company, whereas even if the indie could afford to meet that level of costs they would all be taken into account in determining the net profits.

If he were paid 50% of the company's net profits from the sale of his records, an established artist signed to a major would certainly expect to earn more in this way than if he were paid even a particularly high rate of royalty under the traditional system. It it is important to bear in mind, however, that 50% of the major's net profits would probably be greater than 50% of the indie's net profits from the same sales because the costs incurred by the indie will normally be far higher. The major will have be able to use its own distribution network, for example, and it will have to pay only modest distribution fees to its affiliated distribution company. Indies, on the other hand, will generally have to pay higher distribution fees to their distributors (which can be anything between 15% and 35% of the dealer price).

A deal for a 50/50 split of net profits clearly means that profits are divided in the ratio of 1:1. Typically, under the traditional royalty system, profits are likely to be divided in a ratio nearer 2:1 or even 3:1 in the record company's favour.

the IMF handbook a guide to professional band management

who takes what?

Let us look at the cost structure from a different angle. What happens to the money paid by the customer in the record shop? A full-price CD album might sell for £14.99. The dealer has to account to HM Customs and Excise for VAT, which at the current rate of 17.5% (at the time of writing) is £2.62, leaving the dealer with £12.37. The PPD (Published Price to Dealer) of the record might be £8.45, exclusive of VAT. If a dealer has multiple stores, such as Woolworths and WH Smith, the dealer will have sufficient clout to secure a substantial discount. (For the purposes of this exercise we will assume discounts of 10% across the board, although they are often far greater.) This means that – ignoring VAT for the moment – the record company receives £7.61, which leaves £4.76 for the dealer.

What happens to the £7.61 received by the record company? The company has to pay a mechanical royalty of 8.5% of the dealer price, which amounts to 64p. If the artist wrote the material on the album, a substantial part of this will find its way back to him because of his publishing deal.

The record company is then left with £6.97. Part of this is paid as a fee to the distributor for physically putting the record in the shop. For a major company, distribution will be undertaken by another company within the same group. A fee will still have to be paid, but it will probably be quite low. For an indie, however, this fee will be quite substantial. Assuming a distribution fee for the indie of 20% of the published dealer price, this amounts to £1.70, leaving the indie with £5.27. If the major only has to pay a distribution fee of 10% of the £8.45 PPD, ie 85p, then it is left with £6.12.

The record company then has to pay the manufacturer for any printing, pressing and duplicating costs. Again, the major may pay less than the indie per unit because of the scale on which they operate, but for this exercise we will assume total manufacturing costs of £1 per unit, both for the major and for the indie, which leaves the major with £5.12 per unit. Out of this the major will have to account to the artist for his royalty, and if we assume a rate of 20% of the dealer price (inclusive of the royalty payable to the producer) after the deduction of a packaging allowance of 25% then the artist will receive £7 x 75% x 20%, which comes to £1.05 (see below for a more detailed explanation of this). This will not come into effect, however, until sales are sufficient to reach recoupment, and so the major will be left with a rate of £5.12 per unit for a good many sales which will then reduce to £4.87 per unit. The indie would be left with £4.27 per unit due to its higher distribution fees, and this would be split with the artist after the deduction of any expenses. If, however, the artist and record company are working under a profit-sharing arrangement then it is difficult to see clearly how the unit price for a particular record might be divided. Under the traditional royalty system, based upon the above example, the breakdown for a full-price CD sold by a major (ignoring the fact that the artist royalty will be available for recoupment and remembering that the artist royalty is usually inclusive of the producer's royalty) is as follows:

Customs and Excise	£ 2.62
Dealer	£ 4.76
Publisher	£ .64
Distributor	£ .85
Manufacturer	£ 1.00
Artist and producer	£ 1.05
Record company	£ 4.07
	£14.99

When analysed in this way, the record company takes nearly four times as much as the artist. However, this is an over-simplistic approach, and after taking into account all of the marketing and promotional expenditure (but ignoring the company's overhead costs) the profit ratio might typically be in the region of 2:1 or, even nearer, 3:1 in favour of the record company – a conclusion supported by the evidence shown in the George Michael case. The record companies argue, of course, that they need to retain profits in this ratio in order to support their substantial overhead costs, including all of the A&R costs written off in the pursuit of unsuccessful artists.

advances

how do they work?

An advance is a pre-payment of royalties, and is recoupable from those royalties. However, it is also non-returnable. Royalties take a long time to work through the system and reach a level sufficient to achieve recoupment. The majority of recording contracts remain unrecouped, and the artist never receives a royalty cheque. Therefore, the safest approach for an artist planning his future finances is always to approach a record deal on the basis that any income will be limited to the contractual advances (although there is a danger of cynicism colouring his judgement – see the section on 'The Watershed' later in this chapter).

costs inclusive?

It is usually preferable for an artist's advances to be exclusive of recording costs so that the record company will pay the recording costs (up to an agreed budget and on a recoupable basis) in addition to the advances stated in the contract. The advantage of this is that the artist can plan and budget his general expenditure. In a long-term record deal, part of the advance for the first album is normally paid on signature and the balance on either the delivery or release of the album, so the date on which the balance of the advance is paid is therefore uncertain. Nevertheless, under a costs-exclusive deal the artist can make sensible financial plans more easily than if the advance includes recording costs. Even though a budget for recording costs may be set, these are notoriously difficult to adhere to. A company will often insist on arranging a costs-inclusive deal even though, when the deal is signed and the advance agreed, neither party has a clear idea of what the recording costs are likely to be.

On the other hand, if the artist has control over the recording process and has developed a degree of skill in producing first-rate recordings at a modest cost (for example, he may have his own home recording studio), there may be an advantage in securing a costs-inclusive deal. The costs-inclusive advance may be greater than the aggregate of any personal advance he might have otherwise obtained, together with any actual recording costs. Of course, if the artist does have his own recording facilities the company may use this as a reason to lower the level of advances which might otherwise have been paid.

how much?

In the mid to late 1980s, most of the UK majors signing new artists usually offered costs-exclusive deals. An advance of £50,000 plus recording costs for a new band's first album would not have been thought particularly generous, and an advance of £100,000 along with recording costs was not at all unusual. In the more hyped cases, advances of £250,000 and upwards (exclusive of recording costs) were paid.

During the recession and post-recession years of the 1990s, the majors adopted a different approach. Their position was affected to some degree by the technological revolution, particularly the advent of digital recording techniques, as a result of which it become no longer quite so common for artists to spend extended periods in expensive commercial recording studios, perhaps at a cost of £1,500 per day or more.

Most deals are now costs inclusive. In the case of an album deal, the advance for the first album might fall in the range of £50,000 to £150,000 (depending in part on the nature of the music and the way in which it is recorded). Of course, occasionally exceptional cases crop up which would fall way outside this suggested range.

The size of any advance is usually determined at least in part by the artist's actual financial requirements – for example, a solo artist might expect a lower advance than a group. However, if the artist's negotiating position is strong then the amount of advance may be determined less by actual need and more by a combination of market forces and the record company's sales forecast.

When negotiating an advance, figures should preferably not be plucked out of the air. The artist or his manager should at least attempt to justify what is asked for. A record company does not expect to support a life of luxury for a new artist but it does have to recognise that basic living costs must be covered. Likewise the manager must also be paid, so his commission should be factored into the overall equation. Beyond this, funds may also be required for equipment, stage clothes and perhaps even a van to carry the equipment, and of course lawyers and accountants also need to be paid. It might even be the case that the lead vocalist would benefit from singing lessons, the fees for which will also have to be paid.

The record company will want to know the publishing situation. If the publishing deal is in place, the record company may suggest that it is unreasonable for the record company to underwrite all of the artist's anticipated expenditure and that the artist should approach his publisher for part of the funding. If no publishing deal is in place, the record company will suggest to the artist that he finds one. If the group has perhaps one principal songwriter, there is the problem in that the songwriter will not wish to allow his publishing income to subsidise the group's recording activities.

cross-recoupment

Essentially, all royalties which accrue under an agreement will be used to recoup all advances. For example, if the first album is an expensive flop but the second album takes off, the company can use royalties from the second album to recoup the costs of the first album as well as those of the second album, and possibly the third and later albums. This concept of cross-recoupment is sometimes referred to as cross-collateralisation.

In some rare cases, the artist may be able to impose restrictions on the company's cross-recoupment rights. For example, if the company has control over the artist's back catalogue and a new deal is structured for future recordings, the company might agree that royalties from the back catalogue will be free flowing and will not be used to recoup advances paid for new recordings. As we have seen, a company may occasionally agree to recoup remix costs only from the remix in question. Sometimes, probably only after a re-negotiation, royalties from a particular territory or territories may be free flowing, or they might be available for recoupment only from advances which are paid specifically in relation to sales in that territory. For leaving members there should be limitations on the company's cross-recoupment rights between the original agreement and any leaving member-agreement (see the section on 'Group Provisions' earlier in this chapter).

associated agreements

Today, none of the majors insist on an artist signing a publishing contract with its publishing affiliate as a condition of entering into a recording contract. Even if the artist signs a publishing contract with an affiliated company by choice there would be no cross-recoupment, except in extraordinary circumstances. For example, perhaps in the context of tax planning arrangements, the record company and the publishing company might be persuaded to pay substantial advances during a particular financial year, but only on the condition that cross-recoupment would apply. Smaller companies, on the other hand, still sometimes insist that an artist signs recording and publishing contracts with related companies, and this should usually be resisted. However, if recording and publishing contracts are signed with the same company, or with affiliated companies, it should be made clear that there is to be no cross-recoupment between them.

royalties

retail or dealer price?

Until a few years ago, most UK record deals provided for the calculation of record royalties on the retail price of records sold. Today, however, most deals provide for record royalties to be calculated on the dealer price. In the distant past, record royalties were calculated on the wholesale or dealer price, but as some record companies also owned record shops there was a feeling that the temptation to fix prices might prove irresistible. The artist's best protection was to have his record royalty calculated on the price at which the record was actually sold to the ultimate customer. With the abolition many years ago of retail price maintenance, and more recently the increasing competitiveness of the retail sector, confusion has developed over the prices at which records are sold by retailers. Even though a company may suggest a retail price, this is usually subjected to fierce discounting. Accordingly, for many years there has been uncertainty over the accuracy of the retail prices used for calculating royalties.

Before the current mechanical royalty rate of 8.5% of dealer price was established by the Copyright Tribunal, the rate was set at 6.25% of the retail price. In order to resolve the uncertainty over retail prices, the MCPS and the BPI agreed on a formula to establish a *notional* retail price by multiplying the dealer price by a fixed percentage. Today this procedure is no longer necessary in the case of mechanical royalties, which are now calculated on the dealer price. (See the section on 'Publishing Income' in chapter six.) Many contracts are still in operation under which record royalties (as opposed to mechanical royalties) are calculated on the retail price. This is now calculated on an 'uplifted' dealer price in a manner similar to that previously adopted by the MCPS and the BPI in relation to the calculation of mechanical royalties. The notional retail price is calculated by multiplying the dealer price usually by something between 125% and 132%. In some agreements, the same result is achieved by calculating royalties on dealer prices but by uplifting the royalty rate by a similar margin.

packaging deductions

All majors insist on perpetuating the ludicrous system whereby royalties are reduced by the application of packaging deductions or allowances. Though described as packaging allowances, they bear no relation to actual packaging costs. Many years ago, when packaging allowances were first introduced (at more modest rates), the companies tried to justify them by arguing that the royalty should attach to the music or the record but not its package. Few companies attempt to justify packaging allowances any more, and most will candidly admit that the allowances are merely artificial reductions. For many years, arguments over packaging allowances often generated ill will between the parties. Since the companies have largely given up on their attempts to justify the allowances artists and their advisers have been more ready to accept them. The general approach now is to accept packaging allowances with a shrug of the shoulders and to concentrate on securing an appropriate rate of royalty, having allowed for the fact that the royalty rate will be reduced by the packaging allowances.

An artist may be entitled to a royalty of say 18% of the dealer price, for example. The record company will insist upon a packaging allowance of usually up to 20% for vinyl discs and cassettes, 25% for CDs and 30% or even 35% for videos. Accordingly, in the case of a CD the 18% royalty is not 18% at all: it is 18% of 75% (ie the dealer price less the 25% packaging allowance). In other words, the royalty rate being offered is 13.5%. The company will not offer 13.5%, and will instead insist on offering 18% of 75%. Very few people are fooled by this, however, and one day one of the majors may decide to adopt a more straightforward approach. However, a company which offers royalty rates which appear at first sight to be 25% lower than the rates it has been offering (and are still being offered by other companies) will appear uncompetitive. Another problem is that certain record companies have given 'favoured nations' protection to certain artists on this issue, which might amount to a guarantee that no new artist signing to the label will receive more favourable treatment on packaging allowances.

returns and net sales

Royalties are not calculated on the number of records manufactured, unlike mechanical royalties. Instead they are payable on net sales (records sold, rather than given away, and not returned). In some territories, notably North America, records are sold on a sale-or-return basis, which means that the dealer can send all or any of them back to the distributor if he is unable to sell them. Records are also sometimes sold on a sale-or-return basis in the UK, but only under exceptional circumstances (for example, when there is an expensive TV advertising campaign and the only way for the distributor to persuade dealers to buy enough stock to meet expected demand is to reassure them that they can return unsold records). However, in the UK there is what is known as a 'returns privilege', under which dealers may return up to 5% of the records distributed to them. A dealer might take five records each from 20 artists on the same label, totalling 100 records. Under the returns privilege he may send back a total of five records. If he chooses to return five records by one artist, that artist suffers 100% returns. As well as this, the dealer may also return faulty records.

Until recently, many companies accounted to the artist only upon 90% of net sales. Using the example of 18% royalty, the effective rate for a CD is in fact 18% x 75% (to allow for the 25% packaging allowance) x 90%, which comes to 12.15%. This practice is said to date back to the days when the old 78rpm shellac records were manufactured. In those days royalties were calculated on 90% of records manufactured, on the rough assumption that 10% broke, a practice which has no relevance today. In any event, net sales will be defined in order to exclude faulty products or returns. Some companies, however (most notably Virgin Records), still generally account on 90% of net sales, as do some US companies.

royalty base price

In order to calculate what an 18% royalty of dealer price is worth we need to establish what is usually referred to as the royalty base price. Although we talk of a royalty on '18% of dealer', this royalty is in fact not calculated on the actual dealer price but rather on an artificial price, which is arrived at by deducting the packaging allowance from the dealer price. In addition, the artist should be aware of the possible impact on the royalty base price of discounts. Ideally, the artist's royalty should be calculated by reference to the published price to dealers, less only the packaging allowance. In some cases, however, the royalty is calculated not on the PPD but on the actual dealer price, after discounts. All distributors have what they refer to as 'file discounts', which are different discounts depending upon the category of dealer involved. Woolworths will command bigger discounts than the independent corner record shop. Ideally, these discounts should not affect the royalty base price.

free goods

A further complication arises because of what is known as the free goods policy. In this instance there is confusion over what is meant by free goods. Sometimes it means records which are given away free for genuine promotional purposes to DJs, reviewers and the like. The artist is not paid a royalty on records donated for these promotional purposes, which might be called 'actual' free goods.

In North America records are distributed on the basis that for every ten albums distributed, say, nine are deemed to be sold and one given away for 'promotional purposes'. Sometimes two albums in ten are given away, and in the case of singles usually at least three in ten are given away. These freebies are known as 'automatic' rather than 'actual' free goods. Automatic free goods, of course, are merely a disguised discount. It would be just the same if all ten records were sold rather than nine, but at a 10% discount. However, if records given are away for free then the artist receives no royalty. This is a separate issue from calculating the percentage of net sales. If a US company pays a 16% royalty on 90% of net sales but gives away an average of 20% of its records as free goods and applies a 25% packaging allowance, the real rate of royalty is 16% x 90% x 80% x 75%, which works out at 8.64%. Unfortunately, artists are generally unable to do much about this.

what rates?

UK RATES
A new artist signing to a UK major would expect to receive between 15% and 20% of the published price to dealers, although there would usually be a number of embellishments added to this. Again, let us assume a rate of 18% for UK sales (sometimes called the headline rate).

OVERSEAS RATES
The artist should try to secure the same rate of royalty for the major overseas territories, but the 18% might reduce to 16% for sales in major overseas markets such as Germany, France, the USA and Canada, Australia and Japan. Elsewhere, in the lesser markets, this rate might further reduce to 14%. This royalty would usually be inclusive of any royalty payable to a third-party producer. Producers are dealt with more comprehensively in chapter five, but if we assume that the producer is paid 3% of dealer price then this would give a net rate for UK sales of 18%, less 3%, standing at 15%. If the artist experiences territorial reductions then he should try to ensure that the producer accepts similar (pro rata) territorial reductions, so that, if the artist receives a 16% rate in the major overseas territories rather than 18%, the producer should receive only $^{16}/_{18}$ of his UK rate for those territories.

Territorial reductions tend to be more dramatic under US contracts. If the headline rate for US sales under a recording contract with a US major were 16% (and US recording contracts tend to provide for marginally lower rates than those which usually apply in UK recording contracts), then very often the rate in the major overseas territories, including the UK, might be $^2/_3$ of the US rate (ie 10.66%), and in the remaining countries of the world this might be 50% of the US rate (ie 8%).

ESCALATIONS
These rates will often escalate automatically for later recordings. If the rate is 18% for the first album under a six-album deal, then this might also apply for the second album but rise to 19% for the third and fourth albums, then perhaps 20% for the fifth and 21% for the sixth, with similar increases in relation to the overseas rates. Very often, perhaps in addition to the automatic escalations, there may also be sales-based escalations. For example, the 18% rate in the UK might increase to 19% on sales in excess of 300,000 copies and perhaps to 20% after 1,000,000 copies. Any escalation of this kind would normally apply only to the excess sales of that album, and would not be retroactive. In some cases, the higher rate might automatically apply for all sales of the next and later albums. Escalations based on sales would normally work on a territory-by-territory basis, with different sales targets in each case.

FORMAT REDUCTIONS

There are also likely to be format reductions. Singles might be at a reduced fixed rate of perhaps 12% or 13%, or alternatively the rate for singles might be 3% less than the headline rate. When compact discs were first introduced, most record companies refused to issue records in this format unless the artist agreed to a reduced rate of royalty (usually 75% of the otherwise applicable rate). The rather flimsy justification given for this was that production costs were very high. Some companies even tried to plead a need for a 'break' in view of the costs of research and development, but of course none of the record companies had to bear any of these costs in the first place as they were incurred by the hardware manufacturers. It is only comparatively recently that the reduced rate for CDs has disappeared from most contracts, although the reduced rate will continue indefinitely in relation to numerous back-catalogue items. The great CD rip-off involved a double whammy in that not only was the royalty rate dropped but the packaging allowance was increased, generally to 25%. Most artists and their advisers are now so relieved no longer to have to suffer a reduced rate that they accept the 25% packaging allowance without complaint, even though the costs of duplicating CDs are now minimal.

real royalty rate

One of the aims of the IMF is to hasten the demise of the misleading system by which record companies seek to confuse the royalty issue. One suggestion is that record companies should be compelled to state what the IMF would refer to as the RRR (Real Royalty Rate), in much the same way that lenders when offering an interest rate have to state the APR (Annual Percentage Rate). If it becomes common practice for artists and their advisers to talk in terms of the real royalty rate in discussions with record companies, the charade will become more transparent. Contrary to popular belief, lawyers have no wish to perpetuate the current system and would prefer to concentrate on the real issues. Moreover, more and more record company executives express dismay over the current system. By the real royalty rate, the IMF means that rate obtained by expressing the amount in pence per unit received by the artist as a percentage of the dealer price, less VAT. This automatically takes into account packaging allowances, territorial and format reductions, the applicable percentage of net sales and all other accounting provisions in the agreement. Ideally, every contract should specify the RRR for each format in each territory.

further reductions

As we have seen, the RRR will be only a fraction of the royalty rate apparently offered by the record company. The story does not end there, however, and further reductions will apply for particular types of sale.

BUDGET SALES

The company will generally offer half-rate royalties on records sold at anything less than full price. Most labels have a published full-price category (which might have a PPD of £8.45, in the case of a CD), a separate mid-price category (in which CDs might have a PPD of £5.95) and a low-price or budget category (with a PPD of perhaps £4.95 or less for a CD). The costs of manufacturing and distributing low-price records are the same as those for full-price records (except that there may be a small saving on packaging costs), so that the company's margin will be considerably reduced. It will argue that the artist's royalty should reduce in line with the reduction in the company's profit, and that this is not achieved simply by calculating the royalty on a lower-sale price. The artist should investigate the company's pricing policies and ensure that the definitions of full, mid and budget price are sensible, and do not allow room for abuse. The company will usually wish to pay half-rate royalties on anything less than full price. If this is the case, one compromise is to accept $^3/_4$ rate royalties on mid-price sales and half rate only on genuine low-price sales.

RECORD CLUBS

A significant number of album sales by established artists, perhaps between 15% and 30%, are made through record clubs, and record club sales attract half-rate royalties. Most contracts provide that, for example, no royalties are payable on records given away by the club to attract new members. However, record companies rarely conduct their own record club operations, and instead merely grant manufacturing licences or sell finished records to the record clubs and allow them to get on with it. The company will not know whether the club has given away the records or sold them, and will generally be paid for all records supplied to the club. However, because of the volumes involved, the clubs will receive substantial discounts. In practice, the company may only have to deliver large quantities of records to the club's fulfilment centre and will not have to worry about distributing those records to the shops. The clubs can drive a hard bargain on discounts, and so a reduced royalty rate may be justifiable, although a 50% reduction is almost certainly not. Nevertheless, half-rate royalties on record club sales remain standard.

COMPILATIONS

The compilation album market has grown steadily over the years, and most record companies now derive a substantial part of their income from compilation sales. At one time artists and their advisers were sceptical about the benefits of compilation licensing. The concern was that, if a successful track were widely available on multi-artist compilations, the public would prefer to buy a compilation featuring the recording rather than the artist's own album. The view now is that exposure of an artist on a compilation creates a greater awareness of that artist, and stimulates sales of the his own recordings. At one time there was a general feeling that the widespread availability of an artist on compilations rather cheapened the artist. Some artists still subscribe to this view, and there are still major artists who still refuse to allow their recordings to be used on compilation albums.

The artist's record company may put together its own multi-artist compilation album, either comprising entirely of its own artists or, more likely, a combination of its own artists together with repertoire licensed in from other record companies. In such cases, there is no convincing reason why the artist should not receive his full headline rate of royalty, which will be pro-rated between the number of tracks on the album. If the headline rate of royalty is 18% and the artist has only one of 20 tracks on the album, he might expect to receive $1/20$ of his normal rate for the album, ie 0.9%. Nevertheless, the companies' standard position is to offer only a 50% rate in relation to compilation use. Again, a headline rate of 18% compilation use would therefore attract a pro rata share of 9% (ie 0.45%) on a 20-track album. The artist should resist any reduction in the headline rate for compilation use on the company's own releases.

The situation is different with third-party compilations, which account for most compilation activity. In these cases, the company grants a licence to a compilations specialist in return for a royalty. If the royalty received by the company equates to the headline rate which it pays to its artist, the company will be left with nothing. The companies' standard position is therefore to offer the artist 50% of the headline rate. This is not necessarily fair to the artist, and as we have seen it may reduce his rate to, say, 9%. For first-rate current repertoire licensed for inclusion on something like the 'Now' series, at least, the company is likely to receive a royalty of 20% or perhaps even 25%. If the company receives 25%, out of which it pays the artist 9% (which will only be paid if the artist has recouped), the company earns nearly twice as much as the artist. The company will consider this to be entirely reasonable – after all, this equates to a ratio of nearly 2:1. The record company will claim that, in order to support its substantial overhead costs and the various A&R costs which have to be written off in respect of unsuccessful artists, it needs a ratio more in the region of 3:1 (see the section on 'Who Takes What?' earlier in this chapter).

The artist may reluctantly accept a ratio of 2:1 or 3:1 on full-price sales of the artist's own album, given that the record company has a significant role to play. However, different considerations should perhaps apply in situations where the company merely licenses its rights for what are often referred to as 'secondary marketing activities'.

the IMF handbook a guide to professional band management

An artist will sometimes succeed in securing 50% or more of the company's receipts for third-party compilations; the contract might provide that the artist receives half-rate royalties or, if greater, half of the company's receipts. Alternatively (although this amounts to the same thing) the artist may receive his full rate of royalty or, if less, half of the company's receipts. In extreme cases, the artist may receive a share of any advances received by the record company from the licensee.

TV ADVERTISING

In the early 1980s, record companies introduced half-rate royalties if the company paid for a television advertising campaign. They thought it unfair that the artist should benefit from the company effectively buying extra sales. As time went by, artists' advisers found more sophisticated ways of limiting the impact of this. The reduction should only apply at all if the television advertising campaign is 'substantial', and this has led in turn to complex definitions of what is meant by this. The reduction should only apply for a limited time, usually from the start of the campaign until the end of the next accounting period following the end of the campaign, or perhaps the accounting period after that. Sometimes, the company imposes a reduced royalty on all sales during the accounting period in which the campaign starts, even if that happens several months into the accounting period. However, this doesn't alter the fact that the total reduction in royalty might be greater than the cost of the campaign, so that the artist may end up paying more than the entire cost of the campaign.

For a while, the companies argued that this arrangement was fair because television advertising campaigns are expensive and involve considerable risk. However, market research is now so sophisticated that any risks have been more or less removed. In effect, the record company will usually only spend money on TV advertising if it is confident that the additional sales will justify the cost, and the trend now is for full royalties to be payable, but with all or part of the costs of the campaign (usually 50%) being recoupable.

performance income

Every time a record is broadcast or played in public, the broadcaster or venue owner needs a licence from two distinct copyright owners: the PRS and the PPL. The PRS (Performing Rights Society) grants licences on behalf of writers and publishers for use of the performance right in the words and music. The PPL (Phonographic Performance Limited), however, grants licences for the use of the performance right in the sound recording.

recording contracts

There are important differences between the way in which the PRS and the PPL operate. In order to understand these differences properly a little history lesson is necessary, and those interested only in the current position may skip the next few paragraphs.

Copyright law was slow to recognise the existence of rights in sound recordings. Although Thomas Edison applied for a patent for his sound recording machine in as early as 1877, sound recording copyright was not recognised in English law until a case in 1934 brought the matter to light. To this day, copyright in sound recordings lasts only for 50 years from the year of release, whereas musical and literary copyright lasts for the life of the creator plus 70 years.

Performers did not receive any right to control the use of sound recordings on which they played until the Performers' Protection Act was passed in 1963. This Act was supposed to give effect to the rights granted to performers by article twelve of the Rome Convention of 1961, which the UK ratified in 1963. However, the law gave UK performers no right to obtain income from this. Infringement of the Performers' Protection Act merely gave rise to criminal penalties.

In 1934, the PPL agreed to pay featured performers 20% of the net income collected on behalf of its members, who were (and still are) exclusively record companies. This payment was made *ex gratia*, meaning that the performers had no legal right to demand it. In 1946, the PPL agreed to pay a further 12.5% of its income *ex gratia* to the Musicians' Union in recognition of the contributions of unknown session players. The UK government argued that these *ex gratia* arrangements complied with the Rome Convention.

However, the Musicians' Union made no attempt to distribute its 12.5% share of this income to the session players whose performances appeared on sound recordings. Instead, the money was paid into a special fund in order to benefit musicians in general. Somewhat ironically, some of this income from sound recordings was used to finance the Musicians' Union's 'Keep Music Live' campaign.

In 1988, the Monopolies and Mergers Commission investigated the PPL's activities, declaring that the arrangements for the payment of performers were unsatisfactory and failed to meet the UK's obligations under the Rome Convention. The MMC recommended that performers should be paid equitable remuneration in proportion to the use made of each recording in broadcast or public performance.

the IMF handbook a guide to professional band management

The most significant effect of the MMC's ruling was that the PPL stopped paying 12.5% of its income to the Musicians' Union, refusing to pay until the Union could distribute income equitably to those individuals who had played on sound recordings. Finally, in 1994, the PPL paid the Musicians' Union some £22 million in accumulated payments, which the union distributed among its members.

In 1992, the EC Commission issued a directive on Rental and Lending Rights and Piracy (92/100/EEC). The directive also dealt with public performance income for sound recordings. Unlike article twelve of the Rome Convention, the directive gave performers a legal right to income from public performance of sound recordings. Article eight of the directive grants performers a right to a "single equitable remuneration", to be paid by the user every time a sound recording is broadcast or played in public.

Most EC states passed laws granting such economic rights in the early 1960s. Nearly 40 years later, the UK has still not done so. The UK chose to enact the directive not by an Act of Parliament but by means of a statutory instrument, the legislative equivalent of flat-pack furniture. This resulted in the Copyright and Related Rights Regulations issued in 1996 (more than two years outside the deadline laid down in the directive). Instead of granting performers a right which they could enforce separately against users, the regulations give performers a right against copyright owners – in other words, the PPL's members.

This is where the most significant differences between PRS and PPL lie: performers may not be members of the PPL; the PPL alone may negotiate with users; the PPL alone may decide the division of the income it collects; the PPL's members (record companies) may leave the PPL on six months' notice or wind up the organisation altogether, leaving performers no recourse but to claim directly against their record company; the PPL's members may license certain rights directly to users, as they have done with interactive rights. Without the PPL's intervention between the user and the record companies, performance income is likely to be used to recoup advances. The Copyright and Related Rights Regulations fail to implement the directive because they do not ensure that performers receive the remuneration to which they are entitled.

Two organisations have been formed to look after performers' rights under the new legislation: PAMRA (the Performing Artists Media Rights Association) and AURA (the Association of United Recording Artists). PAMRA is backed, and to some extent directed, by the Musicians' Union, the actors' union Equity, the record producers' association Re-Pro, the Incorporated Society of Musicians and other organisations. AURA is an independent organisation promoted initially by the IMF.

The principal difference between AURA and PAMRA lies in the types of performer that each seeks to represent. AURA looks after featured performers, whereas PAMRA claims to represent all performers. However, since all of PAMRA's members have equal voting rights and the vast majority are session players, PAMRA's emphasis is on the rights of non-featured players. This is hardly surprising, given the organisations which participate in PAMRA.

Whilst PAMRA administers only performance income rights, AURA aims to collect related income such as CD rental and blank-tape levies, and to act as a lobbying and campaigning organisation on behalf of featured (and especially contracted) performers.

There is a further distinction between the associations in their attitudes to collection of performance income from overseas. AURA favours direct membership of overseas societies for its featured performer members, which allows performers and their advisers to negotiate directly with the society collecting the income in the territory concerned. It also reduces administration costs by removing one tier of administration. The most significant disadvantage of this system is that certain funds of unattributable income (so-called 'black box' income) are accessible only to collecting societies and not to individuals. AURA's response to this is that the rules should be changed to allow individuals to claim a share of such income.

PAMRA discourages direct membership of overseas societies by depriving members who join these societies of their right to vote. PAMRA is a member of SCAPR, an informal international association of collecting societies. SCAPR lays down rules for its members concerning the exchange of performance income. One of these rules stipulates that SCAPR societies must distribute to their members 100% of the income they receive from overseas. Members of SCAPR meet their own administration costs with deductions from the money they send to overseas societies. The level of these deductions is within the exclusive control of the society making the payment and is not disclosed. AURA believes that the lack of transparency in this system disguises inefficiency.

As far as UK income is concerned, featured performers may claim this directly from the PPL by registering their details at the Performers' Registration Centre. However, many featured performers prefer to authorise either PAMRA or AURA to collect on their behalf. The cost of doing so is a flat rate of 15% for PAMRA members and a negotiable 5-10% for AURA members. It seems that non-featured performers may not claim directly from the PPL.

Before the regulations were passed, 67.5% of PPL income went to record companies, 12.5% to the Musicians' Union and 20% to featured performers. Under the new law, PPL purports to pay 50% of its distributable income to performers, 32.5% of which goes to featured performers and 17.5% to session players. Income will in future be distributed on a track-by-track basis so that every performer's income should reflect the popularity of the tracks on which he played.

Where there are no session players, 100% of the distributable income will go to the featured performers on the track. Where there are session players, each session player's income is capped at a maximum of 3.5%. So, for example, where there are only two session players only 7% of the possible 17.5% non-featured performers' income will be paid out to them. The distribution of the remaining 10.5% is still the subject of negotiation, with PAMRA arguing that it should be paid to session players on other tracks and AURA contending that it should be paid to the featured performers on the track.

Although the PPL's decision to pay 50% of its net income to performers appears to be a concession, in reality performers are unlikely to receive any more income under the new system than under the old, because of the way in which the income of US performers is treated. Because the US does not recognise rights to income from the public performance and broadcast of sound recordings, US performers are not entitled to claim income from the PPL for the use of their sound recordings in the UK. Under the old system this income was simply shared between the record companies and the performers, but under the new system the PPL has decided that all of the US performers' income will go straight to the record companies. AURA interprets this as a direct result of the UK government's failure to implement the EC directive.

The PPL also refuses to pay performers any share of the income collected by its related company, Video Performance Limited, from the broadcast of videos, claiming instead that videos are films. Since soundtracks of films (ie dialogue and sound effects) are exempt from the regulations, the PPL claims that sound recordings are exempt from the legislation when they are combined with images in videos. The PPL also refuses to pay performers any share of the £3 million it collects from the sale of high-priced CDs which

recording contracts

are licensed for public performance to aerobics instructors and the like. The PPL claims that such income is collected for a dubbing service, and not for the public performance of sound recordings.

Contrary to European Court rulings which date from the mid 1970s, the PPL has indicated that it will not accept direct claims from performers who are based outside the UK. In order to discharge its obligation to overseas performers, the PPL paid all income due to overseas performers to PAMRA. PAMRA deducts its administration costs from that income before paying it to the overseas collecting societies with which it has reciprocal arrangements. AURA, on the other hand, continues to insist that overseas featured performers should be permitted to claim directly from the PPL.

The first distribution of income under the new law took place in June/July 1999 for income relating to the year 1996-7. Income for the following year, 1997-8, was distributed in November 1999. Thereafter, income is distributed regularly in November of each year, a year in arrears. The interim distribution agreement reached between AURA, PAMRA and the PPL only applies to the first two years' distributions, so at the time of writing (June 1999) negotiations are about to begin for the system, which will apply in the next few years.

other uses

Record contracts usually contain provisions dealing with the artist's income from any use of the recordings beyond the manufacture and sale of records. Many agreements give the artist 50% of the company's net receipts from such uses. Those receipts are sometimes referred to as flat-fee receipts.

This might extend to any 'premium' use – ie the exploitation of the recordings in connection with another commercial product or service. For example, the record company may supply records to Kellogg's to give away free to anybody sending in a set number of tokens from packets of Corn Flakes. Kellogg's will pay for the records, even though they are then given away free. The artist should not accept that no royalties are paid on premium sales. Sometimes the company offers half-rate royalties on premium sales, which might mean that an artist on a headline rate of 16% would receive 8% of whatever Kellogg's pays for the records. There seems to be little justification for this, and a fairer system would be for the artist to receive a percentage (say 50%) of the company's receipts. As a precaution, the artist should always insist on a right of approval over premium use, which would allow him to insist on full disclosure of the financial arrangements so that, if necessary, the royalty provisions may be modified before approval is granted.

The most typical example of the flat-fee receipts scenario is income generated by the grant of synchronisation licences (the use of a recording in the soundtrack of a film, or in an advertisement of some kind). Again, the artist would typically expect to receive (or at least be credited with) 50% of the fee.

new formats

When compact discs were first introduced, the record companies looked for ways of reducing their artist royalty liabilities (see the section on 'What Rates?' earlier in this chapter). They argued that compact discs were more expensive to manufacture than vinyl or cassettes, which was probably true only for a very short time when compact discs were first introduced and when they were manufactured and sold in relatively small numbers. The most common device was to offer a royalty on compact discs equivalent (in terms of pennies per unit) to the royalty on the sale of the equivalent vinyl disc version of the same record. In the event, the public wholeheartedly accepted the compact disc format and was persuaded to pay substantially more per unit than the vinyl or cassette equivalent. Nevertheless, for several years all new contracts included provisions for reduced-rate royalties in the case of compact discs. Sometimes the rate itself was lower (perhaps three quarters of the otherwise applicable rate), sometimes the royalty was calculated on the vinyl or cassette price rather than the compact disc price, and sometimes there was a higher packaging allowance.

In the case of existing repertoire, which the record companies had acquired under the terms of contracts entered into before compact discs were contemplated, the companies would usually refuse to release that repertoire in compact disc format unless and until the artist granted a royalty break of some kind. As a legacy of all of this, even though full-rate royalties are now invariably paid for sales of compact discs, a higher packaging allowance normally applies. Typically, there may be a packaging deduction of 20% for sales of cassettes but 25% for those of compact discs.

There is a widespread feeling amongst managers and artists that they were out-manoeuvred by the record companies in relation to compact discs. For this reason, it is unlikely that the record companies will be given such an easy ride with any new formats introduced in the future. Many new recording agreements now make provision for new technology and provide for reduced-rate royalties. Perhaps in the hope of pulling off a similar stunt, some contracts state that, if at any time records are sold in an as-yet-uninvented format, a reduced rate will apply. If pressed, most companies will accept that this provision should either be abandoned altogether or that the reduced rate should only apply for a very limited period. This is sometimes linked to the point at which the format is no longer new, which might be defined as the end of the accounting period during which sales in the new format first exceed a given percentage of total sales.

the digital revolution

Technology is moving so fast that physical formats may be of less relevance in the future. Digital technology enables the delivery of music by telephonic transfer, and records may be purchased over the Internet. For the moment, more often the transaction is effected over the Internet and the record is then sent by mail, but in some cases it is possible to purchase music which is delivered by direct download. Some recording contracts are worded so that (intentionally or otherwise) any income from exploitation by means of digital transfer will be dealt with under the provisions of secondary exploitation so that the record company will be obliged to pay one half of its receipts to the artist.

Increasingly, the major record companies are more and more alert to this and feel very uncomfortable about the position in which they find themselves. Record companies argue that they need to maintain a ratio of profits between the record company and the artist of something like 3:1. Without a profit ratio of this kind there is a fear among record companies that they will be unable to sustain their current overhead costs and the same level of investment in new talent. The majors therefore now offer to pay a percentage of their receipts from downloading equal to the equivalent rate of royalty on ordinary retail sales prices. Artists are unlikely to be impressed by the suggestion that, despite the fact that (in the case of sales by download) most record companies have nothing to do in terms of the physical manufacture and distribution of records, only perhaps 15%-20% of any income should be paid to themselves, the artists. Of course, by definition a major record company is a company which owns or controls its own facilities for the manufacture and distribution of records so that, if those facilities are no longer needed, there may no longer be any need in the new world order for major record companies.

the watershed

It is perhaps unsurprising that there is widespread cynicism about the current system. Many managers believe that recording contracts are laughable and not worth the paper on which they are written, and those of this school of thought concentrate on getting maximum possible advances as often as they can, paying little attention to the terms of the contract. This, however, is a rather short-sighted approach. While a degree of cynicism is healthy, managers must pay full attention to all of the provisions of any recording contract, not only during negotiations but indeed at all times. As the case involving George Michael has shown, recording contracts will generally be enforced by the courts. Most recording contracts contain the potential for the artist to earn fabulous riches, and it is a dreary task to argue about reduced royalties on budget sales and the like when the artist is only concerned with getting signed and into the studio, when recoupment is still distant. However, there is no point in approaching negotiations over any new recording contract on the assumption that the artist will not be successful. Sooner or later, if enough records are sold, the artist will recoup. This is a watershed moment, a point after which royalties come gushing through. Suddenly all of those boring provisions have real and dramatic impact. The unfair terms which might with greater effort have been avoided will now stand out and mock the artist and his advisers.

accounting

accounting periods

The majors generally account to their recording artists twice a year. On sales for which the company is paid between 1 January and 30 June the artist will usually receive a statement 90 days later, at the end of September. On sales for which the company is paid between 1 July and 31 December the artist will receive a statement at the end of the following March. Some record companies account for UK sales on the basis of sales *information*. These companies include, on an accounting statement, any sales notified during an accounting period. Other companies only account for sales for which the company has actually been paid. Obviously, the busiest month of the year for record sales is December, and the record company will probably not receive payment from its distributor for December sales until the following January. If the company only accounts for sales for which it has actually been paid then those sales will not appear on an accounting statement until the end of the following September.

There are more significant delays on overseas sales. Most companies receive accountings from overseas licensees every quarter. For example, the overseas licensee might account to the UK company in February for sales between 1 October and 31 December. These sales will only appear on the artist's royalty statement delivered at the end of the following September, nearly twelve months later. Some companies have even slower arrangements than this, partly for tax reasons. For example, these companies might insist that all overseas licensees account to a particular group company with a centralised accounting function, which will subsequently accounts to each of the other companies in the group. For an artist signed to Warner Bros. in London, Warner France will account to Warners International in London, which will then account to Warner Music UK. For an artist signed to one of the UK Universal Music companies, as another example, Universal France may account to Universal International in the Netherlands, which would then account back to the UK operating company. The artist should always check with his record company exactly how his royalties are to be routed and what delays he can expect.

reserves

Most record companies insist upon provisions which enable them to make reserves against returns. Although a particular royalty statement will disclose a given sales figure, the record company will hold back the royalties in relation to a proportion of those sales in case the dealer returns some of the records. In the UK and in most overseas territories, dealers are not usually allowed to return records unless they are faulty. If faulty records are returned the record company must then replace them, and this should not impact upon the artist's royalty. In the UK, however, most distributors operate what is known as a 5% returns privilege (see the section on 'Returns and Net Sales' earlier in this chapter), by which the dealer may return up to 5% of any unsold stock. It would therefore seem unreasonable for the record company to make a reserve of more than 5% (although, as explained earlier, it is theoretically possible for an artist to suffer returns of more than 5% under the privilege scheme). In fact, in practice most record companies do not impose a reserve on account of a 5% returns privilege or any similar scheme.

The issue of reserves assumes more importance if records are distributed on the basis of sale or return. In some territories (notably the USA and Canada), most records are sold on a 100% sale-or-return basis. In the UK and other territories some records are distributed on this basis, but usually only when there is a special campaign involved. Many companies insist upon the right to maintain a reserve of, say, 25% but will agree that the reserve should only apply to records sold on a sale-or-return basis. Most companies will agree that reserves should be liquidated either in the next accounting period (ie the reserve is then released after deducting any royalties in respect of records actually returned) or perhaps liquidated equally over two accounting periods.

the IMF handbook a guide to professional band management

Most UK record companies will accept that they may only impose reserves in respect of UK sales, and for overseas sales the company may not impose any reserves beyond those imposed upon the company by its overseas licensees. That said, it is prudent in this case to insist upon the disclosure of the relevant details. The most important territory in this respect is the USA and Canada. The artist should ascertain what reserves the company's North American licensee may impose against the company and over which period those reserves are to be liquidated.

withholding taxes

Most recording contracts include an express provision to the effect that the company may deduct, from royalties and advances due to the artist, any sums which the company is obliged by law to deduct by way of withholding tax. In the case of a UK company paying royalties to a UK resident, no tax is required to be withheld so that withholding generally only becomes an issue if a record company and an artist are situated in different territories. If withholding tax does apply then, if a double taxation treaty is in force between the two territories, the artist should be entitled to a tax credit against his own taxation liabilities. A provision should be inserted into the contract to the effect that the company must give the artist all reasonable assistance in obtaining such credit, which would involve the company supplying an appropriate certificate of deduction and dealing with any queries raised by the revenue authorities.

Sometimes this is of no use to the artist because his tax affairs may be such that he has insufficient tax liabilities against which to offset the benefit of any tax credit. In these circumstances, if the record company has had to pay withholding tax in respect of royalties received from its overseas licensees and has deducted a proportionate share of the withholding tax from the royalties payable to the artist but has then obtained the benefit of a tax credit, the company should, in fairness, pay back to the artist a proportionate share of that benefit. With some recording agreements, it may be worth spending time and effort in investigating the record company's overseas licensing structure in order to ensure that the artist will not suffer unduly from withholding tax problems. At best, the artist will secure a provision to the effect that any foreign withholding tax will be ignored for the purposes of calculating the artist's royalties.

audit rights

Most record companies will offer the artist a right of audit. If they do not, the principle of an audit right will never be resisted if asked for. However, the record company will seek to impose certain restrictions, so that, for example, audits may not be carried out more than once every twelve months and may only be carried out by a reputable firm of chartered accountants. Most UK record company audits are carried out by one of the limited number of firms of accountants specialising in auditing music industry royalties. Of course every audit will be different, but for a relatively successful artist auditing a UK record company concerning sales of records over a relatively successful period of three years, for example, then typically perhaps two or three auditors will be involved for perhaps a week at the offices of the record company. They will prepare a report and then spend more time with the record company in an effort to clarify any areas of confusion. Consequently, audits are expensive affairs. The auditors will normally try to spend only that amount of time which is likely to be justified by results, but an audit might cost between £5,000 and £10,000, or even £15,000 and £30,000 if the artist concerned is particularly successful, there have been large sales, and the amounts of money involved justify the accountants spending as much time as is needed.

Some record company personnel still tend to interpret an artist's request for an audit as an allegation that there has been some financial irregularity, but it is increasingly accepted as a sensible and prudent precaution for any successful artist to carry out regular audits. As we have seen the accounting function is a complex one, and mistakes – together with disagreements over points of interpretation of the relevant contractual terms – are therefore inevitable. In fact, the more enlightened record companies welcome regular audits. A successful artist should probably audit every two or three years, perhaps after each album cycle. The contract will usually state that all accounting statements are to be considered as having been accepted and no longer subject to any objection, unless such objection is made within a specified period from the rendering of the statement (usually two, three or perhaps four years). If the artist does not carry out an audit within the prescribed objection period then he, or his lawyer or accountant, should write to the record company and secure an extension. Most record companies will readily agree to this rather than pressuring the artist to carry out an audit before the expiry of the objection period.

Most companies will accept that, in the event of a discrepancy (but in practice only if the discrepancy is around 5% or 10% of the sums properly payable), they will reimburse the reasonable costs of the audit. In most cases, the auditors will find a number of arithmetical errors which the company will readily accept and will also make a number of additional claims based on how the contract should properly have been interpreted. Royalty auditors have a reputation for sometimes making some rather extravagant claims, and the auditors will typically prepare a report detailing numerous separate heads of claim. The aggregate claim will usually be a substantial sum in excess of the

5% or 10% limit, which may be specified in the contract as the amount of underpayment which triggers a liability on the part of the company to reimburse the audit costs. Accordingly, the report will include a claim not only for the aggregate unpaid royalties but also for the auditors fees. This is then followed by a sometimes protracted negotiation, which will invariably result in the audit being settled on the basis of a round-sum payment representing a fraction of the overall amount. If the settlement is higher than the amount of the audit fees then, from the artist's point of view, the exercise has been worthwhile. It usually is.

AFTER THE DEAL

contract administration

filing

A recording contract is like a living thing: it adapts and grows, and somebody needs to look after it. During the life of a recording contract, there will usually be side letters adding to or modifying parts of the agreement. These might deal with the purchase of equipment, arrangements for tour support in various territories, or royalty breaks for campaigns in particular territories. Somebody (usually the lawyer) needs to be responsible for the contract's housekeeping. The housekeeper should maintain a file which will include the contract itself and any correspondence concerning it. In particular, it is sensible to fix to the contract all formal amendments, together with copies of option notices.

dates

Somebody – the manager, the lawyer or the accountant – has to keep an eye on important dates, such as option dates, to ensure that there is no delay in invoicing for any advance which is due. Record companies rarely pay advances unless prompted. If they are late in paying they will seldom agree to pay interest. It is also worth noting option dates in case the record company mistakenly fails to exercise an option in time. Mistakes do happen, although missing an option is the only cardinal sin in a business affairs department and is likely to lead to instant dismissal. A careful note should be made of exactly when masters are delivered.

recording contracts

re-negotiations

when?

The more cynical manager relies heavily on the fact that recording contracts are probably unenforceable and, in any event, will always be re-negotiated in the event of success. Basically, this is nonsense. Some years ago, similar cynics were to be found in record companies issuing recording contracts which were quite unfair and which they assumed were probably unenforceable. Following any success, and sometimes even if there was only the smell of success, they were prepared to offer improvements to keep everybody happy. Fortunately, the industry does not really work in quite the same way any more. If the record company is in profit in relation to a particular deal, an aggressive manager can usually extract more advances on one pretext or another. However, such concessions would rarely come close to what is generally meant by a re-negotiation.

how?

A proper re-negotiation is difficult to achieve, as record companies are generally confident that their contracts can be enforced. Whilst a record company will do what is necessary to keep a successful artist happy, within reason, this rarely extends to giving away anything valuable. Accordingly, if a contract is to be re-negotiated it has to be a two-way street: the artist has to provide something tangible in return for the improvements he seeks.

The bulldozer or blackmailing approach to re-negotiation involves explaining to the record company that the artist is desperately unhappy for one reason or another, and that he cannot bring himself to finish recording the new album until something is done to make him happier. It is best to leave this approach until quite late (preferably until the album has already been scheduled for release and the record company has cleared its decks in anticipation of starting work on the album). If this tactic fails – and it usually does because the record company knows that the artist is in fact desperate to release the record – then probably the only bargaining chip the artist holds is to offer options for another album or two. This is why, during the negotiations over the original contract, so much significance is attached to the number of options. If the artist achieves success early on and is resentful about the terms of his deal, and if the company already has the right to call for another four or five albums, there is little incentive on the record company to re-negotiate. The record company will probably not feel insecure until the penultimate album is delivered.

If the artist can manoeuvre himself into a position strong enough to re-negotiate he will usually look for higher royalties, more substantial advances (perhaps with a non-recoupable bonus payment as an additional reward for past success), the exclusion of long-form video rights, perhaps the exclusion of particular territories (usually North America if the performance there has been poor), the reversion at some point of the copyright in his masters (a particularly difficult nut to crack), and perhaps (in the case of a group) a specific solo recording commitment or the exclusion of solo recordings from the deal.

chapter 4
enforceability of agreements

by Andrew Forbes

The enforceability of music industry agreements is an emotive subject. The high-risk and speculative nature of the business leads those who invest in talent (ie record companies, music publishers and managers) to seek long-term exclusive arrangements from their artists. The reason for this is obvious: if a substantial amount of money, time and energy is to be invested in an artist, the investor will obviously want to be sure that he will be able to reap the rewards of this, should success follow.

This desire for protection by those who effectively work to build an artist's career has to be handled sensitively, particularly in view of the relative youth and lack of business experience evident in many artists. This, coupled with an artist's keen desire to find someone who can help them to succeed, can create a situation ripe for exploitation by the unscrupulous.

It is for these reasons that the courts have seen a steady stream of cases in which artists seek to challenge the enforceability of agreements into which they have entered with record companies, music publishers and managers. In general, the courts are extremely reluctant to interfere with contracts – the 'freedom to contract' on such terms as one wishes is one of the cornerstones of English contract law. However, the music industry has succeeded in making significant inroads in this respect by pursuing a range of potential rights which can be used to challenge the enforceability of an agreement. This is the subject of this chapter, which will cover three areas of law relevant to the enforceability of music industry agreements: restraint of trade, undue influence and European Community law in the form of Article 85 of the Treaty of Rome.

RESTRAINT OF TRADE

how the courts approach restraint of trade

the policy behind the restraint of trade doctrine

The court does not interfere with bargains between artists and their management, publishing or record companies lightly. As Lord Reid stated in a case called *Esso* v *Harper*, "in general, unless a contract is vitiated by duress, fraud or mistake, its terms will be enforced though unreasonable or even harsh and unconscionable…in the ordinary case the court will not remake a contract". Parties will generally be held to agreements into which they enter, no matter how unbalanced the terms may appear. You could agree to sell your house for £1 if you wished to; you would be held to your bargain.

The doctrine of restraint of trade, however, is an exception to this approach which has been developed by the court. The rationale behind the formulation of the doctrine is to preserve the perceived public interest in free trade. It aims to achieve this by breaking down unreasonable contractual restrictions which seek to stifle competition. There is therefore a tension between the court's desire to uphold the freedom of parties to contract on whatever terms they consider appropriate and, on the other hand, to promote free trade.

It is important to bear in mind the what exactly the court is doing when it applies restraint of trade principles to an agreement. It is generally accepted that the aim of the agreement is not to protect the weak and vulnerable from transactions which the court considers unfair – that is the role of the doctrine of undue influence, which is considered later in this chapter. However, in cases pertaining to the music industry there has been a blurring of the distinction between restraint of trade and undue influence. Lord Diplock stated in *Schroeder* v *Macaulay* (1974) that the public policy behind restraint of trade was in fact the protection of those whose bargaining power is weak from being forced to enter into bargains that are unconscionable by those whose bargaining power is stronger. In the context of music industry agreements, at least, this reflects the fact that both restraint of trade and undue influence are used to protect the interests of artists who enter restrictive agreements when they are in a position of poor bargaining power.

the Nordenfelt test

The essential mechanism which the court uses to determine whether a restriction is an unenforceable restraint of trade is what is known as the Nordenfelt test. This was set out by the House of Lords in its definitive analysis of the doctrine of restraint of trade in the case of *Nordenfelt v Maxim Nordenfelt Guns and Ammunition* (1894). Lord Macnaghten stated that "all interference with individual liberty of action in trading, and all restraints of trade themselves, if there is nothing more, are contrary to public policy and void". However, restraints may be justifiable if they are reasonable. Lord Macnaghten identified a two-stage approach to be applied, to the effect that a restriction will only be enforceable if it is both reasonable between the parties and it does not offend against public policy. These will be referred to from now on as the two limbs of the Nordenfelt test.

The Nordenfelt approach has been clarified in a number of subsequent cases. The last definitive statement as to way in which the doctrine applies to music industry agreements was contained in *Schroeder v Macaulay*. In the well-known cases which have followed *Schroeder* (ie *Zang Tumb Tuum v Johnson* [1993, the Frankie Goes To Hollywood case], *Silvertone v Mountfield* [1993, the Stone Roses case], *Panayiotou v Sony Music* [1994, the *George Michael* case] and *William Nicholl v Shaun Ryder* [1998, the *Shaun Ryder* case]), the courts have merely been applying the principles stated in *Schroeder* rather than developing any new principles of law.

when should the test be applied?

Before applying the Nordenfelt test, the court must first decide whether the contract in question attracts the restraint of trade doctrine at all. There is no rigid definition to determine whether a contract will attract the doctrine. The court has stressed that the doctrine is "to be applied to factual situations with a broad and flexible rule of reason".

The most recent case, *George Michael*, clarified the approach to be taken. The doctrine only applies to contracts which are in restraint of trade in the sense that this is used "as a term of art covering those contracts which are to be regarded as offending a rule of public policy". There are two elements to this: the contract must be in restraint of trade as the term is used in ordinary parlance; and, if it is, the court must then consider whether there is some reason to exclude the contract from the application of the doctrine. The Nordenfelt test will only be applied if the contract passes this two-stage test. The court effectively defined the ambit of the doctrine by determining those situations that were covered by the doctrine rather than those which were not.

In *George Michael*, the court held that the recording agreement between the artist and his record company was a "compromise agreement" (ie an agreement settling a dispute). For reasons of public policy, the court considered compromise agreements to be beyond the scope of the doctrine of restraint of trade, and therefore decreed that, in this instance, the doctrine of restraint of trade did not apply. The artist's case fell at the first hurdle. The court nevertheless went on to express what its decision would have been if the doctrine had applied, providing further guidance on the way in which the court should approach the enforceability of music industry agreements. What is clear from the cases is that the court is willing, in principle, to apply the restraint of trade doctrine to recording, publishing and management agreements containing restrictions on artists.

reasonableness between parties

If the court decides that the doctrine applies to a contract currently under consideration, it will then go on to apply the first limb of the Nordenfelt test: are the restrictions reasonable between the parties?

considerations

The burden of proof is on the party who is seeking to enforce the contract (ie the manager, publisher or record company), who must show that the restrictions are reasonable between the parties. The restrictions are therefore presumed unreasonable unless the manager, publisher or record company can demonstrate to the contrary.

In considering this, the court will look at two areas: whether the restrictions go further than providing adequate protection for the legitimate interests of the party in whose favour they are granted (ie the manager, publisher or record company); and whether they can be justified as being in the interests of the party restrained (ie the artist).

providing protection for the restricting party

Esso v *Harper* formulated a two-stage test to determine whether a situation attracted the doctrine. Firstly, what are the legitimate interests of the party seeking to enforce the contract which it is entitled to protect?

enforceability of agreements

Secondly, are the restrictions more than adequate for that purpose? These are questions of fact depending on the business and circumstances of the case in question.

It has long been established that restrictions are examined as they would have applied to both parties at the date of formation of the contract. The court should consider from this standpoint what may happen under the contract, rather than looking at what actually has happened. However, the court made it clear in *George Michael* that a realistic approach should be taken, rather than a search for far-fetched effects which are divorced from reality.

The legitimate interests of a record company which is seeking to rely on restrictions contained in a recording agreement have been set out in *Frankie Goes To Hollywood* and *George Michael*, details of which appear later in this chapter. In *Frankie Goes To Hollywood*, the court was not particularly impressed by the legitimate interests raised and thought that any validity that they might have possessed was outweighed by the one-sided bias of the contract. In *George Michael*, the court commented that all of the interests listed were valid aspirations for any record company, though some interests had more bearing on justifying the contract in question than others. The court thought that the restrictions in the contract went no further than was necessary to protect the record company's legitimate interests.

justification of restrictions

The court will consider whether the restrictions were justified in view of the artist's interest in obtaining the benefit to him available under the contract in question, and will look at the net effect of the entire sweep of provisions in the contract. The aim is to balance the parties' interests. The artist will wish to obtain the benefit of the contract without restricting himself unduly, while the manager, publisher or record company will wish to maximise its benefit under the contract. The exercise carried out by the court will be to balance the benefit of the transaction against the burden imposed. In *Stone Roses*, the court thought that the contract was so entirely one-sided and unfair that no competently-advised artist in the position of the Stone Roses would ever have agreed to sign it. Note, however, that in *George Michael* the court specifically stated that "the restrictions contained in [the contract being considered] are both reasonably necessary for the protection of the legitimate interests of Sony Music and commensurate with the benefits secured to Mr Michael under it".

Again, each decision will turn on the detail of the contract being considered and the facts of the particular case. However, it is possible to draw out various factors which the courts will take into account. These include the following.

GEOGRAPHICAL SCOPE OF RESTRICTIONS

The ambit justified in a particular case will depend on the nature of the business concerned. In view of the international nature of the music business, the courts are prepared to countenance worldwide restrictions in recording agreements, although they have not fully considered whether there is a distinction to be drawn between recording agreements (in which international protection may properly be given to copyrights) and management agreements (in which this consideration will not apply).

DURATION

There is no concrete ruling on the time-span of the contract. It is not possible to say, for example, that five years is fine but eight years is too long. The duration of particular restrictions must be considered in the context of the rest of the contract as a whole, including other provisions such as amount of consideration.

In *Frankie Goes To Hollywood* the court thought that the possible eight- or nine-year duration of the contract was unreasonable, and that five years was too long in relation to the publishing agreement. It should be noted, however, that the court was clearly considering the cumulative effect of the restrictions in both agreements, such as that which demanded that the artists sign to sister record and publishing companies.

In *Stone Roses*, there was a potential period of seven years, or possibly even an indefinite period of duration, coupled with no release commitment. The court thought that this was unreasonable, and was particularly influenced by the fact that the band's career could have been 'sterilised' for this period.

In *George Michael*, duration was defined by the artist's obligation to deliver masters within various option periods subject to a 15-year 'cap'. In the context of the contract as a whole, the court did not think that its potential duration was unreasonable.

In the context of a management contract, the court held in *Shaun Ryder* that a seven-year term (comprising an initial term of three years and two two-year options) was unreasonable. It also observed that it is usual in the music industry for an earnings target to be included to legitimise a further period which is the subject of an option, and that it was unreasonable for an option period not to be tied to an earnings target.

AMOUNT OF CONSIDERATION

The more money an artist receives under an agreement the more extensive the restraints by which he can expect to be bound. This was a major influence on the court in the George Michael case in deciding that the restrictions in the contract were reasonable.

BARGAINING POWER OF THE PARTIES

If one party exerts commercial strength over the other to take unconscionable advantage of the other's weakness, restrictions imposed as a result may well be unreasonable. To an extent, this blurs the distinction between restraint of trade and undue influence. In the *Stone Roses* case the court emphasised the difference between the parties in terms of experience and expertise, although in *George Michael* the court took the view that this was of only limited relevance.

BROAD APPROACH TO FAIRNESS

It is often argued that, as breaking new talent in the music industry is such a high-risk business, wide restrictions are justified, although this proposition was not accepted in *Frankie Goes To Hollywood*. However, it will form part of the factual matrix by which the court considers the restrictions in question, and the proposition will therefore have some relevance in the court's balancing of the parties' interests.

AVAILABILITY OF LEGAL ADVICE

The fact that an artist has taken expert independent legal advice will not of itself render restrictions reasonable (although it will assist a manager, publisher or record company in demonstrating that this is the case); the court must also ask itself in each case whether the contract was fair at the time that it was concluded. If legal advice from a lawyer experienced in matters concerning the music industry was unavailable, this may well be relevant to any consideration of inequality of bargaining power. In the *Stone Roses* case, for example, the court stressed that the knowledge of industry lawyers would extend to the state of the market, an appreciation of the impact of various terms and the state of the law on entertainment contracts generally. The availability of expert independent legal advice is also an important factor in determining whether to apply the doctrine of undue influence.

RELEASE COMMITMENT

In the context of a recording agreement, the absence of an obligation to exploit the product of an artist's services may arouse the court's suspicions that the exclusive nature of a recording agreement could sterilise the artist's career and therefore increase the likelihood of the court arriving at a finding of unreasonableness. In *Schroeder*, the court thought that some positive obligation on a publisher was necessary: maybe not as much as a positive commitment to publish the work of an unknown composer, but possibly a statement to the effect that the publisher would use their best endeavours to promote the composer's work. In *Frankie Goes To Hollywood*, the court was critical of the absolute discretion given to the record company by which it could refuse to release records and yet still have the copyright in unreleased recordings assigned to it.

In *Stone Roses*, the record company would not have been saved by an amendment which it had proposed, requiring it to allow a third party, "chosen by mutual agreement", to release records if it had later declined to do so. There was still no guarantees in place, in this case, that records would ever be released.

In *George Michael*, the record company's only obligation was to release three singles in the UK and US. However, if it did not release albums in the UK the artist could serve notice requiring release, and if this release was not carried out the contract would terminate. Elsewhere he could compel the record company to enter into good-faith negotiations with third parties to license unreleased albums. The court took the view that there was no real risk that the record company would not release the artist's records, and that to recognise any such risk would be a "distortion of commercial reality".

TERMINATION
If the manager, publisher or record company alone has the right to terminate an agreement, this could be viewed as having the effect of making restrictions unreasonable. In *Schroeder*, the publisher could terminate whenever it wished but the composer had no right of termination by contract at all. This was also the case in *Frankie Goes To Hollywood* and *Stone Roses*.

RIGHTS OF CONSULTATION
In the context of a recording agreement, if the artist has a right of consultation concerning the choice of material to be exploited, the producer, the recording budget and the acceptance of masters etc, this will improve the chances of the agreement being found to be enforceable. Compare *Frankie Goes To Hollywood* (in which the record company had the last word), *Stone Roses* (in which the artists had no artistic control whatsoever) and *George Michael* (in which the artist had wide artistic control).

LEAVING-MEMBER PROVISIONS

In the context of a recording agreement, these may be considered to unreasonably restrict the artist (see, for example, *Frankie Goes To Hollywood*, in which a clause required both a leaving member's new band to be acceptable to the record company and to be procured to enter into an agreement on same terms as the band, and also that any new member could only be allowed to join if approved by the record company and would then sign the same deal as the rest of the band. Although this issue may be relevant to management agreements, it is generally dealt with differently in those cases and is a point on which the courts have yet to provide guidance.

POST-TERMINATION PROVISIONS

In the case involving *Stone Roses*, the court thought that the inclusion in a recording agreement of a ten-year post-term restriction on re-recording was excessive. In the *George Michael* case, the court took the view that a three-year restriction was reasonable and was usual in recording agreements. In the *Shaun Ryder* case, the court was strongly critical of a provision included in a management agreement which gave the manager a right to commission on an album both recorded and released after the end of the term of the management agreement. It observed that it could see no legitimate basis for this, and also stated that it was not persuaded that commissioning post term indefinitely, at the full rate of commission, was reasonable.

UNLIMITED RIGHT OF ASSIGNMENT

In the *Stone Roses* case, the court was critical of the record company's right to assign its interest. However, in *George Michael* it decided that the right of assignment involved a remote risk of detriment to the artist. This point may have some significance in relation to an agreement with a management company (rather than an individual) in which a right of assignment granted to the company is not linked to an appropriate 'key-man' provision.

public policy

If the restrictions pass the first limb of the Nordenfelt test, the court should go on to consider the second limb: are the restrictions reasonable as a matter of public policy? The person challenging the contract (ie the artist) will have to shoulder the burden of proving that it is unreasonable on this basis. The restrictions will therefore be presumed to be reasonable on grounds of public policy unless the artist can demonstrate to the contrary.

Almost all cases concerning the enforceability of music industry agreements are fought on the basis of reasonableness between the parties (ie the first limb of the Nordenfelt test rather than the second). However, in practice it is very difficult to separate the two. It is in the public interest that contracts containing restrictions which are reasonable between the parties should thus be enforceable, and it is therefore difficult to envisage a situation in which the terms agreed by an artist are found to be reasonable between the parties and yet objectionable on grounds of public policy. An artist will consequently face considerable difficulties in satisfying the burden of proof under this limb of the Nordenfelt test once the manager, publisher or record company has demonstrated that the restrictions are reasonable as between the parties. In the *George Michael* case, no grounds which pertained to the second limb of Nordenfelt were put forward by the artist. However, as noted above, the court relied on a consideration of public policy in deciding that the contract would not attract the restraint of trade doctrine at all.

severance

the doctrine of severance

Where a restriction is in fact a combination of several distinct promises, the court will be prepared to sever (ie strike out) those parts which are excessive in scope, the deletion of which will leave the remainder of the contract intact. However, any words which are to be removed must be 'clearly severable', which means that they must be independent of the rest of the clause in question and must be severable without their removal affecting the remaining part of the clause. For severance to be possible the remaining wording must not need to be added to or modified, the remaining terms must continue to be supported by adequate consideration, and the character of the contract must not be changed by the removal of the wording in question so that it becomes wholly different to the contract into which the parties originally entered. This was stressed by the court in the *Stone Roses* case; the court would have changed the nature of the contract entirely if it had started introducing limitations or if it had shortened the term of the contract (for example, by severing the last two option periods). In the *Shaun Ryder* case, the manager tried to shorten the term of the agreement by severing one of its two option periods, but the court was not prepared to accept this.

use of severance clauses

Parties who contract with artists often seek to use a clause which states that the parties agree to such modification of the contract as is necessary to render it valid and effective (ie inviting the court to sever objectionable clauses and leave the rest standing). While such clauses have received some support from the courts there is a serious risk that they will be ineffective as they amount to little more than an invitation to the court to rewrite the agreement if it is ever subject to litigation concerning its enforceability. They may also offend against the rule concerning certainty, in that the parties are agreeing to such terms as the court may consider enforceable at some time in the future. In the *Stone Roses* case, the court thought that this type of clause was objectionable on grounds of public policy, constituting an attempt by the record company to secure the enforcement of a contract which would otherwise be unenforceable.

effects of unreasonable restrictions

different terminology

Cases use various terms to describe the effect of contracts which constitute an unreasonable restraint of trade. They have variously been described as being 'void', 'voidable' or 'unenforceable'. The distinction is important because, if a contract is void, it will strictly speaking be of no legal effect whatsoever. If it is voidable, it will be enforceable until a right of avoidance is exercised. If it is unenforceable, the contract will be valid in all respects with the exception that one or both parties cannot be sued on it.

unperformed obligations

In *Nordenfelt* the court regarded offending restrictions as void, in line with the approach that the restrictions are to be considered at the date on which the contract was signed. However, the modern approach is that the obligations are unenforceable insofar as they remain unperformed (see *Esso* v *Harper*, *Schroeder* and *O'Sullivan* v *Management Agency and Music* [1985, the *Gilbert O'Sullivan* case]). This approach is open to criticism in that the restraint is to be considered at the time at which the contract was signed, and also because it will allow the party seeking the restriction to obtain the contract's benefit up to the point at which the court determines that it is unenforceable. Nevertheless, this appears to be the current state of the law.

In the first-instance hearing in the *George Michael* case the artist accepted the approach in *Schroeder*, although he reserved the right to argue on appeal that the agreement was void. The court's decision therefore did not address this point.

UNDUE INFLUENCE

general approach

Undue influence is a doctrine developed under what is known as the court's 'equitable jurisdiction', under which the aim is to achieve a level of fairness between parties to a dispute rather than the application of strict legal principles. The court will apply the principles of equity to set aside an unfair bargain. This is different to the doctrine of the restraint of trade in that, in this case, the court is concerned not with striking down clauses which amount to an unreasonable restraint of trade but instead with applying rules of justice to protect those in a weak and vulnerable position. Undue influence is based on a notion of moral reprehensibility rather than the unenforceability of unreasonable bargains in order to preserve free trade.

There are two categories of cases in which the court will set a transaction aside, as set out in the case of *Allcard v Skinner* (1887):

- Where influence was expressly used by one party to secure conclusion of an agreement ('express' or 'actual' undue influence, where the court will strike the agreement down on the basis that it will not allow a person to benefit from their wrongful act).

- Where the relationship between the parties was such that a presumption of influence was raised ('presumed' undue influence, where the court will seek to prevent abuse of particular relationships on the basis of public policy).

In those cases which cover restraint of trade under music industry agreements, we are generally dealing with the principles applicable to the second example here. The main music industry precedents are *Gilbert O'Sullivan, Armatrading* v *Stone* (1984) and *Elton John* v *Richard Leon James* (1991, the *Elton John* case). The exertion of undue influence was also considered in *Shaun Ryder*, which was mentioned earlier in this chapter.

the court's approach

An artist will need to prove two things to bring the presumption of undue influence into operation:

(i) That the relationship between the parties was such that the manager, publisher or record company was in a position to exert influence over the artist.

The court will consider the particular facts of each case to determine whether such a relationship exists (see *Joan Armatrading*). General guidance was given in a case called *Goldsworthy* v *Brickell* (1987), in which the court stated that it was necessary for there to be a degree of trust and confidence such that the party in whom it is focused is in a position to influence the other into effecting the transaction in question, either because they are the adviser of the other, they have become entrusted with the management of the affairs of the other, or for some other reason.

The relationship required has been found to exist in relation to a recording artist's manager and music publisher. In the *Gilbert O'Sullivan* case, the artist signed a management agreement with an individual who also controlled companies with whom the artist signed publishing and recording agreements. It was held that there was a fiduciary relationship between the companies and the artist, in view of the level of involvement which the former had in the management of the latter's career. This was sufficient for the artist to found a claim for undue influence. In the case of *Elton John*, the artist was unknown at the time of signing a publishing agreement and completely in awe of the publisher, who was a giant in music publishing. There was no negotiation, and the artist received no legal advice on the terms proposed. The artist had trusted that the publisher would treat him fairly on the basis of the publisher's stature in the industry.

It is interesting to note that in *Shaun Ryder*, the manager did not even attempt to dispute that the necessary relationship existed.

(ii) That the artist entered into a transaction which was so manifestly and unfairly disadvantageous to him that this could not be reasonably explained by the ordinary motives on which people ordinarily act.

It is necessary to show that the manager, publisher or record company has obtained an unfair advantage by acting in a morally reprehensible way. The court has stressed that this goes beyond showing that terms were objectively unreasonable. In *Elton John*, the artist was exclusively bound for a period of six years and assigned copyright in all of his output during this period to the publisher (even though there was no commitment on the part of the publisher to publish any of the artist's work). In exchange, the artist had a right to modest royalties. The court regarded this as an unfair bargain, even though the publisher had acted in good faith and had not intended to act unfairly regarding the terms imposed as the industry standard at the time.

In *Shaun Ryder*, the court identified one particular provision which, in its view, demonstrated manifest disadvantage to the artist. This was a clause entitling the manager to commission an album which was both recorded and released after the expiration of the term under the management agreement.

In the event that the artist proves that these two criteria have been met, the transaction will then be set aside unless the manager, publisher or record company can rebut the presumption of undue influence by proving that the artist was acting in circumstances which enabled him to exercise an independent will, free from the influence of the manager, publisher or record company, and that the artist had a full appreciation of what he was doing. The fact that an artist has had independent legal advice will not necessarily be sufficient to rebut the presumption, although this is likely to assist the manager, publisher or record company. It should also be noted that, if the artist misunderstands the advice or is given possibly erroneous advice, the court will not set aside the agreement if he otherwise understood the nature of the transaction and acted with a free will. The manager, publisher or record company will be assisted in rebutting the presumption if it can show that the independent legal adviser used by the artist was expert in the negotiation of music industry agreements.

In *Shaun Ryder*, the artist was not overtly pressurised to sign the management agreement, yet the court considered the following circumstances to show that the manager had failed to rebut the presumption of undue influence: the artist's lawyer had amended a draft of the management agreement proposed by the manager's lawyer; the manager took a draft which omitted those amendments to a studio to get the artist to sign it; and the manager knew that the artist had difficulty with paperwork and was likely to be under the influence of drugs, and hoped that the artist would simply sign it without consulting his lawyer further – which, in fact, he did.

finding undue influence

If a finding of undue influence has been established, the agreement will be held to be voidable (ie enforceable only until a right of avoidance is exercised). The artist will therefore be entitled to have the contract set aside and seek to be restored to his original position, and in principle the court be prepared to order that this should happen. However, as undue influence is part of the court's equitable jurisdiction, the court will seek to obtain justice between the parties on the facts of the particular case. This may involve the manager, publisher or record company accounting to the artist for any profit obtained under the agreement, although in an appropriate case the court may permit retention of reasonable remuneration for work done (see *Gilbert O'Sullivan*, in which the defendant was permitted to retain some profit to reflect its contribution to the artist's success).

equitable defences

A claim for undue influence will be subject to defeat by various defences available under the court's equitable jurisdiction (known as 'equitable defences'). The most relevant of these for our purposes are the defences of laches and acquiescence.

laches

Laches are essentially delays in the time it takes to prosecute a claim, such that it would not be reasonable to allow the claim to be raised against the other party. If an artist delays in taking action once he becomes dissatisfied with their agreement, a defence may be available to the manager, publisher or record company on this basis. The artist will be at particular risk if he delays taking action once the agreement in question has expired (see *Elton John*).

acquiescence

This is essentially what happens when a party to an agreement – by its clear, unequivocal and deliberate conduct – induces the other party to believe that the agreement will not be challenged. Conduct by an artist which indicates that he or she will not seek to challenge a manager, publisher or

the IMF handbook a guide to professional band management

record agreement may provide a manager, publisher or record company with a defence on this ground.

THE TREATY OF ROME

Article 85 (1)

The Treaty Of Rome is a piece of European legislation which is applicable under English law. The provision which could potentially be used to seek to challenge the enforceability of music industry agreements is Article 85 (1), which is aimed at promoting free trade within the European Community. The relevant wording from Article 85 (1) is as follows:

> "The following shall be prohibited as incompatible with the common market: all agreements between undertakings…which may affect trade between Member States and which have as their object or effect the prevention, restriction or distortion of competition within the common market …"

music industry agreements

We do not yet have a case on the application of Article 85 (1) to a management or publishing agreement. Its application to a recording agreement, however, was considered the *George Michael* case, although in that particular case the artist relied considerably on the evidence which he had gathered in relation to his case on restraint of trade rather than producing any further evidence to support his case on Article 85. The court therefore made its decision in the absence of evidence directed to the various issues raised. The outcome of the case – ie that Article 85 did not apply to the agreement in question and that, even if it had applied, the artist's claim on this basis would have failed – could well have been different if any evidence had been specifically provided to support the point.

The burden of proof will be on the artist to establish that the contract in question contravenes Article 85 (1). The artist will have to show:

(i) That both he and the manager, publisher or record company are 'undertakings'.

The application of Article 85 (1) to performers' agreements was considered in the *Rai/Unitel* case (1978). It is clear that an artist will be an undertaking when he exploits his performances commercially. There was no dispute in *George Michael* that the artist was an undertaking.

(ii) That the agreement may affect trade between member states of the Community.

Trade must be affected to an 'appreciable extent'. The contract must be considered in each case in its legal, economic and commercial context, which will require a detailed examination of the surrounding facts and, in particular, the operation of the market in question. It is important to note that, while under the restraint of trade doctrine a contract is examined as it applied on the date it was signed, Article 85 is perambulatory; the court will look at its effect in practice.

In *George Michael*, the court took the view that this was a preliminary requirement which the artist had to establish before looking at 'object' and 'effect' (see [iii] below).

It is important to consider the market which is being addressed when considering whether trade may be affected. In *George Michael*, two distinct markets were considered: the market for the artist's services themselves (the 'raw material') and the market for recordings of the artist's performances (the 'end product' of the artist's services). The court found that "the market for the services of UK recording artists in the pop field...is a purely national and domestic market", and that "there is no Community-wide market for the services of UK recording artists in the field of popular music, since...only in exceptional cases will UK recording artists sign to a non-UK recording company". There was therefore no market (and no trade) between member states which could be affected by the agreement in question, and the artist's claim under Article 85 fell at this first hurdle.

The court nevertheless went on to consider whether (assuming that there was a Community-wide market for UK artists' services) the agreement in question would have affected trade between member states. It held that it would not, on a number of bases. As far as the 'raw material' was concerned, this was because there was insufficient evidence provided by the artist to show that trade would be affected in either a legal, commercial or economic context. In addition, the court had to look at the position in the market for the agreement in question. As the artist had not attempted to challenge a prior recording agreement by which he was bound, his claim on this point could not even get off the ground because, if the agreement in dispute had not existed, he would still have been restricted by the earlier agreement. With regard to the 'end product', there was no evidence of the record company's distribution system and the court therefore could not conclude that trade between member states would have been affected.

> (iii) That the agreement must have as its object or effect the prevention, restriction or distortion of competition within the common market. In considering the 'object', the court applies an objective test. It will not look at the intentions of either parties, but will instead try to discover whether as a matter of fact the agreement has an anti-competitive effect.

In *George Michael*, the court again went on to consider this aspect, even though it had already found that the artist would fail under Article 85. It held that the object was in fact the promotion of competition (ie the release of a new end product onto the market). The court thought that the artist's suggestion that the recording agreement was intended to prevent anyone exploiting the artist's recordings was a distortion of commercial reality.

The court should look at all of the surrounding circumstances in considering the 'effect' of the agreement in question. There is a substantial overlap with the considerations in (ii) above.

The artist also failed on this ground in *George Michael*. This was on the basis that there was no market for raw material outside the UK, and that the restrictions on exploitation of masters in the agreement were no more than was reasonable and did not have an anti-competitive effect and that, because Article 222 of the Treaty Of Rome excludes property ownership from the ambit of Article 85, the rules concerning competition would not apply to the provisions relating to assignment of copyright in masters to the record company.

effect of Article 85

The agreement is rendered void automatically (see Article 85 [2]). In addition, there is a risk of substantial fines being imposed by the European Commission.

clearing an agreement with the EC

It is possible to apply to the Commission for a declaration that Article 85 does not apply to an agreement ('negative clearance') or to apply to the Commission for an exemption under Article 85 (3).

English courts

Despite the decision in *George Michael*, it is clear that the court continues to regard recording contracts as agreements to which the principles of restraint of trade and undue influence are readily applicable. The balance between the interests of a record company and its artist therefore continues to be a very delicate one. Record companies cannot rely upon the sanctity of a contract which will apply to most of their contractual dealings with third parties, and they therefore make absolutely sure that in each individual case with each artist every effort is made to ensure that they take no more protection than is adequate to safeguard their legitimate interests and that any restrictions to which artists agree are commensurate with the benefits which they receive. It is undoubtedly the case that agreements with management and publishing companies containing restrictions will also continue to attract the attention of the courts, as has been demonstrated by the *Shaun Ryder* case). Again, a delicate balancing exercise of the parties' interests is required if the risk of a finding of restraint of trade or undue influence is to be minimised.

While there is a clear distinction between the principles of restraint of trade and undue influence, the courts on occasion use language more appropriate to the latter when discussing the former. We do not yet have a sufficient body of cases to be see whether the courts are in fact using the restraint of trade doctrine to achieve the same end as undue influence (ie protection of the weak). However, this is certainly consistent with the decisions to date. When young, inexperienced musicians have been involved, the courts have refused to enforce the agreements in question (see the *Schroeder, Frankie Goes To Hollywood* and *Stone Roses* cases). The case involving *George Michael*, on the other hand, involved an artist who had already achieved a considerable measure of success in his own right. The court appeared to have little sympathy for his position, and the agreement was thus held to be enforceable.

The availability of expert legal advice to the artist continues to be of great importance, in relation to the application of both restraint of trade and undue influence. If expert legal advice is not provided, there will be a serious risk that agreements will be found to be unenforceable and voidable. The fact that the artist's lawyer's input was 'sidelined' in the

Shaun Ryder case (ie the manager obtained the artist's signature on a contract which omitted the artist's lawyer's amendments) undoubtedly weighed against the manager.

Article 85 of the Treaty Of Rome may yet prove to be a potent weapon in the hands of artists. In the *George Michael* case, the court was presented with very little evidence on this issue. In this case, the court found that Article 85 did not apply, as the specific market for the services of UK recording artists was limited to the UK. If evidence had been presented on this aspect it could well have been demonstrated that this was not in fact the case, and if evidence had been presented on the further requirements of Article 85 it is possible that a claim under this could have been sustained.

practical aspects of enforceability

In an ideal world, a manager, publisher or record company would have regard to the following with each contract signed. In practical terms this is likely to be a counsel of perfection. They are, however, points worth bearing in mind.

- When a draft contract is prepared, the manager, publisher or record company ideally should be in a position to demonstrate that it has considered what it regards to be its legitimate interests and has designed the restrictions contained in the contract to provide no more protection than is necessary to adequately safeguard these.

- It is important that draft contracts should be tailor made to each signing. If a smaller deal is proposed, more limited restrictions are likely to increase the manager, publisher or record company's chances of making them stick.

- The manager, publisher or record company runs a serious risk of a successful challenge to the contract if there is no negotiation of the main terms set out in it, or if the artist is not represented by a lawyer with experience of the music industry.

- The agreement is more likely to be found to be valid and enforceable if the artist is given rights in relation to artistic matters.

- Post-termination provisions are very sensitive, particularly if they are likely to have the effect of sterilising an artist's career after termination has taken place.

schedule

This section will investigate those legitimate interests which record companies seek to protect by use of restrictions in recording agreements in relation to those cases in which they became major factors.

the Frankie Goes To Hollywood case

- For every successful artist there are a multitude of failures. It is therefore reasonable and in the interests of everyone in the music business that successful artists should be tied to the record company so that the company can over time be compensated for the costs of unsuccessful artists.

- The second record by an artist has much more chance of being successful if the first has been. The record company should therefore have the right to subsequent records to justify its investment in earlier ones.

the George Michael case

- The desire to sell as many records as possible.

- The desire to ensure that there is an even and adequate flow of product.

- The desire to be able to plan ahead.

- The desire to have proven successful product available for as long as possible.

- The desire and need to be able to compete on equal terms in an international environment against other record companies which have long-term signings.

- The desire to be known for continued high-calibre releases by long term successful artists in order to maintain a reputation with consumers, dealers and new unsigned artists.

- The desire to maintain morale and enthusiasm amongst employees.

- The desire and need to recover the investment made in a particular artist.

- The desire to make a profit on that investment.

- The need to have available sufficient product to finance losses on unsuccessful product and the fixed costs of the infrastructure (including overheads).

- The desire to accumulate property rights as an asset.

- The desire to have a supply of successful product in the future at reasonable and predictable prices.

chapter 5

producer contracts

by Andrew Thompson

This chapter deals with the typical agreement between a major record company and a producer in relation to the production of a given number of tracks by a particular artist. It also looks briefly at the type of arrangements which may be made when a major record company is not involved.

In terms of legal issues, a producer contract is more straightforward than a recording contract or a publishing contract, as there is no exclusivity and there are no restraints. Essentially, the producer contract deals with what the producer has to do and what he should be paid. Nevertheless, in practice it is often hard to resolve these issues, and it is therefore sometimes difficult to secure a signed contract. Whilst it is rare for a record company to put an artist in the recording studio without him having signed a recording contract this cannot be said of producers, and it is too often the case that producer contracts are only signed after the event.

the IMF handbook a guide to professional band management

PRODUCERS

the problem of delay

confusion

There are several reasons for the frequent delays experienced by producers when concluding deals. One reason is poor communication between the record company's A&R department and its business affairs department. The business affairs person may only come to hear of the deal after the pre-production work has started, and even if he is aware of the situation he may have difficulty in obtaining clear instructions from the A&R man concerning what the producer is required to do and what he is to be paid.

This is not necessarily the fault of the A&R man; there is often a reluctance on everybody's part to commit to and define the parameters of a particular project until the producer and the artist are seen to be able to work together effectively. The position is sometimes made worse by poor communication between the producer, the record company and the artist, and the preliminary discussions will concentrate mainly upon artistic issues. Most artists – and many A&R men – exhibit an in-built reluctance to discuss money or anything businesslike, and indeed many producers suffer from the same malaise and tend to be shy when discussing their deals, particularly when talking to artists. Most such producers will engage a manager, and eventually a business-like discussion with the A&R man may take place. The producer or his manager may consequently think that they have agreed something in principle, but too often they will subsequently find that the record company's business affairs man thinks otherwise.

inertia

It is important that any confusion is dispelled at the earliest opportunity before the deal-making process gets bogged down by its own inertia. The risk of inertia arises partly because nobody, including the producer, is prepared to treat the matter of the deal as a priority. The producer is usually too busy building his relationship with the artist, and in any event may well be in the studio day and night. For his lawyer, the producer's agreement is a dull affair when compared with the relative excitement of a recording contract or publishing deal for a 'hot' artist. Similarly, the business affairs manager will view his batch of producer agreements as the most dreary part of his workload. He may be pestered by record company executives demanding why the latest hopeful has not yet signed his recording contract, but he is not likely to be under any internal pressure to deal with a producer agreement, other than in the rare event when a much-needed producer refuses to work until his contract has been properly arranged. Moreover, there is no incentive for the record company to hurry over the producer's contract because generally it will refuse to make any final payment until the contract has been signed. The various methods of dealing with this kind of inertia are investigated later in this chapter.

the role of the producer

the scapegoat

The producer is the translator of the artist's ideas. He may be the best person to decide how to approach a particular recording because the artist may be too close to his art to do this. A&R departments display great antipathy at the idea of artists producing themselves because this too often leads to over-indulgence. In one sense, therefore, the producer's role is to deal with any conflict of interest arising between the record company's commercial motives and the artist's creativity. This will often mean that the producer is in a no-win situation. He cannot please both the artist and the record company, and whatever goes wrong he will always be the most convenient scapegoat.

pre-production

The ways in which producers interpret their role and how they carry it out vary considerably. Some producers may not wish to spend all day and night in the studio and may prefer instead to delegate some of the technical aspects of production to the technicians and engineers, restricting their involvement to that of selecting and rejecting songs and judging how those songs should be arranged. They will involve themselves in rehearsal sessions and in selecting the various backing musicians and other musical criteria. Some producers view this whole pre-production phase as the most crucial part of their responsibilities, although most producers will accept that they should be in charge of the whole process in a hands-on sense and will wish to be in the studio at all times.

budgetary control

The record company will invariably impose upon the producer the responsibility for budgetary control. In a more mundane fashion, the producer will usually also be responsible for booking the studio and for completing all of the paperwork (including filling out the Musicians' Union session forms and notifying the record company any samples that may have been used).

samples

The record companies have been quick to ensure that their position in relation to the use of samples is protected as fully as possible. The artist will be required in the recording contract to give certain warranties in relation to the use of samples. Separately, the record company will require additional protection in its contract with the producer, and it will generally be the producer's responsibility to notify the record company immediately in the event of the use of any samples. Sometimes it will be the producer's responsibility to obtain clearance for the sample in question, but usually the record company will accept responsibility for obtaining these clearances. Nevertheless, the record company will invariably insist that, for contractual purposes, a particular master will not be considered to have been delivered until all of the necessary clearances are in place. To the producer, this will often mean that the 'delivery' (usually the trigger for payment of the producer's fees) is in the hands of the record company. In order to overcome this difficulty, producers will sometimes prepare different versions of a track as a contingency: one with the sample and one without it.

songwriting

If the producer is involved in the arrangements for a particular song in such a way that the recorded version of that song is substantially different from the original demo prepared by the songwriter, then the final version will arguably represent a new arrangement and the producer, as the arranger, will have an interest in the copyright. For this reason, some producers insist on being credited as a co-writer of the material. Generally, however, this practice is frowned upon. The producer's advance and his entitlement to any royalties compensates him for all of his work. While he may argue that his work strays into the area of musical composition, nevertheless it is rarely accepted that the producer's involvement is of a sufficiently creative nature that he should be treated as a co-writer or composer as well as the record's producer.

Sometimes, of course, the producer may enjoy a genuine involvement in the songwriting: either his songs will be recorded or perhaps he will co-write the material with the artist. In these circumstances the producer will earn from the exploitation of the publishing rights separately from his contribution to the musical material. In this event, there is one common pitfall which the producer should try to avoid. Most producer agreements contain controlled compositions clauses (see the section on 'Controlled Compositions' in chapter three), and as we have seen the effect of controlled compositions provisions is generally to reduce a writer's income from mechanical royalties in respect of record sales in the USA and Canada. On some occasions the producer may succeed in avoiding provisions of this kind, but this may simply have the effect of transferring the problem to the artist. If the controlled compositions provisions in the recording contract include material written not only by the artist but also by any producer, then if the producer succeeds in securing full mechanical royalties for himself the reduction will instead be applied against the artist's share of the mechanical royalties.

mixers

Some producers are not really producers at all, belonging instead to that special breed known as mixers. These people have little or no involvement with the artist but are technical wizards. They take the tracks and remix them to create a better, or at least different, sound. All material needs to be mixed in this way, and mixing is simply one of many functions generally carried out by the producer. Some producers prefer to hire a specialist mixer to carry out the mixing function, although usually the producer would wish to supervise this. In some cases the record company will be unhappy with the work undertaken by the producer, and may therefore refuse to pay the advance due on delivery. Rather than start again, the company may instead decide to keep the existing material but arrange for another producer or a specialist remixer to rework it. On other occasions there may be no criticism of the original producer but the record company may decide that, for marketing reasons, it requires a specialist remix of a particular track. With dance music, of course, numerous remixes of the same basic track may be released.

delivery standard

Ultimately the producer's responsibility will be to deliver finished recordings to the record company of a technically-acceptable standard, and often of a standard which is 'commercially' acceptable to the record company. This is an area of considerable controversy. Usually, all or part of the producer's advance will be deferred pending delivery of the masters. If the record company insists upon commercially-acceptable masters, then the producer will be nervous that, at the end of the day, the record company will decide that the masters are of insufficient quality and may therefore refuse to make payment. Many producers are not prepared to accept this, but equally some record companies adamantly refuse to give up this protection. Some companies have a reputation for being difficult over the final payment and will refuse to make this unless until the A&R department is completely satisfied with the work. Accordingly, the argument over this issue may continue until the work has been completed, at which point – with luck – the record company will decide that it is satisfied with the finished result. An acknowledgement to this effect is then inserted in the contract, which is then signed, and the advance is paid.

the producer's rights

financial entitlement

The record company will usually take the convenient view that the producer has no rights in relation to the recordings. It is for precisely this reason that the record company is rather relaxed in allowing the work to proceed despite the fact that there is no signed contract. As far as the record company is concerned, the producer has no rights other than the right to be paid for his work, the entitlement to receive such payment as has been agreed. If there is any confusion concerning this, the producer is nevertheless entitled to payment on what is known as a *quantum meruit* basis (ie a fair and reasonable payment for the work done).

the 'maker' of the recordings

The record company, as far as it is concerned, is the 'maker' of the recordings, to the effect that it is the owner of their copyright. The record company does not require any performer's consents from the producer because his performance is usually not featured upon the recordings. Neither, usually, has the producer contributed to the writing or composing of the musical material featured, so the producer therefore has no legal interest in that material. Accordingly, the record company would argue, there is nothing the producer may do to prevent the company from exploiting the material beyond suing for the payment of any fees due.

the Re-Pro argument

It could be argued that the producer does indeed have an interest in the recordings, and so the attitude generally adopted by the record companies is perhaps dangerously complacent. Under the provisions of the Copyright Act of 1956 the person who owned the copyright in a recording was the person who had commissioned that recording. The position changed, however, with the introduction of the Copyright Designs and Patents Act of 1988, under which the owner of the copyright is stated as the "person by whom the arrangements necessary for the making of the recording are undertaken".

The following is an extract from the submissions by Re-Pro (the trade organisation representing the interests of record producers) made to the Monopolies and Mergers Commission in 1994 in relation to its enquiry into the supply in the UK of recorded music.

> "We have recently taken the opinion of a leading QC who specialises in copyright law in order to determine the question of authorship of sound recordings which are subject to the 1988 Act. His unequivocal view is that a record producer is a person who undertakes the arrangements necessary for a recording to be made. If a record producer undertakes all of these arrangements alone then he or she is the sole author of the recording concerned. Where those arrangements are undertaken jointly by the record company and the record producer authorship is shared between them. In any event, whenever a record producer is engaged by a record company he or she will always be at least joint owner. Section eleven of the 1988 Act provides that the author of a sound recording is the first owner of the copyright in that sound recording. In passing the 1988 Act, Parliament also decided to drop the provisions in the 1956 Act which vested copyright in sound recordings in any person who commissioned their making. The fact that the record companies commission and pay for the making of sound recordings is now irrelevant to the question of ownership of copyright in recordings made after the introduction of the 1988 Act. It follows that, under the new law, record producers are at the very least one of the authors and first owners of the copyright in recordings produced by them."

A prudent record company would therefore ensure that, prior to commencement of recording, the producer makes an unequivocal assignment in writing of his interest in the recordings, if he had any. If the record companies were to recognise such a requirement this might introduce a note of greater urgency into the whole negotiating process.

credit

This matter is usually of great importance to the producer. The form of credit should be agreed at the outset, and an obligation should be imposed on the record company to ensure that all records bear the proper credit. The company may also be persuaded to feature the credit on paid advertising material. A record company will sometimes accept that it may not engage another producer to carry out work on the recordings without the producer's prior consent, although if there is no such restriction then the producer should insist upon being provided with a listening copy of any recording which features his work together with that of another producer, and he should insist on the right to have his credit removed.

THE CONTRACT

the parties to the contract

UK and US approaches

A producer's first contact is usually (although not always) with the A&R man rather than with the artist or the artist's manager. It is usually the record company which pays all of the recording costs and, of course, ultimately owns the recordings. Invariably, the form of the contract is generated by the record company's business affairs person, and it is therefore automatically assumed that the producer will enter into a contract with the record company. However, this is not necessarily the case: US record companies will refuse to enter into any contract with a producer, insisting instead that the artist, or the artist's production company, enters into the agreement. Thus the record company shrugs off any responsibility for the producer and neatly sidesteps any potential contractual difficulties. With luck, the company will even be able to persuade the artist's lawyer to deal with the paperwork. Fortunately, in most cases, UK record companies have not yet abrogated for producers in this way, and will still enter into contracts with them directly.

direct accounting

The producer will always prefer to contract with the record company rather than the artist, as he is then more likely to be paid. This is not to suggest any dishonesty on the part of the artist, but simply a matter of cashflow and financial stability. Also, taking out a right of audit against an artist is a more or less worthless exercise; a right of audit needs to be accompanied with the right to inspect the record company's books and records of account. This problem is partially solved if the producer's agreement is made with the artist or with some intermediary production company, but only if this is supported with suitable direct accounting arrangements. The producer should not be satisfied with a simple letter of direction from the artist to the record company requesting that the company pays the producer's royalties and deducts them from any royalties payable to the artist; if the producer's financial interest is to be properly protected, there needs to be a separate contract made between the producer and the record company. The best solution is a tri-partite agreement, taking the form of an irrevocable letter of instruction from the artist to the company, countersigned by the producer, in which some 'consideration' is shown to move from the producer to the record company (perhaps £1) in order to create a legally-binding commitment.

standard forms

The IMF Producer Managers Group and Re-Pro have introduced a preferred form of producer contract. The intention is that the various record companies should be persuaded to adopt this form of contract in an effort to reduce the delays and aggravations generally involved in agreeing up a suitable form of contract. There has already been some limited success with this. With many well-established producers, a contract will be agreed upon in relation to a particular project with each company for whom the producer regularly undertakes work . Therefore (again as a short cut) each time the producer undertakes work for that company the same form of contract will be used as a template for the new deal, although the principal terms will vary in each case.

the deal memorandum

driving the deal

How does the producer avoid any preliminary confusion over his deal? He needs to know with certainty what he is to be paid, when he will be paid and by whom. In order to overcome the inertia which is usually involved with contracts, a strong-minded character is needed to seize the deal and then needs to show some tenacity in driving it through. It is difficult, and probably inappropriate, for the producer to attempt to do this himself, and the artist will usually be of no use. The artist's manager may go through the motions, but he has no authority to make any commitment on behalf of the record company,

the IMF handbook a guide to professional band management

and the record company cannot be relied upon at all. The best person to drive the deal through is either the producer's manager (if he has one) or his lawyer.

paying the lawyer

If the task falls to the producer's lawyer then it should initially be decided who pays the lawyer's fees. The record company will not contribute towards them at all, and it is usually the producer who is liable for them in the first instance. However, there should perhaps be an arrangement of some kind between the producer and his manager as to who bears the costs.

Arrangements between producers and their managers will vary considerably. The manager will often charge 20% commission but will provide a complete service, in the sense that the manager will not only secure the work and negotiate the principal terms but will also drive the deal through with minimal or even no involvement from an outside lawyer. Other managers charge 20% but rely heavily upon a lawyer's input, and agree to bear the legal fees out of that commission, while still others charge 10% (which is rare) or 15% but expect the producer to pay any legal fees. What is considered fair and reasonable in a particular case will depend entirely upon the nature of the relationship and the value to the producer of the particular services provided. However, it is generally considered to be unfair for a manager to charge 20% commission and then rely heavily upon the producer's lawyer to drive through the deal, because the producer will then have to pay the legal fees as well as the commission. Time is money for a lawyer, and if he is charged with the responsibility for negotiating the principal terms and of then driving the deal, instead of progressing with the paperwork at a more gentlemanly pace, he will spend a lot of time and his fees will reflect this.

distribution of the deal memorandum

The person charged with responsibility for the deal should issue a deal memorandum at the first available opportunity. The lines of communication will still be tangled at this stage, however, and it is therefore important that everybody is provided with a copy: the artist's manager, possibly the artist himself, certainly the artist's lawyer, the head of business affairs at the record company, the A&R person responsible and, for good measure, the managing director of the record company. The trick is to secure an agreement on the deal memorandum as quickly as possible so that the producer can then start work in the studio without undue risk. If the producer cannot be persuaded to hold back until there is clear agreement on all material terms before he starts work, as is usually the case, then this is all the more reason to secure an agreement on the principal terms of the deal, before work progresses too far.

contents of the deal memorandum

It is important that the memo is not bogged down with details, but it should still cover all material terms together with those aspects of the deal which often prove controversial. It should therefore deal with the following points:

- The contract must be with the record company itself.

- The number of tracks to be recorded.

- The advance per track, or the overall advance for the entire project.

- The date on which the advances will be paid.

- The royalty rate, along with any escalations in this rate and whether the royalty is to be calculated at that rate by reference to the dealer or the retail price.

- For the purposes of clarification, that the royalty rate is to apply worldwide (if this is the case) rather than being subject to the same pro rata territorial reductions suffered by the artist (likewise format reductions).

- The royalty is to be paid subject only to recoupment of the advance and is neither to be subjected to the recoupment of any recording costs nor deferred pending such recoupment.

- The recording budget should be specified but it should be stated that the producer will have no responsibility for any excess costs, unless they have been incurred because of wilful neglect or default on his part.

- The producer will require A- and B-side protection.

- The royalty is not to be reduced by the amount of any royalty payable to any other producer or mixer engaged in relation to the recordings in question.

- The credit requirements.

urgency

The producer may have to compromise on some of these issues, but if he is to secure his position in relation to them then he has to do so quickly. It is no good arguing any of these points after the work has been completed; the record company will simply dig in its heels. When the deal memo is circulated it should be accompanied by a request for copies of the relevant extracts from the artist's recording contract showing the detailed royalty calculation and payment provisions, but perhaps also indicating that the producer will be willing to accept that his royalties will be calculated in the same manner, providing that the provisions are reasonable. It is usually a mistake to relax and wait for a response to the memo, as there very often will be no response for some time. The next stage of the process is to hound all of those concerned on the telephone. If there is both a lawyer and manager involved then they should both be involved in this.

MONEY

what is the producer worth?

basic concepts

The producer is generally entitled to a royalty so that his efforts will be rewarded according to the success of his work. The producer will rarely have any involvement in the promotion or the marketing of the record, and so the level of that success is not within his control. Of course the producer will require a fee for his work, which will usually be treated as an advance against his royalty entitlement. Producer royalties range usually from 2% to 5% of the dealer price, and most producers are paid 3% or 4%. Most producers think that they are underpaid, although many people take the opposing view. However, while it is certainly true that successful producers are very wealthy, few should begrudge them their rewards. Sometimes a producer will be persuaded to work on the basis that no royalty is payable, although this is rare and is generally restricted to production for superstar artists, who may resent having to pay a substantial proportion of their royalty income to a producer in circumstances in which the reputation of the artist is already established. The superstar may notice that his royalty earnings from his last album were around £4 million but that £1 million of this was paid to his producer. Having a superstar's ego he will wonder whether the producer's input on the last album justified so high a reward, and he may be unwilling to pay him another £1 million for spending six weeks with him in the studio recording the next album. The superstar may remember that the producer was paid an advance of £50,000 for the last album, and he may decide that, on this occasion, he will generously offer £250,000 (which is in itself not bad for six weeks' work), but only on the basis that this represents a buy-out of all of the producer's rights so that no further royalties will be payable. Given that the artist is a superstar, no doubt the producer is also from the top of the pile. If this is the case, he will be insulted by the suggestion that he should work on a record and have no royalty entitlement and will reject the proposal out of hand. If the superstar persists in denying the producer his royalty entitlement, and if the producer needs the £250,000 badly enough, the superstar may succeed in this.

artist versus producer

On balance, producers are probably valued more highly by record companies than they are by artists, and too often artists end up resenting the amount which the producer earns. If, for example, the gross artist royalty is 16% and this is inclusive of a producer royalty of 4%, then (in the case of a solo artist) that artist will earn three times more than the producer, although the artist's royalty will be available for recouping recording costs whereas the producer's will probably not. The solo artist may feel reasonably comfortable with this, but if we look at a band with four members then the producer's 4% will exceed the 3% available for each of the band members. Moreover, the band's work does not end once the recordings are completed, and they may then be engaged in perhaps two years of hard slog in promotional work and touring. Also, of course, the band may have time to record only one album every two or three years; a producer, however, may be able to produce perhaps three or four each year. On the other hand, the producer might argue that his work helps the artist to establish his reputation and that the artist is able to profit from this by the release of further material, whereas the producer derives no benefit at all from the artist's future activities (although in extreme cases producers have been known to ask for an override royalty on the artist's next album).

the artist pays

The artist, or his manager, should be aware of these issues and should be diligent in negotiating the producer's deal. Too often, in a wave of enthusiasm for a particular producer, percentages are agreed in haste and with little thought as to how they may pan out in the future. Still more dangerous is the tendency shown by many record companies to secure the services of the producer and agree to the terms of his deal without any involvement from the artist, because ultimately (assuming recoupment is achieved) it is the artist's money which is being generously handed out by the record company to the producer. If the record company is determined to use a particular producer, and he insists upon a royalty of 5%, then on some rare occasions the artist may persuade the record company to make a contribution, so that perhaps only 3% or 4%, instead of the full 5%, is deductible from the artist's gross royalty.

the IMF handbook a guide to professional band management

the European approach

These days, more and more UK producers are undertaking work for European record companies. Under a typical European-style deal the producer's deal is unrelated to the artist's deal (ie the artist's royalty payable under the recording contract tends is not inclusive of the producer's royalty). The royalty payable to the producer, therefore, tends not to be subject to the recoupment of recording costs. This is certainly true in France and Scandinavia, although Germany is increasingly adopting the UK model. Nevertheless, royalty rates payable to producers in Europe tend to be similar to those payable to producers in the UK. European record companies generally adopt a more flexible approach than their UK counterparts, and they may sometimes be persuaded to allow the producer's lawyer to prepare the contract (a distinct advantage!), and even to contribute towards meeting the cost of legal fees.

royalties

royalty rates

Most producers used to command royalties of between 2% and 4% of the retail price, and the most common rate was 3% of retail. However, now that royalties are generally calculated by reference to the dealer price (see the section on 'Royalties' in chapter three), most producers command 3% or 4%. (3% of the retail price roughly converts to 4% of the dealer price.) When negotiating his rate, the producer should check that his royalties are payable by reference to 100% of sales, and if not then the rate should be adjusted in order to take account of this. He should also try to ensure that the agreed rate applies to all sales worldwide, although he may still have to suffer territorial reductions. If he is offered, say, 4% for UK sales and 3% elsewhere, he should reject this but perhaps be prepared to compromise, on the basis that he will suffer the same pro rata reduction as the artist. If, for example, the artist's gross rate of royalty is 16% in the UK but 13% elsewhere, the producer might accept 4% for UK sales and $^{13}/_{16}$ of 4% in relation to foreign sales. The producer might also try for royalty escalations based upon sales targets of some kind, so that perhaps the 4% rate will increase to 4.5% for sales in a particular territory in excess of that number required in that territory to achieve gold or platinum status. As an alternative, the producer might benefit from a pro rata share of any royalty escalation enjoyed by the artist, although the record company and the artist will usually resist this.

method of calculation

Most producers will accept that their royalty should be calculated at the agreed rate in accordance with the same royalty calculation and payment provisions as those which apply between the record company and the artist concerned. Some refuse to accept this, however, and insist upon the negotiations extending to a full-scale review of the detailed royalty calculation provisions. There is some merit in this, particularly in the case of a sought-after producer who is producing a recently-signed artist, who may not have been in a particularly strong negotiating position in relation to his recording contract. If the principle is accepted, then the person driving the deal for the producer should insist that he is provided with relevant extracts from the recording contract at the soonest available opportunity so that these may be reviewed. If they contain provisions which are unfair or unusual, then the producer should of course object to them.

a-side protection

Most producers insist upon what is known as A-side protection so that, if a track by the producer is featured as the A-side, the producer will suffer no pro rata reduction in his royalty rate, even though he may not have produced the B-side. The record company will sometimes only accept this on the basis that they will not have to pay a royalty to the producer if he has produced the B-side and not the A-side. A producer is normally reluctant to accept this, but he may do so if this is limited to those instances in which the producer of the A-side also has B-side protection, in which case the record company is at least protected against having to pay twice for one track.

secondary exploitation

Some record companies are careful to word their producer agreements to ensure that the producer is only entitled to a royalty in relation to record sales, so that they have to pay nothing in relation to any other form of exploitation. However, the producer should insist that he is also paid for other exploitation, and will usually accept a pro rata share of whatever is payable to the artist. For example, in the case of income from synchronisation licences, the record company is usually obliged to account to the artist for 50% of its receipts. Using the previous example of a 16% gross artist royalty and a 4% producer royalty, the producer should receive a $1/4$ share of the 50% payable to the artist (12.5% of the gross). The producer should also ensure that his royalty entitlement extends not only to records but also to videos and other audio-visual devices, as well as interactive formats. He will often accept a pro rata share of whatever is payable to the artist in relation to the exploitation of

the IMF handbook a guide to professional band management

audio-visual rights. It may be argued that this is inappropriate because the producer has only been involved in the audio and not the visual element. On this basis the producer's entitlement may be halved so that, with reference to our example, he would be entitled to 12.5% of that payable to the artist.

performance income

The question concerning the proportion (if any) of the performance income which should be paid to the producer is currently subject to some controversy. Under the new regulations, the PPL will collect all performance income (which is derived from licensing to broadcasters and others the right to perform the recordings publicly) on the basis that 50% of it will be distributed to the record companies and 50% to the performers. It is still unclear how the performers' share will be divided between the featured artists and any session musicians, but it is unlikely that any part of this will be distributed to the producer, and neither will the record companies allow producers a part of their own 50% share. Accordingly, if producers are to be excluded from any industry-wide collection and distribution arrangements in relation to performance income, the best they will be able to achieve is a contractual right to participate, by inserting a provision in the producer's contract to the effect that the record company must pay the producer a proportion of the record company's 50% share. The current indications are that the record companies will resist this.

advances

successful producers

A successful producer may command an advance of £40,000 or £50,000 per album. Depending upon his working methods and the type of artist with whom he works, he may be able to complete four album projects in a year. He might therefore earn £200,000 per annum by way of advances, although this will be inclusive of any commission he has to pay, and he will also have certain professional expenses (ie legal and accountancy fees). Of course, in extreme cases a producer may be able to command fees far higher than this – some top producers sometimes charge up to $100,000 per track. A mid-range producer (one with a reasonably strong track record who has recently produced one or two successful records) may command, say, between £30,000 and £40,000 per album, and he may manage to complete three album projects per year, together with the occasional track for other artists, in which case he might gross perhaps between £100,000 and £125,000 per annum.

However, producers have to work hard for their money. They are under pressure to deliver the goods on time and within budget, and unfortunately the creative process does not always work according to plan. Producers have to deal with temperamental artists and demanding A&R men, and quite likely they will end up in the studio around the clock. Nevertheless, in most cases, once a producer is well established, his ability to command hefty advances is likely to last for only a few years, and there is a natural temptation to make hay while the sun shines. Producers are continually coming in and out of fashion, and a producer is often only as good as the last album he produced.

A recognised producer who is not yet in the top league may command around £1,000 or £2,000 per track. A producer will on some occasions be prepared to accept less than this, for instance if only a limited budget is available and if the producer is particularly enthusiastic about the artist with whom he is working.

mixers

A specialist mixer usually charges anything between £2,000 and £10,000 per track, a figure which is usually inclusive of studio fees, while high-profile remixers have been known to command as much as £20,000 for a single track. A successful mixer will usually be offered more work than he is able to handle, even though he will often complete a mix within the space of one day. (The normal rate is probably a day and a half per mix.) If he is a high-profile mixer in sufficient demand he may also be able to secure a royalty entitlement, which will usually be 0.5% but might be a full 1%. A mixer brought in to work on an album would not usually secure a royalty entitlement, however; it is normally specialist club or dance remixers who will insist upon a royalty entitlement. This might be offered for a 12" dance version of a song, but some remixers will argue that their royalty entitlement should also extend to any 7" version, and will sometimes push for a co-production and/or co-publishing credit. Record companies will often insist that the original producer accepts a reduction in the rate of his royalty if the record company then has to pay a royalty to a third-party producer or mixer, although if the original producer is in a reasonably strong negotiating position he should be able to successfully resist this. As a compromise, he may accept that his royalty will be reduced if a third party is brought in to rework his material prior to its initial release, but he may also insist that any special mixes produced for specific marketing purposes should be paid for entirely by the record company. If the producer ends up having to accept a reduction in his royalty, he would seek to limit this to maybe a half of whatever is paid to the third party, so that the cost is then split between record company and producer. Alternatively, he may accept that the entirety of third-party royalty is deducted from his royalty, provided that he receives at least half of the royalty rate to which he would otherwise be entitled.

per-track advances

A producer will usually quote his rates on a per-track basis, perhaps asking for £4,000 per track. If he is working on an album, the chances are that he may be asked to produce 13 or 14 tracks, and the conventional compromise which is reached in these cases is that he may be paid his full per-track rate but for only ten tracks (£40,000 for the entire album), irrespective of the number of tracks.

advance or fee?

The company will generally insist that the entirety of any fee paid to the producer is treated as a recoupable advance. If the record company pleads poverty or is not prepared to pay the producer's usual advance for some other reason, it may sometimes be persuaded to treat the producer's fee (or perhaps 50% thereof) as non-recoupable. This may be dressed up on the basis that the non-recoupable element is attributable perhaps to the producer's engineering services. Likewise, if the producer also plays instruments on the recordings he may be able to persuade the record company to treat part of the advance as a non-recoupable fee in respect of his playing services.

bonus advances

The producer may also be able to secure bonus advances, which may be triggered by particular sales targets. Normally, this would simply improve the producer's cashflow in that, depending on how it is calculated, his bonus would simply amount to an accelerated payment of those royalties which may have accrued but are not yet due for payment.

payment schedule

Usually, half of any agreed advance is payable on commencement of the producer's services, with the balance payable upon completion. Nevertheless, most record companies refuse to make any payment until there is a signed contract. However, it is sometimes possible to accelerate payment of the final instalment so that perhaps 50% of it is paid on the completion of recording but prior to mixing, and the final balance is paid only upon the delivery of the finished, fully-mixed masters. Producers should always resist any suggestion that part of the advance is delayed pending the record's commercial release.

expenses

The producer will also expect his expenses to be reimbursed, and will often be entitled to a *per diem* payment of some kind to cover subsistence costs.

recoupment and deferment

UK and US approaches

Most UK record companies will agree to account to the producer for his royalty subject only to the recoupment of his advance. However, some UK companies are following the example shown by the record companies in America, which invariably refuse to pay any producer royalties until the recording costs have been recouped. In the worst cases, the producer's royalty will actually be used towards recoupment of those costs. In most cases, however, the record company will simply agree to a deferral of the producer's royalties, so that they will be paid after being calculated from the first record sold (subject, of course, to the recoupment of the producer's advance), but only if the record sells enough to enable the company to recoup the recording costs from the artist's royalty.

example

As a way of illustrating this point, let us again assume a gross artist royalty of 16%, inclusive of a 4% producer's royalty. Let us assume that the producer receives an advance of £20,000 but that there are additional recording costs of £100,000. What will be his position if the 16% gross royalty generates £100,000 of royalties, for example? The 4% producer's royalty would be worth £25,000, and so at this stage, after the recoupment of his £20,000 advance, he is due the payment of a further £5,000 in royalties. However, if his contract with the record company contains a provision to the effect that his royalties are to be deferred pending recoupment, then no royalties will be payable to him until the recording costs, net of the producer's advance (£100,000 in this case), have been recouped from the net artist royalty (12%). In this example, the net artist royalty amounts to only £75,000 at this stage, and so there is an unrecouped deficit of £25,000. Therefore, no royalties will yet be payable to the producer.

If the next royalty statement discloses an aggregate royalty income (calculated at the 16% gross rate) of £200,000, so that the producer's 4% is at that stage worth £50,000, then the full £50,000 will then be payable by the company, minus only the £20,000 advance, because recoupment will by then have been achieved (ie the 12% net rate will have given rise to £150,000, which is therefore more than sufficient to recoup the £100,000 recording costs).

pitfalls

If the producer is forced to accept deferment provisions of this nature, he should be careful to avoid certain pitfalls: firstly, he should ensure that he only suffers from a deferment, and that his royalties are not used actually to recoup a share of the recording costs; secondly, recoupment for this purpose should be calculated either by reference to the net recording costs (after deduction of the producer's advance) from the net artist royalty or by reference to the gross recording costs, inclusive of the producer's advance, from the gross artist royalty. Also, for the purposes of calculating recoupment, there should be a strict definition of recording costs. Most importantly, recoupment should not extend to any other costs which may be recoupable from the artist (ie the costs of promotional videos and tour support).

accountings

method

The producer will usually accept that he will be accounted to in the same way and on the same dates as the record company accounts to the artist.

audit rights

The producer should ensure that he has a suitable direct right of audit against the record company. Ideally, the record company should be obliged to reimburse the audit costs in the event of a discrepancy of some kind (perhaps where there is an underpayment of 5% or 10% of the total amount properly payable, in relation to the accounting periods under review). As we have seen in the section on 'Audit Rights' in chapter three, more and more recording artists undertake regular audits. However, the producer usually has a lesser financial interest than the artist. Producers are also reluctant to incur the considerable costs involved in undertaking a proper audit, even if the contract provides that those costs are to be reimbursed if a discrepancy arises. In practice, the most sensible course for the producer is to maintain contact with the artist and to occasionally discuss with the artist whether they should jointly carry out an audit, with the artist and the producer contributing to the costs involved on a pro rata basis – to the extent that those costs cannot be recovered from the record company. In any event, it is worth trying to obtain a provision to the effect that, if the artist carries out an audit as a result of which a settlement of some kind is made, the producer's royalty account then should automatically be adjusted on the same basis.

INDEPENDENT PRODUCTIONS

independent record companies

royalty or profit share?

A producer may have to accept that he will be paid on a rather different basis if he undertakes work for an independent record company or for a production company. The first difference is that the independent companies generally do not have the same level of funding as the majors, and so he may be squeezed harder in terms of his advance. Many independent record companies have turned away from the traditional royalty system and instead pay their artists usually 50% of any net profits. Although there is some logic to this joint venture between the artist and the record company, it is less logical for the producer to be tied to this arrangement. The producer will have no involvement in a record once his work in the studio is finished, and he will certainly have no control over what expenses are incurred. Usually, therefore, the producer will insist that his royalty is calculated in the normal way. In fact, if he has had to accept a reduction in his advance because of budgetary constraints, he may require his royalty to be enhanced in some way in order to compensate for this.

what percentage of profit?

If the producer is still persuaded to accept a share of net profits, what percentage might he expect? Our example of the 16% royalty under the traditional system, inclusive of a 4% producer royalty, gives a ratio of 3:1 – ie the earnings of the artist are three times greater than those of the producer (although this does not take into account the fact that the artist suffers recoupment of recording costs from his share). If the gross royalty is at the higher end of the scale, say 21%, and the producer commands only 3% then the ratio increases to 6:1 in favour of the artist. If the artist is to receive 50% of net profits then the producer might ask for between 10% and 25% of the artist's 50% share. Although this does not affect the producer, it then has to be decided whether the producer's share comes 'off the top', leaving the balance to be split equally between the record company and the artist (which is the more usual arrangement), or whether the artist's 50% should be inclusive of the producer's share.

speculative work

basic protection

Sometimes the producer will be persuaded to carry out work on a speculative basis before an artist has even signed a record deal, when the artist may have a manager or publisher prepared to fund the costs involved. Ideally, the producer will still secure a fee of some kind, although very often he will be persuaded that there are no funds available for this purpose. In order to protect his position he should consider imposing a contractual obligation upon the artist to the effect that any record company which may become involved will account directly to the producer for royalties at an agreed rate. The rate should be fairly high in order to reflect the element of speculation and risk. The producer might also insist that he owns the copyright of the recordings until any record deal has been struck, and he should also either impose a re-recording restriction upon the artist or make it clear that his royalty is payable not only on the recordings which he has produced but also on any other recordings of the same songs which may be made by the artist.

studio deals

Most speculative work of this nature will involve a studio deal of some kind. Sometimes, of course, the producer will have his own studio or at least facilities at his disposal to make some quality demos. If his own facilities are used, he will need to factor this in when calculating his payment. More often, he will carry out the work during down time at a commercial studio (those few hours between bookings when the studio is idle), as most commercial studios offer special deals for people wishing to use them at this time. The deal with the studio might involve obtaining cut-price rates, or paying the studio a royalty of some kind in the event that the recordings are commercially released in lieu of a guaranteed payment. In this situation, the producer may have to fight the studio to protect his own position. For example, he will probably not be able to own the copyright in the recordings because the studio will almost certainly insist on owning the tapes. In this way, the studio may then assign the copyright of the recordings to the record company, when one is found, in return for an agreement with that company either for the payment of an override royalty or for the reimbursement of the studio costs. The producer's first task, if he attempts to extract the best possible advantage from the use of any commercial studio in this way, is to ensure that there is no ambiguity involved and that it is clearly understood that the producer will not be liable for any studio fees. If the studio requires a deal of some kind, that deal should be made with the artist and not with the producer.

chapter 6
publishing contracts

by Andrew Thompson

Whilst the recording contract is the principal means by which a recording artist pursues his trade if he writes his own musical material, then next in financial importance will be his publishing arrangements. Under his record deal, he will earn from the exploitation of the physical recordings, but he will earn from the exploitation of his songs separately. 'Publishing' in the context of the music industry means the arrangements by which a song is exploited. When we refer to a publishing contract we usually mean the agreement under which the writer agrees to write material for his publisher. This is more accurately described as a songwriting agreement, or what the MCPS and the PRS refer to as an ESA (an Exclusive Songwriter Agreement). When a publisher enters into an agreement with another publisher (perhaps for the exploitation of particular songs overseas) that agreement is usually referred to as a sub-publishing agreement.

In this chapter we will consider whether a songwriter should enter into a publishing contract and, if so, when. Later, we will analyse the different types of publishing income and look at how a particular deal may be valued. Then we will look more closely at a typical publishing contract, and briefly consider alternative contractual arrangements. Finally, we will review those factors which need to be borne in mind even after the deal is struck.

the IMF handbook a guide to professional band management

WHO NEEDS A PUBLISHER?

the nature of a publishing contract

copyright

Stated in the simplest terms, a publishing contract involves the writer giving the rights to his songs to the publisher, in return for which the publisher collects all of the income accrued from the exploitation of those songs and then accounts to the writer for an agreed share of that income. The writer usually transfers the copyright in his songs to the publisher, although generally only for a limited period of time. A song is generally considered to be a very precious and personal thing, and some writers therefore have some difficulties with the idea of giving away their songs, preferring instead to retain ownership of their songs and make their own arrangements for the collection of any income. If the writer does not assign the copyright of his songs to the publisher, but instead merely grants him a licence of some kind, then the agreement would probably be called an administration agreement, or perhaps a licensing agreement, rather than a publishing contract. This issue is considered in greater detail later in this chapter

the publisher's services

All publishers will emphasise a number of positive reasons why a writer should enter into a publishing contract. The publisher will claim that, with the various systems it has in place, it is better able to collect efficiently any available income than a writer operating on his own. Moreover, the publisher is more skilled in negotiating fees for the licensing of certain rights in the writer's songs. The publisher will also have a professional manager or team of managers searching for additional ways in which to exploit the writer's material. He may even be able to offer help and guidance in the songwriting process, although this is very rare these days and the publisher's creative involvement is usually limited to suggesting potential co-writers. The publisher may also have facilities which the writer may use, either at a subsidised cost or for free (ie for recording demos). The publisher may also be prepared to invest in the writer's career by paying advances to him, even before there is any sight of any publishing income from which to recoup them. The funding which is supplied by the publisher may prove vital during the early stages of the writing process.

when should the deal be done?

the significance of the record deal

The conventional wisdom used to be that, for a singer/songwriter, the publishing deal was delayed until the record deal was in place. It is the record deal which lends value to the publishing rights, and there was a fear that, if he concluded a publishing deal before signing a recording contract, he would sell himself short. However, this view is no longer as common, and publishers are now far more competitive. A publisher will often be the first to recognise a particular talent, even before a record company, and may enthusiastically seek an involvement with the writer with a view to then helping him to secure a record deal. Some publishers will even finance master-quality recordings for independent release as a step towards securing a major record deal.

funding

Publishers are skilled at selling themselves, but like all salesmen they tend to make exaggerated claims. The plain fact of the matter is that, in the vast majority of cases, writers look to publishers for one overriding reason: money. If there is no difficulty in securing a record deal for a particular recording project, the prudent approach is would probably be to conclude the record deal so that it could then be used to secure the best possible terms from a publisher. Otherwise, if reasonable terms are available from a publisher, there is no reason in principle why a publishing contract should not be concluded without delay.

the publisher

choice of publisher

As we saw in chapter three, if a number of record companies compete to sign up a particular artist then the choice of which company to run with may prove difficult. However, if there is competition between a number of publishers, the choice (at least for singer/songwriters) is more often determined simply by the financial terms offered.

Some singer/songwriters are sometimes reluctant to sign a publishing deal with a publisher who is affiliated to their record company. Ordinarily the accounting statements received from the publisher may serve as a useful source against which to check on the accountings received from the record company. If the record company and publishing company are related then there is a greater risk of concealment. This should not be a problem with the major companies, all of which ensure that there is a proper separation between the recording companies and their publisher affiliates. There is perhaps a greater risk when signing to smaller companies, and even then most smaller publishers are entirely reputable.

efficiency of administration

Before concluding any deal the writer should be satisfied that the publisher has efficient collection systems in place. Every publisher will say that his arrangements for collection and accounting procedures are impeccable, so the writer should ask other people, such as other writers signed to the publisher and the writer's professional advisers.

professional management

A songwriter who does not have a separate career as a recording artist and instead relies on persuading other artists to record his songs or persuading television and film companies to commission his work is bound to attach more significance to the ability of his publisher to seek out commissions for him, obtain covers for him and introduce him to appropriate co-writers. As with every aspect of the music business, personal relationships count for a great deal.

PUBLISHING INCOME

types of income

performance income

In this country, the PRS has a virtual monopoly in relation to performance income, which is generated by the public performance of musical works on the radio, on the television, in clubs, restaurants and other places of entertainment, in shops, or in any other public place. The PRS collects substantial licence fees and, after payment of its administration costs, divides up whatever is left for distribution between its various members. Unless the writer is a member of PRS he cannot receive any of this income, and in order to be accepted as a member the writer has to assign to the PRS the performance right in all of his musical works. The PRS will then pay $^6/_{12}$ of any performance income attributable to the writer's songs directly to the writer (for some reason the PRS still thinks in terms of fractions rather than percentages) and will pay the remaining $^6/_{12}$ to the publisher. If the writer does not have a publisher then the entire performance income will be paid directly to him. The manner in which the PRS calculates performance income for distribution among its members is complicated, but there are some specific rules. For example, the fee exacted by the PRS in June 1999 for a three-minute slot on Radio 1 is £49.21. For a three-minute slot on BBC Television the fee is approximately £136, and a three-minute slot on Capital FM is worth £15.76. These fees may appear small, but a successful single which enjoys considerable airplay will generate substantial performance income.

mechanical royalties

In order to manufacture records, the record company requires a licence known as a mechanical licence from the owner of the song. Under the terms of the licence, mechanical royalties are payable at the statutory rate (for records manufactured in the UK) of 8.5% of the dealer price. So what is the 8.5% mechanical royalty worth? For a full-price CD album with a dealer price of £8.89, excluding VAT, the 8.5% royalty is worth 75p. The mechanical royalties are generally collected by the MCPS on behalf of its members. The MCPS deducts commission at the rate of 4.75% for mechanical royalties payable by the major record companies and those other record companies operating under what the MCPS refers to as its AP1 scheme (which applies to record companies with a proven track record), and 12.5% in all other cases.

synchronisation fees

The consent of the copyright owner is required in order that a piece of music may be used in a film. The consent is given in the form of what is called a synchronisation licence, and the fees payable under the terms of that licence are referred to as synchronisation fees. Hence a synchronisation fee is payable by an advertising agency for the use of a piece of music in a television advertisement, by a television company for the use of music to be broadcast on television and by a film company wishing to use music in a film. Unlike performance income or mechanical royalty income, in which neither the writer nor his publisher have any control over the method of calculation, synchronisation fees are freely negotiable so that the writer will rely upon his publisher to secure the best possible fee in each case. Even then, though, some instances are covered by what are known as 'blanket' licence agreements, including for example any background music used on television, which will be covered by the general licences granted periodically by the PRS and the MCPS to the broadcasters.

print income

The most traditional form of music publishing is the printing of sheet music. Before records were available publishers made their money by printing sheet music, for which there was a great demand. There has recently been something of a resurgence in sales of sheet music, although more for compilation song books than single pieces of music, and for some writers this is a material source of income.

the value of publishing income

past income

It is impossible to predict how much money is likely to be generated from any particular publishing rights, and the publisher will therefore agree to account to the writer for a given percentage of the amount which is actually generated. But how does the publisher calculate the advances which he is prepared to pay? If the deal relates to specific songs which have generated earnings in the past, it is a relatively simple task for the publisher to calculate the average annual earnings over the previous few years and then calculate how much to offer as an advance against anticipated future earnings. Past earnings are by no means a guarantee of future earnings, as the profitability of a particular song will ordinarily decrease with the passage of time. However, the publisher will make assumptions to compensate for this based on his knowledge of any future marketing plans.

future income

So how does the publisher decide what to pay for a new writer, for example a singer/songwriter who has not previously released a record? The more sophisticated publisher will have the benefit of complex financial models, which he will employ to predict the speed and size of his financial return. However, these models are of limited use because they depend upon the accuracy of numerous assumptions. By using a few crude rules of thumb, therefore, let us take a fanciful look at what the publisher might offer a particular writer. We will take as an example a band which has just signed a record deal with a major record company which guarantees the release of an album. They intend only to record their own material and do not co-write, so that 100% of the publishing rights for the album will be available.

the piggy-back approach

The publisher who adopts this approach likes this setup. He knows the record company, and he rates them highly. He also knows that the record company has paid the band £150,000, inclusive of costs. He has also discovered that this is a priority signing and that the record company intends to pull out all the stops, and decides that he is prepared to take a similar financial risk. He predicts they will make at least two promotional videos at an aggregate cost of £50,000 and he has heard that there is a commitment for independent promotion. After taking into account the band's advance, along with remixing costs, videos, independent promotion and the like, he judges that the record company will be investing around £300,000. He assumes that, after paying manufacturing and distribution costs (including mechanical royalties), the record company will make an average of £4 per unit on all UK sales over all formats, before paying artist royalties, and will receive a royalty of £1.50 per unit on overseas sales. He assumes that the record company has taken a long-term view when calculating its investment, but thinks that it will probably break even on 60,000 UK sales and 40,000 overseas sales, and calculates the income that he might expect from those sales. After allowing for the subtraction of the MCPS's commission, he still reckons on receiving say 60p per unit for UK sales (averaged between cassette sales and CDs), giving rise to £36,000, and after sub-publisher deductions he reckons on receiving 50p per unit for the overseas sales, which would gross another £20,000. In addition to the £56,000 in gross mechanical royalties, he predicts that there will also be a fair amount of airplay. After checking the records of his comparable writers, he discovers that their gross performance income is around 30% of their gross mechanical income, which in this case would mean £16,800, although he will only receive $^6/_{12}$ of this. All in all, if the record company breaks even he reckons that, by that stage, he can expect at least £60,000. He is not too keen to pay out this much, however, because he knows that he will have a long wait for the money to come through the pipeline, and instead decides to offer the band a 75/25 deal and pay them £45,000 as an advance. However, he will try and stagger payment so that £15,000 is payable immediately, £15,000 on UK release and £15,000 on US release. They just might go for it!

the scientific approach

The publisher working this way needs to build up his market share. He is prepared to take a risk, but it has to be a calculated one. He knows that there is competition to sign the band: the lawyer is already touting them around

the IMF handbook a guide to professional band management

town, and they signed their record deal in a blaze of publicity. He knows that he will have to pay at least the going rate. He doesn't think, however, that an investment of £50,000 on signing will be enough. He has pitched in at this level for several new bands this year and every time he has lost out. He wants to offer £75,000 but he needs approval from the Board for this. He provides the financial director with some projections, in a similar manner to the first publisher, and asks him to come up with some figures. The financial director then takes his laptop home and comes back the next day with the answer: he can offer £30,000 for the first album. After lunch with the band's manager, the publisher once again calls in the financial director. He has since discovered more about the band, and he wants to revise the projections. He doubles the anticipated sales and asks the financial director to factor in the singles sales and some income from compilations. He has also heard the remix of the first single, and he now wants to increase the projected performance income. He also wants to include a provision for some synchronisation income, because the manager has told him that Disney are looking to use some of the music in their new film. The financial director reworks the figures, and on the next day the Board grants approval for an initial investment of £75,000.

the maverick approach

This publisher will kill for the band. He thinks they are the next big thing, and that even if the band does not hold together the principal songwriter is a genuine talent. He does not care what they cost. He is prepared to offer £100,000 and will double it if he has to. He doesn't give a stuff about his Board because the company has already made £1 million from his signings from last year, and he has just signed a lucrative new three-year employment contract.

THE CONTRACT

the term

contract periods

Most contracts will run for a period of twelve months, at which point the publisher will have a number of options to extend for a successive number of twelve-month periods. Typically, the publisher will require two or three options so that the agreement runs for a total of three or four contract periods.

extensions

If the publisher is prepared to pay an advance (and without this there would usually be little incentive for the artist to sign a long-term publishing deal) then, quite reasonably, the publisher will expect a minimum commitment of some kind from the writer (see the section on 'The Minimum Commitment' below). Each contract period will therefore be extended, if necessary, until a given period after the commitment has been met. The contract will usually enable the publisher to extend the relevant contract period until, for example, three months after the commitment has been met, which will allow the publisher sufficient time in which to assess the situation before deciding whether or not he wishes to exercise his option to continue into the next contract period. In order to avoid problems involving restraint of trade, most publishers are advised to put a limit on the period of extension of perhaps two or three years. For a four-year deal, therefore, if there is a maximum period of extension of two years then each contract period will run for a maximum of three years, so that the contract might then theoretically run for a maximum of twelve years.

exclusivity

A publishing contract will invariably be exclusive, in that the publisher will have control of all of the songs written and composed by the writer during the term of the contract. In addition the publisher will expect to acquire any other existing material, unless of course rights in that material have already been granted to another publisher. Sometimes, in order to prevent a writer from holding back songs towards the end of the term of the contract, the publisher may insist that the contract also extends to any songs commenced during the term but only completed after the end of the contract.

the minimum commitment

delivery or release?

With an ordinary songwriter, as opposed to a singer/songwriter, the publisher may simply require a minimum number of songs to be completed and delivered. Nevertheless, if substantial advances are paid, then (the absence of a recording contract notwithstanding) the minimum commitment may be expressed in terms of the minimum number of songs which must be commercially released. In the case of a singer/songwriter, certainly, the publisher will require the minimum number of songs to be released by the writer's record company, and for this purpose the songs will often only qualify if they have been released by a major.

extent of the commitment

It is important that the minimum commitment is realistic, ie achievable within a reasonable timeframe. For example, the commitment for a singer/songwriter who co-writes all of his material and usually includes one or two songs on his albums which are written by other writers should be for around 40% of an album (which leaves him to write 50% of eight out of ten songs). Sometimes, however, the publisher may insist that the minimum commitment is only met when the minimum number of songs has been released by a major record company, not only in the UK but perhaps also in one or more specified overseas territories. Before agreeing to provisions of this nature, however, the writer should review his record contract and assess the chances of being able to comply with the commitment within a reasonable period.

failure to comply

If the commitment is not met then the extension provisions will apply. Also, the publisher may seek to reduce the writer's advance if the commitment is not met in full. For example, the contract may specify that the writer must procure the release of an album at least 90% of which has been written by him. However, the contract may be structured so that the commitment will be considered to have been met provided that at least 50% of the album has been written by the writer (in which case the extension provisions no longer apply) but so that the advance is reduced. For example, if 50% of the album qualifies then $5/9$ of the advance would be paid, and if 70% of the album qualifies then $7/9$ would be paid.

territory

overseas exploitation

Most publishing agreements are made on a worldwide basis, so that the publisher will enjoy rights for the songs in question throughout the world. Most of the major publishers have companies affiliated to them located in all of the important territories, while the independent publishers have appropriate sub-publishing arrangements in place throughout the world. Generally, therefore, all reputable publishers are in a position to exploit songs on a world-wide basis.

limited territory

Some publishing agreements are restricted to a limited territory. As we have seen in chapter three, a number of practical problems arise when recording arrangements are made on a territory-by-territory basis. However, those practical considerations do not arise in the case of publishing arrangements.

pros and cons

A UK publisher may be prepared to pay higher advances for worldwide rights than the writer would be able to achieve by securing individual advances for each territory. The UK publisher would then enjoy the protection that the income from all worldwide territories would be available for recoupment purposes, which would therefore spread the publisher's risk. Conversely, entering into territory-by-territory deals accords the writer the advantage that, if there is particular success in one territory, once the advance for that territory has been recouped then royalties will begin to flow immediately, and those royalties will not be available to recoup advances paid for other territories. The writer may also expect to receive his overseas royalties more quickly in this way than if they were routed back through a UK publisher. On the other hand, if a number of deals are entered into separately rather than one worldwide deal, this is likely to inflate the legal fees to be paid by the writer, and of course the writer, or his manager, will then have to monitor and liaise with a number of different companies. In some overseas territories it is common practice to create an incentive for a record company by granting publishing rights to a publisher affiliated with the record company. Accordingly, if an artist controls his own recordings and licenses these throughout the world on a territory-by-territory basis then it might make sense to deal with any available publishing rights in a similar manner. Generally, however, territory-by-territory publishing deals are unpopular, and the typical UK writer – and certainly the singer/songwriter – will prefer to conclude a worldwide deal with a UK publisher.

advances

relevant factors

For most writers the advances are critical, and these will vary dramatically. A would-be recording artist struggling to find a record deal but still able to attract the interest of a publisher may be pleased to secure an advance on signing a publishing deal of £10,000, and perhaps even less, as this may provide vital funding at a crucial time. If he has secured a valuable recording contract, however, then he might expect to receive ten times as much. There are various factors involved which will affect the amount which the publisher is prepared to pay. We saw earlier in this chapter how the approaches adopted by publishers vary considerably, and looked at the piggy-back approach, the more scientific approach and the maverick approach. Of course, these are only extreme examples. The publisher will calculate the amount of advance based on his assessment of the writer's talent. If there is an element of competition for the writer, the level of any advance will largely be dictated by market forces. Otherwise, the most crucial factors are likely to be the needs of the writer and what he is prepared to accept. The publisher will assess the entire arrangement, including the proven abilities and track record not only of the writer but also of those close to him, including his management team. If a record deal is not yet in place then the publisher's assessment of what should be risked by way of an advance payment will largely depend on the nature of the record deal he believes that the artist is capable of obtaining.

payment schedule

Having agreed on an advance, the publisher will then try to minimise his risk by spreading its payment. He may suggest that 25% of the advance for the first album is payable upon signature, along with a further 25% on commencement of recording, a further 25% on UK release and a final 25% perhaps on release in the US or in some other overseas territory.

deferred advances

If a singer/songwriter signs a publishing deal before a record deal is in place then he will probably receive only a relatively modest advance. However, this will usually be followed by a more significant advance on the signing of a record deal with a major record company, with a further advance usually being paid on the release of the first album.

option advances

As far as any option periods are concerned, the advance for each period will typically be calculated in accordance with a formula (often two thirds of the royalty earnings from the previous album), subject however to a minimum and a maximum payment. The minimum payment will usually be not less than the advance for the first album, and the maximum figure is often double the minimum figure. In the case of a four-album deal, for example, if there is an advance of £75,000 for the first album then the advances for the subsequent albums might be calculated in accordance with this formula, but subject to a minimum payment of again perhaps £75,000 for the second album (with a maximum of £150,000), a minimum of perhaps £100,000 (with a maximum of £200,000) for the third album, and a minimum of maybe £125,000 (with a maximum of £250,000) for the fourth. Alternatively, the option advances are sometimes fixed amounts and with generous increments, but so that each advance may be reduced by the amount of any unrecouped balance. On this basis, if the advance for the first album is £75,000 the publisher might agree on advances of £100,000, £150,000 and £200,000 respectively for the three option albums. Using this as an example, if the first album generates only £25,000 in royalties (leaving an unrecouped balance of £50,000 from the initial £75,000 advance), the publisher might exercise its option to continue with a second album on payment of a reduced advance (ie £50,000, comprising the £100,000 specified for the second album minus the £50,000 unrecouped balance).

royalties

rates of royalty

It was usually traditional for publishers to account to their writers for 50% of their income, and a 50/50 split is still more or less a standard arrangement with television and film companies when commissioning writers to compose music for a specific use. However, a songwriter can generally now expect a far more lucrative deal, which will usually fall within the range of between 60% and 80%, while a singer/songwriter, whose own efforts will generate most of the publishing income, would expect to receive royalties at the top end of the scale, usually at around 75% or 80%. Sometimes royalties of even 85% or 90% are payable. However, there is an obvious correlation between the royalty rate and the amount of any advance payable so that, for example, a publisher prepared to pay a writer an advance of £100,000 against a royalty of 75% of the publisher's receipts might be prepared to increase the 75% to 85% or even 90%, but perhaps only if the publisher insists that no advance is payable. An 85% or 90% royalty rate will more often be seen in the context of administration arrangements, and this area is investigated later in this chapter.

Under a typical publishing contract a new writer would often expect to achieve a 75/25 royalty split. He may be persuaded to accept a royalty of, say, 70/30 in relation to the songs delivered during the initial contract period, but if the publisher exercises the first of its options then the split will be 75/25, which might apply for the second and third contract periods. If the publisher has an option for a fourth contract period then it is likely that this will be granted only on the basis that, at that stage, the split increases to 80/20.

In the case of performance income, if the royalty rate is 75% then the writer will receive 50% directly from the PRS – although, of course, they would refer to it as $^6/_{12}$. The remaining $^6/_{12}$ will be paid to the publisher, but the writer will require 50% of this (so that, in effect, he receives 75% of the gross performance income). However, his 50% share of the publisher's $^6/_{12}$ will be available to the publisher to apply towards recoupment of any advance. As far as mechanical and synchronisation income is concerned, the writer will receive 75% of what the publisher receives (refer to the section on 'Methods of Calculation' below for what is meant by receipts for this purpose). For sales of sheet music, the publisher will generally license rights to a third party and will simply pay the writer 75% of its receipts pursuant to any such licence. If the publisher itself publishes the music in sheet form, the contract will usually include a provision that the publisher will pay the writer between 10% and 15% of the retail price.

reduced royalties for cover recordings

Publishers will often seek a reduction in the rate of royalty for income derived from cover recordings (ie a recording of a performance of the song in question by a recording artist other than the writer). If we again assume that the basic split is 75/25, the publisher may insist that a split of 60/40 should apply if the income is derived from a cover recording. This is a dubious practice, although quite common. In our example the writer would receive 75% of the income generated by his own recordings of his songs but perhaps only 60% of the income generated from recordings of those songs by other people. The task of collecting the income from a cover is no different from that of collecting the income from the writer's own recordings, and so this in itself does not justify the income being treated in a different manner. The publisher will argue that a reduction in royalty is justified because of the work performed by its professional manager in securing the recording. The vast majority of covers are recorded because the artist concerned makes a unilateral decision to record, and the first that the publisher will know about this is when the artist's record company applies for a mechanical licence. To be fair, most publishers will therefore accept that the reduced rate should only apply for covers which have been obtained as a result of the direct efforts of the publisher. Even in these cases, however, the practice of paying a reduced royalty is a questionable one. All publishing contracts will contain an express provision to the effect that the publisher must use all reasonable endeavours to exploit the songs in question. It is therefore difficult for the publisher to argue that, if it achieves some success in doing what it is obliged to do, it should then be more handsomely rewarded. Using the same example, the logical approach is that the basic rate should be

60/40, but that if the writer makes his own recordings of his songs then for those recordings the split should increase to 75/25. Obviously this amounts to the same thing, but it might be more palatable for the writer if the contract were presented in this way. What is clear, however, is that a writer who is not a recording artist should not be fooled into thinking that he has a 75/25 deal if this provides for a 60/40 split in relation to covers. Clearly, he has a 60/40 deal.

method of calculation

Royalties are either calculated on what is known as a receipts basis or on an at-source basis. This has particular relevance when applied to overseas income. An overseas sub-publisher, whether he is affiliated to the UK publisher or not, will naturally be entitled to retain part of the income arising in its territory before remitting the balance to the UK publisher, and will usually be entitled to deduct 10% or 15%. However, in some cases (particularly with the smaller independent publishers), the UK publisher may have negotiated a substantial advance from the overseas sub-publisher (in which the writer will not share) on the basis that the overseas sub-publisher is entitled to as much as 25%. If we look again at our publishing agreement which provides for a 75/25 split then, if we assume that the publisher's overseas sub-publishers are each entitled to retain 20%, it follows that the UK publisher will receive 80% of any foreign income. If the writer's publishing agreement is a receipts deal then he will receive 75% of 80% of foreign income (60% of the gross). If the deal is at source then he will receive 75% of the gross, so that for every £100 arising in the territory concerned the sub-publisher will retain £20, remitting £80 back to the UK publisher, who will then account to the writer for £75, retaining a margin of only £5. Most publishing contracts – certainly those with the major publishers – are now at-source deals. Some publishers try to distinguish between major and minor territories, calculating royalties at source in the major territories (ie those in which the publisher has its own affiliated sub-publishers) but accounting for royalties only on a receipts basis in the minor territories.

If the writer has to accept a receipts deal, a cap of some kind should be imposed so that a ceiling is set whereby the maximum a sub-publisher can deduct might be 15%, for example. If the publisher actually suffers a 25% deduction then, for every £100 which arises in the territory concerned, £75 will be remitted to the UK publisher. However, out of this the publisher will have to pay the writer 75% of £85, which equates to £63.75.

The writer should also ensure that there is no double deduction in relation to locally originated covers. What happens, for example, if the sub-publisher in France procures a local cover recording? Again, let us assume that the writer's deal is 75/25 but that this reduces to 60/40 for income resulting from cover recordings. If the writer's royalties are to be calculated at source then his entitlement will be clear: 60% of the at-source income. If, however, the writer's royalties are calculated on a receipts basis then problems may arise. The foreign sub-publisher may be entitled to deduct, say, 20% in ordinary circumstances but 40% in the case of a locally-originated cover. If there is no cap set on the sub-publisher's deductions then the writer is entitled to 60% of 60% (ie 36%) of the income arising at source. This is unfair – the writer should either receive his full 75% of the UK publisher's 60% share (ie 45% of the income arising at source) or the cover rate of 60% calculated upon deemed receipts of 80% (which would entitle the writer to 48% of the at-source income).

accountings

statements

Most publishers will account to the writer on a semi-annual basis and usually within 90 days of this so that, for the six-month period ending on 30 June in each year, a statement will be delivered at the end of the following September, and for the six-month period ending on 31 December a statement will be delivered at the end of the following March. The writer will, of course, receive his share of performance income directly from the PRS, who account on a quarterly basis, although there are only two main distributions in each year.

delays

As was explained in chapter three, in the case of a record deal there may be lengthy delays before foreign royalties trickle through the pipeline. Publishing income is prone to still longer delays, mainly as a result of the inefficiencies of the collection societies concerned. The record company in the appropriate territory will pay mechanical royalties to the local mechanical copyright collection society, and this in turn will then pay the sub-publisher affiliated with the UK publisher. The sub-publisher should then pay the UK publisher, although the writer should establish that the UK publisher's sub-publishing arrangements are structured so that the UK publisher will receive accountings direct from the overseas sub-publisher, so that no unnecessary link has been added to the chain. For example, in Germany the local record company responsible for a record sold in December may only account to GEMA, the German collection society, in January the following year. GEMA accounts quarterly within 30 days, so the payment would fall within the first quarter of the year and be due to be paid by GEMA to the local sub-publisher in April. If the German sub-publisher accounts to the UK publisher on a quarterly basis, the money received during the second quarter will be due within, say, 60 days of the end of that quarter, and the UK publisher would then receive payment at the end of August. If the UK publisher accounts to the writer on a semi-annual basis, payment would not be due until the end of March in the following year. Due to inefficiencies and delays, two years or more often passes before foreign royalties finally work their way through the system.

audits

The writer should also ensure that he has appropriate rights of audit. An audit of a publishing company tends to be a far less complicated affair than that of a record company, but it is nevertheless prudent to carry one out periodically. If a writer's royalty account is unrecouped, so that the audit is unlikely to give rise to any additional payment, then it may be sensible to delay the audit. However, the writer should be careful not to fall foul of any limitations in the agreement to the effect that accounting statements are accepted and no longer subject to any objections after a given period (usually two or three years). Generally, however, it is a simple matter to persuade the publisher to extend any objection period, therefore allowing any audit to be deferred.

retention period

Under a typical publishing contract the publisher will acquire the copyright in the songs in question. Sometimes, however, the writer may retain the copyright and instead grant the publisher an exclusive licence. This effectively places the publisher in a position no worse than before, because an exclusive licensee of copyright has the same rights as the copyright owner. As a rule, however, the publisher will wish to own the copyright and be able to register the copyright in his own name.

Traditionally the publisher insisted on owning the copyright outright for the full period of copyright, which is currently the life of the writer plus a further 70 years thereafter. Some publishers still insist on owning songs for the full period of copyright, but this is generally restricted to those cases where a publisher commissions a writer to compose music for a specific purpose, such as for a film or a TV programme. A singer/songwriter signing a publishing contract should expect to assign the copyright in his songs to the publisher only for a limited period, usually the term of the agreement – which, as we have seen, will generally be three or four years but may be extended if necessary until the fulfilment of the minimum commitment – and then for a further period.

This tends to be one of the more controversial areas involved in any negotiation. In the 1980s competition was so fierce that publishers were persuaded to accept very limited 'retention periods', often the term plus five years, and sometimes even shorter. A retention period of the term plus five to ten years was quite common. Towards the latter part of the 1980s there was a great deal of activity in the sale of various music catalogues, many of which were sold for stunningly high prices. The reason for this was that the catalogues contained successful songs, or standards, which were owned by the publisher concerned for the life of copyright and from which it was clear that income would continue to accrue for many years to come. As a result, the trend towards shorter periods of retention was reversed, and ever since then publishers, having re-learned the value of copyright, now fight hard for longer periods. The publishers have lost too much ground to be able to claw their way back to their position of being able to demand the full period of copyright, but a new deal now will typically provide for a retention period of the term plus a further period of between five and 20 years. Sometimes, if a writer agrees to a longer retention period, the publisher may be persuaded to improve the royalty rate for income received after the expiration of a given number of years, perhaps from 75/25 to 85/15, and at some point he might even be persuaded to pay a further advance. For example, perhaps the writer will agree to a retention period of the term plus 15 years, provided that, at the end of five years after the expiry of the term, the publisher pays a further advance equal to perhaps three or four times the average annual royalty earnings over the preceding three years. (This is not a standard formula, by any means, but is one example of the many compromises which may be reached).

rights

As the owner of the copyright in the songs the publisher will have the exclusive right to control their use, even to the exclusion of the writer. As we have seen, the copyright will not extend to the performing right in the work because this right will have been assigned by the writer to the PRS by virtue of his PRS membership. In practice, therefore, the publisher will only have limited control over the songs. For example, any third party wishing to record one of the songs will be entitled to do so under the terms of the compulsory mechanical licensing system, which operates in a similar form in all of the major territories of the world. However, as far as other forms of exploitation are concerned, the writer may wish to impose various contractual restrictions. For example, the publisher will usually accept that certain synchronisation licences will only be granted with the writer's approval.

exploitation

All publishing agreements include a provision to the effect that the publisher must use reasonable endeavours to exploit the songs. However, if the publisher fails to exploit a particular song within a particular period, machinery will be available to the writer (perhaps after a cure period) to demand all rights in the song to be re-assigned to himself, irrespective of the duration of the retention period, so that he may then exploit them by other means. The primary reason for the inclusion of provisions of this nature is to protect the publisher from any claim that the agreement is unenforceable because it constitutes an unreasonable restraint of trade. The courts would not be prepared to enforce an agreement under which a publisher is theoretically able to hold a writer to an exclusive contract for a lengthy period but then refuse to exploit his work.

warranties

Publishing contracts generally contain a number of warranties which are required from the writer. Perhaps the most significant of these is the warranty to the effect that all of the compositions will be original and will not infringe the rights of any third party. There is an increasing number of copyright disputes, many of which arise from the current fashion for sampling so that, if a singer/songwriter wishes to incorporate a sample of any kind into a recording, it is vital that he immediately seeks advice and ensures that any necessary clearances are obtained. Given the risk of copyright disputes, it may be prudent for a writer to enter into any publishing contract through a public limited company by means of an employment contract of some kind. The writer should assign copyright in his songs to the company so that, if disaster then strikes, he will at least be protected from bankruptcy. The writer should also consider taking out insurance against copyright claims.

group provisions

The publisher will require all members of a band to sign the publishing contract, even if it is expected that only one member will be writing the songs. This is simply a security measure on the publisher's part. Of course, this will not be possible if one member is already a party to a publishing contract of some kind. A group's publishing contract will contain complex leaving-member provisions. The important point for the writers to bear in mind is that, if one of them should leave the group and the publisher then elects to continue with that leaving member, he should then have a separate contract which has its own minimum commitment provisions so that the duration of his contract is not governed by the fulfilment of the group's commitment. Also, the leaving-member provisions need to deal sensibly with the issue of cross-recoupment; the principles which apply here are the same as those with any recording contract (see the previous section on 'Group Provisions' in chapter three).

other arrangements

The writer may not wish to give away his songs, and therefore choose not to enter into a publishing contract at all. Even so, some arrangements must be made to collect his publishing income. There are three basic choices available to him: firstly, to join the PRS and the MCPS and do nothing further; secondly, to employ somebody to administer the songs directly for him; and thirdly, to enter into an administration agreement with a third-party administrator.

reliance on the PRS/MCPS

Both of these organisations have international relationships, so a writer may wonder why he should bother to make any other arrangements. Why not simply wait for the monies earned overseas to flow through via the appropriate organisation? There are two main problems. Firstly, the system itself is not that efficient; neither the society automatically notifies its affiliates of its claim to royalties, although they will make such requests by a system of international 'fiches' on the copyright owner's request. Unfortunately this system is not wholly computerised, and there is some doubt that the overseas societies will always act once notified. Worse still, there may be local cover recordings of which the copyright owner is unaware and who, therefore, is never notified.

The second problem is that, even if the societies manage to collect the funds in the first place, there is a significant delay in the remittance of those funds. The theory is that if the writer were instead to be represented by a publisher in the relevant overseas territory then that overseas publisher would then be charged with the responsibility of registering its interest and ensuring that the local collection society makes payment directly to that publisher. Because the local publisher has a vested interest, this generally results in funds being paid through rather more efficiently than in cases when the local society is left to pass funds back to PRS/MCPS of its own volition. Moreover, there may not be such a saving in relying on the PRS/MCPS because two sets of commission will then be charged, as the overseas society will deduct its commission before

publishing contracts

accounting to the PRS/MCPS and the PRS/MCPS will then deduct its own commission before accounting to the copyright owner.

self-administration

This is the process of exploiting copyright without appointing a publisher and its various overseas sub-publishers, with the writer becoming instead a member of the local collection societies. In most major territories this is now a reasonably simple procedure, although it is often helpful to employ an agent in the local territory to deal with the formalities. However it is not possible to join directly in Japan, and it is still difficult in Italy. In theory there should be no obstructions in Italy, but one of the rules dictated by the Italian collection society is that the person wishing to join needs to produce 200 copies of a booklet including 20 Italian compositions which are to be published. A few of these are given to the local society, but the rest have no practical use and are usually destroyed. This is to prove that the applicant is a *bona fide* publisher.

There are significant advantages in the self-administration approach. The first is that the copyright owner will bear the commission only of the local society and will not bear additional commission of a UK collection society or sub-publisher. The second advantage is that the copyright owner will receive any applicable funds immediately on effect that those funds are distributed by the local society, and there will be no further delay during which the funds are processed by a third party. Thirdly, membership of the local societies will normally bring with it the privilege of qualifying for a share of 'black-box' income. This income is comprised mainly of income obtained by the local societies by virtue of various blanket licensing agreements, under which, for example, perhaps a television company will pay a substantial fee for the privilege of performing all of the musical works controlled by the society. Blanket licences of this kind are issued in the UK, although the PRS has a reasonably sophisticated system which enables it to identify particular uses so that its income may be distributed sensibly between the specific titles controlled by them. Many countries (most notably Italy) are far less sophisticated, and societies there end up with vast amounts of money which they are unable or unwilling to attribute to any particular song. This money, or part of it, is thus distributed among its various publisher members, who usually retain their share in any black-box distribution for their own use and benefit without sharing this with their writers. The publisher member's entitlement to a share of black-box income usually increases with the length of time which the publisher has been a member.

One disadvantage of self-administration is that the societies do not generally pay advances. Moreover, it is the publisher's responsibility to notify the local societies of the compositions in respect of which it wishes the society to make claims and the publisher is responsible for checking its own statements. To undertake these tasks effectively the publisher needs to have a reasonably sophisticated administrative system and may thus have higher overheads than usual. Also, under self-administered arrangements there will be no local catalogue promotion. One way around this would be to hire one or more people to undertake specific promotional tasks, but the writer would need to assess whether the cost of doing this would mean that he is then able still to justify direct membership or whether he would be better off paying commission to a sub-publisher. In view of the complexities involved, therefore, only a successful writer with a large turnover should try self-administration.

appointing an administrator

If he wishes to avoid entering into a traditional publishing contract, and if he is prepared neither simply to rely upon his PRS/MCPS membership nor make his own administration arrangements, the most sensible solution available to him is to enter into an administration agreement with a third party. Administration agreements are similar to publishing agreements, although the publisher will generally offer no professional management services. His responsibilities will instead be limited to purely administrative services, such as registering the songs and collecting the money. Generally, no advance will be payable, but the royalties will be higher – perhaps an 85/15 split, or even 90/10. Also, because there is no advance, administration agreements tend not to be for a lengthy fixed term. They will usually continue for at least a year (which would safeguard the publisher from setting everything up only to find that the writer wishes to terminate the arrangements), but the arrangement would then usually be terminable by either party upon reasonable notice (maybe three months). The publisher would administer the songs in the writer's name, so that, if the writer is Joe Bloggs, the songs might be registered under the name Joe Bloggs Music.

AFTER THE DEAL

As with a recording contract, life does not come to an end once the contract has been signed. Here are some practical points which writers should therefore bear in mind.

lead sheets/demos

As soon as a song has been completed it should be delivered to the publisher in the form of a lead sheet, or perhaps a demo tape, or at the very least a lyric sheet. Delivery in whatever form is important, as this may trigger the payment of an advance, or the date of delivery may impact on the publisher's option date. In any event, as soon as a song has been delivered there is immediately additional evidence of its existence, which may be significant in the event of any subsequent copyright dispute.

single-song assignment

The majority of publishing agreements impose an obligation on the writer to execute a short-form assignment for each song, and the publisher may need to carry this out in certain territories for purposes of registration.

releases

The writer should ensure that his publisher receives copies of all records in all formats (singles, albums, videos etc) released which feature any of his songs. This will help the publisher to track the royalty income.

collaborations

If the writer only co-writes the material, this is likely to have implications under the publishing contract. He may be under a contractual obligation to ensure that his co-writer assigns his interest in the song in question to the same publisher. Also, co-writing will invariably have implications concerning minimum commitment. When two or more people collaborate in writing a song they usually do so on the understanding that they have contributed to the musical work in equal shares. The writer should therefore ensure that the arrangements are understood by everybody before the work begins. In the event of a dispute, the publisher may be able to assist in resolving the issue. Also, the PRS has procedures in place for resolving disputes of this nature.

samples

A writer should never make use of samples in a work without obtaining proper written clearance. The sooner the writer notifies both his record company and his publisher the better.

group changes

With a publishing agreement for a group, any change in the line-up will have contractual ramifications. There will almost certainly be an obligation for the group to notify the publisher immediately should any changes occur, but even before this the writer should first consult with his solicitor.

likenesses and biographies

Many writers will have a right of approval over the publisher's use of any autobiographical material and/or photographs and likenesses. The best way to deal with this is for the writer to deliver approved materials from time to time.

the PRS

Any writer signing a publishing contract must ensure that he joins the PRS without delay, and the publisher should be able to arrange this on the writer's behalf. As a member the writer is entitled to designate whether the PRS should appoint either ASCAP or BMI (the equivalent major USA performing rights societies) to represent his songs in the USA, although a prudent writer will wish to meet the UK representatives of both organisations before choosing. Sometimes the UK publisher will insist upon nominating one or the other.

consents

From time to time the writer may be asked by the publisher to give consent to a particular matter, perhaps a synchronisation licence or an adaptation or arrangement of some kind. The writer should not give approval without first insisting upon being provided with full details of the financial implications.

exploitation

As we have seen, the publisher is under an obligation to exploit the writer's songs. If the writer delivers a song which he does not intend to record himself, the writer should then try to bring some pressure to bear upon the publisher to find some other use for the song. Moreover, the writer should not lose sight of the machinery in the contract which enables him, under certain circumstances, to require unexploited songs to be reassigned to him.

accountings

The first few accounting statements received by the writer will invariably not be accompanied by a cheque, as his account will remain unrecouped. Unfortunately, this state of affairs will often continue for an extended period – in many cases indefinitely. This does not mean, however, that the statements may be discarded. The writer should always ensure that the publisher accounts promptly on the due date and that those statements are always checked. If the writer is unwilling to look at them himself, or does not feel that he is adequately qualified, then his manager or lawyer should check them for any obvious errors. Statements should then be referred to the writer's accountant, who should be reminded to check any objection periods in the publishing agreement to ensure that no audit rights are lost.

concert appearances

Every time the writer performs a concert he must ensure that the proper PRS returns are made. Performance fees will be payable by the promoter via the PRS. In fact the PRS's monopoly position has been dented in a few respects after the recent investigation by the Monopolies and Mergers Commission. For instance, a member of the PRS may now elect to collect performance fees in relation to his own live performances directly from the promoter. The promoter is obliged to pay 3% of the gross box office receipts. In rough terms, a full house at a smaller recognised venue might trigger a payment of around £500, while a full house at Wembley Stadium might trigger a payment in the region of £100,000. Remember that half of the performance fees will be paid directly to the writer, with the remaining balance paid to his publisher. The PRS is able to administer these arrangements under its 'fast-track' procedures, but it still requires that two standard forms are filed with the PRS – one signed by the band or its management and the other by the promoter – no later than 30 days after each concert. Similar rules apply outside the UK.

advances

The writer should make careful note of the provisions in the publishing contract relating to the payment of advances. These provisions are often complex, and some effort is required in calculating exactly when advances are due. If the writer fails to spot that an advance is due, as often happens, some publishers will delay payment. No doubt the advance will eventually be paid, but the publisher is unlikely to agree to pay any interest on the late payment. If the royalty account is fully recouped, publishers will sometimes try to accelerate the payment of a particular advance so that it is paid immediately prior to the accounting date. This will then enable the publisher to recoup immediately the advance from the royalties due on that accounting date.

covers

If the writer has had to accept reduced mechanical royalties for cover recordings, the publisher will probably have been persuaded to exclude for this purpose any covers actually procured by the writer. In this event, if the writer has introduced one of his songs to another artist or producer, by whatever arrangement, then he should ensure that the publisher is aware of this.

termination dates

The writer should also monitor all relevant dates. For example, he should be aware of the last date upon which the publisher is entitled to exercise any option. He may also wish to involve his solicitor in monitoring these dates. If the publisher fails to exercise an option properly, it will mean that the writer is free of contract, although many publishing agreements now include failsafe provisions to the effect that, if the publisher fails to exercise an option, the writer must serve a warning notice to give the publisher a few days' grace.

The writer must also monitor the expiration date of the retention period. Publishers will generally continue to exploit a catalogue of songs until they are told that they no longer have authority to do so. Unless there are specific provisions within the contract to deal with this, the implication will be that the publisher has been allowed to 'hold over' on the same terms as before. This may enable a publisher to continue to deduct a substantial commission despite the fact that, if the writer were alerted to the position, he may have been able to secure an advance or better royalties, or he could have entered into more cost-effective administration arrangements.

extra funding

When dealing with writers who already have recording contracts, some publishers are prepared to contribute towards tour support, independent promotion or poster campaigns and the like – although it is true that it is generally difficult to persuade them to do so! If a publisher is persuaded to make such payments, however, he will normally insist that those payments are fully recoupable from royalties. The writer is probably better advised to persuade the record company to bear such costs, even though the record company will likewise want to recoup them. Publishing deals generally recoup more quickly than recording deals, and for this reason it may be preferable to load as much recoupment as possible onto the record company's account so that the publishing royalties will flow as quickly as possible. Also, with a group contract, unless all of the band members contribute to the writing equally, the recoupment of what are essentially record company costs from publishing royalties will merely serve to exacerbate the complexities of recoupment and may fan the flames of a potential dispute between the band members.

professional advice

The writer *must* consult a solicitor at the earliest possible stage in any negotiations over a publishing contract. It also would be prudent for the writer to consult his accountant before rather than after the event.

chapter 7

agents

by Martin Hopewell and Jef Hanlon

The role of the agent is to represent the artist in the field of live performance and seek suitable engagements for the artist to perform in front of an audience or on TV or radio. The agent not only seeks to secure engagements at the best possible fee for the artist but, ideally, also takes into account whether the engagement is constructively contributing to the furtherance of the artist's career and the increasing of his prestige. Many agents have also recently become responsible for bringing offers of sponsorship to artists from commercial entities wishing to identify or ingratiate themselves with the artist's following, in return for fees payable to the artist for his association or identification with a product or service.

the IMF handbook a guide to professional band management

the role of the agent

The agent is effectively a valve between the hundreds of thousands of acts and the limited worldwide body of promoters, whether they be promoters of concert venues, festivals, clubs or colleges. Take away the agent and there would be chaos, and promoters would be overwhelmed with calls from artists or their managers. Modern management is complex and covers many diverse areas, and as the agent is an expert in arranging live performances the manager will often delegate his responsibility in this area to him. The agent is seen as the intermediary between the promoter and the artist, although as he is representing the artist he is like a referee who is wearing one of the teams' colours. He is often required to explain the position held by each side to the other, and must therefore understand what makes both sides tick as well as taking into account the needs of both.

types of agent

The classic perception of the agent is historically 'Mr Ten Percent', the cigar-chewing loudmouth who would sell his granny if the price was right. He is in fact a rarity today, and most modern agents – especially those dealing in contemporary music – do far better business by retaining a reasonable (if not friendly) relationship with promoters, and indeed many pride themselves on a hard-earned reputation for fair dealing. Though sharks undoubtedly still exist, they are mostly relegated to the periphery of the business. These unscrupulous types are rarely the exclusive representatives of some artists and are usually fairly easy to spot because they tend to act as bookers rather than as artists' agency representatives. These bookers are invariably more interested in either buying the artist for the lowest possible fee or selling him to a promoter for the highest possible amount, often with scant regard to the technical staging requirements and whether the performance is constructive and positive for the artist's career.

the skills required

To fulfil his responsibilities to his clients, the agent needs to be able to perform a multitude of tasks. An agent must be a negotiator, and in theory negotiate the best possible deal for the artist in terms of both fees and furthering the artist's career. However, in practice the agent also has to consider the welfare of the promoter in a world in which acts come and go but in which promoters are usually still there in the future, when they may be needed to take a risk on staging shows for new emerging acts. At the negotiating table the ability to shout loudly and sell hard is not usually as important in obtaining the best deal as having a high level of technical awareness of the way in which deals operate, or of commanding an understanding of such subtleties as arranging the artists billing, which must be of a style and size agreeable to the artist on all advertising for the engagement, particularly on those occasions when more than one artist is appearing at the same location on the same show.

Another important function of an agent is as a spokesman for the act in the live music business, and he should attempt to reflect the attitudes and wishes of the artist as accurately as possible to ensure that the final show is as close as possible to that which the artist would have set up themselves.

He must also be an expert at logistics, be able to plan the most effective route for a tour, and be aware of the production and travel limitations, types of venue and the technical limitations of each.

He must also carry out administration, preparing and issuing engagement contracts. These are effectively not only the information summary on the event and the functions that both the promoter and the artist are expected to fulfil but also the binding document that ties each party to their side of the deal. He will also monitor ticket sales, organise schedules of payments, receive and hold deposits and provide the promoter with the details of immigration and work permits concerning the artist's travelling party. He might also make available any information relevant to minimising withholding tax, and will send out artwork, logos, photos and any other publicity material needed to advertise the contracted engagement.

As the middleman, the agent also acts as an information centre. He is often the best contact person for all parties with an interest in the performance, and liaises with the production personnel working for the act, the promoter, the local record company, the public relations company, the accountant and any other interested parties. Most agencies have stockpiled large collections of data over the years on everything from venues and the technical specifications of festivals to the murky personal histories of promoters. Information is the key to setting up successful shows and tours.

As well as this, the agent must also play the role of accountant. It is the agent's role to carry out pre-show financial projections of income versus costs and after-show 'final settlements', in which percentage deals are involved, as well as to provide practical advice on dealing with the vagaries of 'foreign artist tax' and play the international currency game. However, most agents will recommend that the artist's official accountant is also consulted, if only to have someone available as a scapegoat if it all goes wrong!

the agent's reputation

An agent is often considered to be only as good and as influential as the acts he represents. Therefore, if the agent fails to adopt the additional role of talent scout and simply relaxes on the strength of a couple of currently successful acts, he will find himself with a lot of time on his hands when those acts decide to stop touring or split up. Agents need to keep petrol running through the engine and ensure that there is a steady stream of new acts always waiting to be developed through the agency system, finding space on stages that wouldn't otherwise have been available in order to expose these new acts and nurture them into the superstars of tomorrow.

The agent's influence and power plays an essential part in his ability to package acts together in joint shows, tours or festivals. It is common knowledge that, if an agent represents a very popular act, he is more likely to be able to persuade promoters to provide solo shows or opening act slots for the lesser-known artists that the agent represents.

One of the more unnatural but most frequent things an agent has to do is say no, and turn down offers from prospective promoters. This he may do for a number of reasons: the inquiring promoter may not be considered suitable to promote the act, the act may be nabbed by another promoting company, or the act simply may not be available on the date required. This is a role for which no commission can ever be calculated, but is an essential requirement of an agent solely representing an artist.

commission

Historically the agent's commission is 10% of the artist's engagement fee, though there are many variations to this arrangement. It is not unusual for new acts to be asked to pay 15%, for example, as their commissionable fees are so much lower than established acts, and the agent's costs will not decrease if a smaller show is negotiated. A compromise is often reached here whereby the agent sets up a sliding-scale commission rate in which commissions decrease as fees rise, for example 15% up to £2,000, 12.5% on fees from £2,000 to £5,000, and 10% on all fees exceeding this). This arrangement avoids unpleasant re-negotiating later, as long as the scale is reasonable in the first place. Very large acts can often negotiate commission rates that are even lower, although 5% is generally accepted as rock bottom. This is not unreasonable when you consider that large-stadium tours can produce commissionable income in the region of millions of pounds, particularly in cases when the agent cannot claim to have been involved in the development of the act to a level of high income. On the other hand, at the point at which this sort of money is being made by him, the artist is normally in a position to be able to afford to pay high bills. However, few major acts would ever see the merit to this argument. It is also worth noting that an agent's commission is fully tax deductible under all known tax regimes around the world.

All agents will expect to be entitled to commission from any promoters with whom they have previously secured an engagement for the artist. The length of activity for this right of re-engagement is normally at least one year from the date of the first engagement which the agent secured with the promoter. Artists and their managers must acknowledge that they cannot expect an agent to use his contacts and experience to introduce them to viable promoters and then, once the introduction has been effected, that it would be appropriate for them to deal directly with the promoter and cut the agent out of the relationship. Agents will rigidly enforce this principle and their rights to commission on re-engagements.

agency agreements

An old and thorny source of disagreement between agents and their artists is the subject of agency agreements. These consist of contracts between the two parties that lay down the terms and conditions under which their working relationship will operate. Unlike recording, publishing or even performance contracts, the agency agreement rarely involves a financial inducement for the artist to sign it and many managers believe that it will unfairly tie their artist with a single agent for an unreasonable period of time, and at a set commission rate which they might otherwise wish to later re-negotiate. Because the question normally arises at an early stage of the artist's live career, at a point at which income is low and the agent's job is at its toughest, most agents feel that they need some sort of commitment from the artist that will protect them in more successful times when the agent ceases to be the hero of the hour and becomes viewed more as the guy who takes 10% of the money for making a few phone calls. Unless everyone is very lucky they will argue, and it will normally take most of the three to five years comprising the term of the agent's contract for the act's income to reach a level at which the agent can expect a reasonable return on his time and effort.

choosing an agent

Most artists tend to arrive on a particular agent's roster after being recommended or through existing relationships. Along with these introductions, it is fairly easy to ask around and research the reputations of various agents. Many acts try to gauge the skill of the agent by the acts which they already represent and the nature of their touring strategies, the theory being that if they could do that for other acts then they could do the same thing for the aspiring artist. This is probably a reasonable assumption, although it makes no account of how much the other acts and their managers have planned their own live career, or of another important factor: plain old luck. As a result, agents often develop 'boutique rosters' of similar artists, and a snowball effect comes into play as other acts join the family. Several agents have built remarkable careers from having stumbled by accident upon a particular act, which has acted as a magnet for others, irrespective of the skill of the agent.

large agencies

The size of the agency is probably nowhere near as important as other important criteria such as enthusiasm, experience, commitment and business acumen, but it's true that for an agent to be able to perform his responsibilities accurately he must be in command of the relevant information, and the larger organisations are certainly in a position to provide a larger net with which to gather data. They are usually also able to apply more leverage to secure shows and packaging because of the way in which promoters rely on the continued goodwill shown by agencies that represent large-artist rosters. An agent that represents a large number of artists, however, can get rather stretched when large numbers of them decide to tour at the same time. The personal attention from the head of the agency at the start of a relationship can turn gradually into a dialogue with the office junior booker when things get busy, or the artist's career doesn't ignite quite as quickly as he had hoped.

It is of course true that a successful agent will be earning a reasonable income but that the agent, unlike the publisher or record company, only makes money from an act that is actually touring. A famous band on the roster can look very decorative but this is of no use if it never plays live, and as soon as it quits touring or splits up the agent's income stops altogether. In addition, most large offices cost hundreds of thousands of pounds a year to run, which adds up to a lot of ten percents to meet the bill! It's not surprising, therefore, that the number of people who have become very fat cats out of careers in agency alone is extremely small. Most of the people currently filling agents' chairs started their careers just wanting to get into the music business, found an opening in agency and simply stuck to it. Many others have used a grounding in working at an agency as a qualification to help them move into management or a career in a record company. Some have even been tempted into the high-risk world of concert promotion.

codes of operation

Up until a year or so ago, in order to run an employment agency in the UK it was necessary for an agent to hold a licence issued by the government. Things have now changed, however, and this is no longer the case. The operation of employment agencies is now controlled by the Employment Agencies Act of 1976, which is now being thoroughly policed and enforced by the Employment Agencies Standards Section of the Department of Trade and Industry. Under the terms of the Act, any breaches that lead to the prosecution of an agent are considered to be criminal rather than civil offences, and therefore most agents are meticulous in making sure that they work within the parameters set out by the Act. There are certain procedures that an agent must follow under the Act, and the most important points are as follows:

- He must maintain a clients' bank account in a manner by which is entirely separate from his own agency's account in order to receive money due to his artists. This makes it clear that the money held by the agent or passed through his clients' account is in fact the artists' money, not earnings for the agency. A bonded account is most desirable from the artist's point of view but not a legal requirement.

- Under the terms of the Act, an agent must pay any monies that he collects on behalf of the artist to him within ten days of receiving it, unless the artist specifically asks the agent, in writing, to hold his money for a longer period of time.

- An agent should, by law, present the artist with a written copy of the terms of business that the agent charges to and expects from the artist in return for securing engagements for the artist. This can take effect on the artist signing a sole agency contract with the agent at the beginning of their relationship, but if a written contract does not exist then the agent should – again, by law – provide written terms of business to the artist for every contract of engagement presented to the artist. It is essential that the artist is clearly notified in writing of the rate of commission which the agent will be charging with respect to any and all future engagements.

- It is important to point out and always remember that the agent earning commission from the artist is never a party to the contract negotiated for an engagement and therefore is not legally liable for the fulfilment of that contract by the parties entering into the contract, ie the artist (employee) and the promoter (employer).

the IMF handbook a guide to professional band management

Ultimately, the more one discovers about the function of an artist's agent and the more one appreciates the degree of knowledge, experience and skills needed to succeed in this field, it is probably fair to say that the stereotypical image of the agent as a shark is very outdated. The only real similarity between an agent and a shark is their mutual need to keep moving in order to survive.

chapter 8

live performances

by Rusty Hannan, Jef Hanlon and Terry O'Brien

Touring will be an important element in the careers of most artists' and therefore in those of most managers'. Once the manager has decided that the time is right to tour he must start to draw together a team of specialists in each area of expertise required to ensure that the tour runs smoothly.

There are four scales of touring in terms of venue size:

- A small club tour, promotion or personal appearance.

- A small venue, club or college tour.

- A theatre/concert hall tour.

- An arena tour.

Obviously the arrangements will vary enormously in terms of supporting personnel, equipment and the amount of planning necessary according to the size of the tour.

the IMF handbook a guide to professional band management

key personnel

The first port of call is the artist's agent, whose role is discussed in more detail in the previous chapter. The agent will use his understanding of the venues and the types of music appropriate for those venues, as well as his expertise in judging the best price to ask for a performance in those venues. He will also assemble and hold dates in a viable schedule. It will then be the responsibility of the agent to contact and secure the services of the promoters in all territories. It is most likely that the agent will be involved no matter what the scale of the tour.

the promoter

The promoter will be responsible for providing the venue for each show, for advertising and marketing the sale of tickets, for supplying the artist's rider requirements, for ensuring the safety of both the public and the artist during the course of the gig and for conforming with licensing regulations. For small-club and small-venue tours, it is likely that a different promoter will be involved with each show. For a theatre/concert tour, things could be arranged so that one promoter caters for an entire national tour, or the tour could be split between several regional promoters. For an arena tour in the UK one promoter will almost invariably promote all dates, with the possible exception of shows in Scotland and Ireland, which are sometimes given to promoters based in those countries.

the tour manager

The tour manager will be brought in as soon as the dates are confirmed. It will be his responsibility to supervise the engagement of the crew, and he will also start looking at the financing by getting quotes and budgeting for costs. He will also advance the tour to ensure that the items specified in the rider to the contract and all other production requirements are available and will be provided, and that if any of these are impossible to obtain then a suitable compromise can be found to enable the show to be performed. Whilst on tour he will manage the tour crew as well as liaising with the local crew and technical personnel. Careful and realistic planning by all involved should keep costs to a minimum, but often tour support from the artist's record company will be needed to allow the tour to proceed and the manager will need to negotiate the basis on which this money is given, how much the record company will contribute and the proportion of this sum which is recoupable. The tour manager is usually responsible for handling and collecting money on tour and settling the show with the promoter, which involves receiving payment under the terms of the contract along with paying any running expenses and collecting receipts for cash payments etc, organising and supervising travel arrangements, and arranging accommodation.

If the tour is a small-club promotional tour, the function of the tour manager is fulfilled by the manager or, alternatively, by somebody who is also able to supervise sound mixing, basic lighting and who can probably also drive the tour vehicle. This would usually mean that the tour party would comprise the artists and one other person.

On a small-venue tour – and depending on the complexity of the act's technical needs – the supporting tour personnel will usually consist of a tour manager and possibly someone who can supervise sound, lighting and backline, either of which will probably double up as a driver.

On larger tours, in addition to dealing with the artist's needs and comfort the tour manager will also be responsible for supervising guest lists, dealing with press and media enquiries or interviews, liaising with the tour sponsors if they are present, and ensuring that any promotional materials (such as banners, etc) are displayed as promised under the sponsorship deal. He should also make sure that an accurate PRS return is completed and given to the promoter to ensure that the songwriters of the material performed during the tour receive their due income, which in theatres, concert halls, arenas and stadiums is a percentage of the box-office takings and can amount to a very substantial sum of money.

the sound engineer

The sound engineer will probably be the second man on the team after the tour manager. On the two smaller levels of touring he will provide the channel listings for the venues to make sure that they have the necessary right mixing console and equipment, and he will also operating the desk during the show. On the larger tours he will draw up the specification for a sound system of a size and power suitable for those venues, and in liaison with the tour manager and production manager he will submit this as the basis for obtaining a price quotation from a company which will provide the public address system and the crew for the tour.

Unlike the front-of-house sound engineer, who mixes the audio for the general public, the monitor engineer mixes the on-stage sound for the performers, who all have individual audio requirements, including individual mixes through their on-stage monitors. The monitor engineer and mixing console will be positioned stage left in close proximity to the performers so that they can communicate easily throughout the performance. A dedicated monitor engineer is usually employed at the theatre/concert hall level of touring, and is definitely required for performances in arenas and stadia.

the production manager

A production manager will only be employed for shows big enough to require a skilled person to direct the technical side, so his involvement is usually limited to theatre, concert hall or arena shows. His function is firstly that of an overall crew boss, co-ordinating the activities of the sub-contracted PA, lighting rental, trucking and catering companies, and he will work closely with the tour manager in establishing costs, scheduling, loading-in, soundchecking and local crew-call times. He will also deal with the technical advance of the venues to establish that the basic facilities – such as stage size, electrical supply, over-stage loading points, number of dressing rooms, kitchen and catering areas, parking spaces for the tour trucks and buses and extras such as forklift trucks and cherry-pickers – are all of sufficient size and quantity to satisfy the needs of the touring production. He will also liaise with the musicians for the supply of their backline equipment requirements. All of these facilities and requirements generate a cost factor, and therefore constant communication with the tour manager and (if applicable) tour accountant is essential in order to keep these costs within the limitations of the budget.

The quantity of crew will depend on the type and size of the show; if the artist is performing in small night clubs and college bars then only one person may be needed fulfil the roles of sound engineer, driver and backline technician. However, if the artist is playing a major arena, a crew of over 50 people may be required.

the backline technicians

Backline refers to the equipment and instruments that are used by the musicians for the performance and include guitars, keyboards, amplifiers, stands etc. Backline technicians are responsible for all of the instruments, amplifiers, equipment and the stage set and often comprise a guitar technician, drum technician and stagehand-cum-carpenter. It is their responsibility to supervise the unloading of the backline equipment from the truck and set it up on stage, to make sure that the equipment in perfect working order, to have instruments tuned and to fit new strings and drumheads if required. Usually, they will also ensure there are towels, water and set lists on the stage and will help the artist if strings break or equipment fails during the show. Additionally they will look after the maintenance, operation and erection of the stage set.

the musicians

Depending on the type of band, a leader or musical director may be required to arrange the score and backing musicians together for the tour. There are various agencies that provide session musicians for tours for which the artist does not have musicians who are used regularly at his disposal, and at this point it is important to consider backline requirements. It is important to know the backline which the musicians are supplying before the tour so that any extras can be hired, and it often needs to be ascertained who is supplying the instruments. A musician should come fully equipped with personal gear, unless they are required to play an unusual instrument. For example, a guitarist should come with a guitar and an amplifier, but it may be necessary to hire a mandolin if it appears on one song. It is also worth noting that strings, drum sticks and skins and gaffa tape are all classed as consumables and are therefore considered to be tour costs.

the lighting director

On large shows, a lighting director will be appointed to put together a lighting plot, rigging plot and equipment list on which the lighting budget will be based. He will tailor the lighting, and possibly special effects such as lasers or pyrotechnics, to enhance the performance and ensure that the show is as visually appealing as possible, and he will also operate the lighting control board and cue spotlight operators during the show. This will require discussions with the artist at rehearsals to determine specific cues or effects, and as always the lighting director's specifications will be passed via the production and tour managers, who will oversee the costings and logistical requirements, such as truck space and local crew loaders required.

At small venues, lighting and an operator are usually provided if desired. If the budget is limited it may be wise to spend cash on a sound engineer rather than on a lighting technician, as a lighting technician probably won't know the equipment as well as the local operator. However, if one is available then the artist's own lighting technician could either telephone or visit the venues in advance and ask for specific lighting equipment to be made available or, if the budget allows, he could travel on the tour to supervise and cue the house operator, which will certainly improve the appearance of the show.

the accountant

The accountant will require the finalised budget, and if payments are to be dealt with through him it may be necessary to produce a payment schedule with purchase order numbers. The payment schedules will outline when payments are to be made to the various staff on the road, which tend to be staggered throughout the course of the tour. Payments out must be coordinated with payments in to make sure that cashflow problems do not arise. The accountant will help overcome monetary problems, such as withholding tax, and will ensure that tax exemption forms (such as the E101 form necessary for touring in Europe) are completed. On smaller tours the function of the accountant is often fulfilled by the artist's management, whilst on very large arena tours a dedicated tour accountant usually travels with the tour to deal with all financial matters as they arise.

With the team in place there will be many areas of the tour which need to be planned and overseen to ensure that no problems occur either before the tour begins or on the road.

other resources

the rider

The manager, along with the agent, needs to draft a rider to the standard contract that will inform the promoter of what he is obliged to provide at the venue in terms of facilities, supplies and services so that the artist can perform the show. Rehearsals must be booked, along with venues for performances. There are three types of rehearsal that are generally required (band/music rehearsals, dance choreography and production rehearsals), and there are many facilities that can provide these. The first two are self explanatory. Production rehearsals will be required for extremely large shows, and constitute a time allocated as a technical period for lighting directors, technicians and set carpenters to iron out any problems before commencing the tour. The band will probably arrive on the penultimate day of production rehearsals for a practice show run-through with the crew. Ideally, production rehearsals will be in the venue in which the artist will perform the first show of the tour for ease and cost-effectiveness, or alternatively a venue of similar size so that all of the elements of the show can be run exactly as they would be for the public performances.

ground transportation

Transportation for the artist, crew and equipment will need to be booked and coordinated. If the artist is performing personal appearances at night clubs and needs just a couple of singers and dancers then it makes sense to hire a people carrier, as these are roomy and are ideal for getting around quickly. However, if the band are musicians and are carrying backline the ideal vehicle for the touring party would be what is known as a splitter van. These are mostly converted self-drive vehicles which have been split or divided in some way to allow more room for equipment at the back and space for a lounge and basic living quarters at the front, including such essentials as a TV and video. When a tour increases in size, or if great distances are involved, it becomes necessary to have a number of sleeper coaches included in the entourage, which are equipped with bunks and lounges and allow both the crew and artists to sleep while travelling overnight between venues.

flights

If they are necessary, flights and hotels will usually be booked with a specialist music travel company, who will hopefully understand the need to keep costs to a minimum but will also understand the often very specific needs of artists and their touring party. With local flights it is important to check that all flight cases which are carrying equipment and stage costumes will fit into the holds of smaller aircraft before booking the flight, and the airline should be given advance notice of the weight and dimensions of flight cases to be checked in over and above personal luggage.

trucking

If the tour is providing its own production at all shows, trucks will invariably be required. It is important to note that only companies that hire trucks for the music industry should be used, as they will provide air ride trailers, which protect the expensive and delicate equipment to be transported. It also means that the drivers will understand the importance of getting to the next show whatever it takes. It is important to note that trucks cannot travel at the same speed as buses, and this must be taken into account when working out logistics and distances. It is also important to note that both PSV coaches and HGV trucks all carry a tachograph which records the distances and hours driven by the drivers and the amount and length of breaks which they take. Vehicles governed by tachographs are subject to random checks by traffic police, and there are very strict laws governing the hours which the drivers of these vehicles can stay behind the wheel and the amount of rest periods they must take. If the distances and time available between shows is such that the drivers will infringe the regulations, a second driver must be hired.

the stage set

essentials

The stage set will also be transported in the trucks. Not every band requires an elaborate set, but even a drum riser needs to be calculated into the budget. The set will be of the mobile variety made by a company specialising in tour sets, rather than a fixed set used for television and theatre. A tour set must be easily and quickly dismantled, and must therefore be built from materials that are sturdy, light, compact, and which fold up so that they save space on the trucks. There is a lot to consider in this respect, and a good set carpenter is worth his weight in gold. Included within the set are the drapes and backcloths carried by the show and sometimes hydraulic equipment to lift platforms or staircases.

costumes and props

If the artist wears stage clothes or costumes, an adapted flight case is usually carried as a wardrobe in which to transport and store them. Sometimes, if clothes are a major part of the presentation, a full-time wardrobe person is employed to clean, maintain and be responsible for the stage garments. If any specific props are used, these are usually looked after and maintained by either the wardrobe person or the backline crew.

special effects

Special effects, such as pyrotechnics, are usually referred to as simply 'specials'. They are often very expensive, and it will therefore be important to know at an early stage in the planning stages if they are to be used so that they can be included in the budget. The use of pyrotechnics, lasers and strobes are governed by licensing laws, and normally advance notice of their use is required by the local authority health and safety inspectors and fire brigade. These officials will often attend the venue on the day of the show to check and approve the installation and operation of these effects and make sure that the public is not in danger. They will have the power to prevent the effects from being used if they think they could be a danger to the audience, artists or crew, and should therefore be treated with respect and consulted in advance whenever possible. In order for pyrotechnics to be used in Europe they will need to be installed by a licensed technician with an official permit.

video

On a tour the term 'video' refers to the projection and video used in a performance. Most artists will be unable to use this until they experience mega stardom. This is not so much due to the cost (although it is expensive) but due instead to the size of the venue needed to accommodate it. The fixed screens now installed in many larger venues means that video is increasingly used on major tours. The pictures projected for the video can be either pre-recorded and edited tape for effects, live pictures from cameras or a mixture of both.

catering

Feeding crew and artists on a major tour can be a huge undertaking, which is made more difficult if some members of the team have dietary requirements that only specialist tour caterers will understand and be equipped to accommodate. A catering company is hired on bigger tours, on which the crew are unable to leave the venue and the band are not able to move around easily in public. The caterers will travel on the crew buses and their equipment will be transported on the production trucks, along with the lights and sound equipment. If the tour is not large enough to justify the expense of hiring a tour catering company then the crew will usually be given a *per diem* (a small daily payment to cover expenses, including those meals not provided with accommodation).

the IMF handbook a guide to professional band management

security

passes

Passes play an important part of a tour's security and will be used to prevent any unauthorised person going backstage. The ultimate backstage pass is the laminate, which predictably consists of a laminated pass with a photo and which is supplied to tour personnel with a lanyard to wear around the neck. These will almost certainly allow access to all areas, including the onstage backstage areas and the dressing rooms.

However, on some tours an escort pass is issued, which allows access to dressing rooms only and is given only to the tour manager, the security staff, any wardrobe personnel and the person who is responsible for dressing-room catering. This allows the artists an extra level of privacy and security.

Day passes, also known as 'stickies', will be given to visitors such as the press, the staff of the record company, local crew, the families of the artists or crew and any special guests. Depending on the access requirements of the visitor, the day pass may give access to all areas at all times, only certain areas or even backstage access after the show has finished. The colours of the day passes will change each day in an effort to prevent them from being re-used.

signage

On larger tours it is common practice to use pre-printed backstage signs to indicate direction to the stage, dressing rooms, dining room, production office and other areas, to help people those people unfamiliar with the venue to find their way quickly and efficiently around the backstage area.

itinerary

It is normal to produce an itinerary for every tour. This is a schedule for everyone, including the management personnel, the record company and touring personnel, and contains dates, venues, times and other useful contact information. This constitutes the touring bible, and it must never be misplaced because all of the information contained within it is confidential.

live performances

SPRING TOUR 1999

DATE:	MONDAY 30TH MARCH	Place:	**PARIS**
TRAVEL:	**ZENITH**	PROD:	00 33 (0) 1 42 45 99 5
	211 AVENUE JEAN JAURES	FAX/PROD:	00 33 (0) 1 42 45 99 5
	75019	LOAD IN:	**10.00am (APPROX)**
	PARIS	S/C:	**4.00pm**
		DOORS:	**6.00pm**
		SUPPORT:	**7.00pm**
TEL:	00 33 (0) 1 42 45 91 48	MAIN:	**8.00pm**
FAX:	00 33 (0) 1 42 01 42 49		
CAP:	**6000**		

LOCAL PROMOTER

		CONTACT:	**PASCAL**
	PARIS PRODUCTIONS	PROD:	00 33 (0) 1 44 92 45 45
	PARIS	FAX:	00 33 (0) 1 46 06 38 79
TEL:	00 33 (0) 1 44 92 45 48	MOB:	
FAX:	00 33 (0) 1 46 06 38 73		

AFTERSHOW TRAVEL:

    ALL BUSES O/N DRIVE PARIS-LONDON APPROX: 300 MILES 10 HRS
    BAND ARRIVE 10.00am HAMMERSMITH APOLLO
    CREW ARRIVE MIDDAY KINGS CROSS STATION

HOTEL:	**HILTON**	HOTEL:	**NO HOTEL**
	106 RUE ST EMILLION		
	PARIS		
TEL:	00 33 (0) 1 34 56 87	TEL:	
FAX:	00 33 (0) 1 54 98 21	FAX:	

ROOM SERVICE: **24HR**

FACILITIES: **SAUNA/DISCO/PUB**   FACILITIES

ADDITIONAL INFORMATION

NOTE: LAST DAY FOR HANDING IN PASSPORTS FOR VISA APPLICATIONS

An example of a typical tour itinerary

the IMF handbook a guide to professional band management

TOUR CHECKLIST

BAND	TOUR		DATE	
ITEM	PERIOD	QUOTE	TO DO	DONE
TOUR/CONTACTS				
AGENT				
PROMOTER				
VENUE				
TERRITORIES/RIDER				
TOUR ACCOUNTANT				
PERSONNEL				
MUSICAL DIRECTOR/MD				
MUSICIANS				
CHOREOGRAPHER/DANCERS				
TOUR MANAGER/TM				
PRODUCTION MANAGER/PM				
SOUND ENGINEER/FOH				
LIGHTING DIRECTOR/LD				
BACKLINE TECHNICIANS/CREW				
CATERING				
SET CARPENTERS				
DRIVERS/TRUCKS & BUSES				
STAGE REQUIREMENTS				
SOUND EQUIPMENT				
MONITORS/IN EAR MONITORS				
LIGHTING				
SET/HYDRAULICS/DRAPES				
VIDEO PROJECTION				
SPECIAL FX/PYROS				
STAGE PROPS/COSTUMES				
BACKLINE INSTRUMENTS				
TRANSPORT/TRAVEL				
HOTEL/QTY				
BUSES				
SPLITTER VAN				
FLIGHTS				
TRUCKS				
ADDITIONAL				
REHEARSALS/MUSIC/DANCE				
REHEARSALS/PRODUCTION				
ATERING				
ITINERARIES/PASSES				
MERCHANDISING				
PROMOTION				
RADIO/TV				
POSTERS/FLYERS				
MEET & GREETS				
SPONSORSHIP/BUY-ON FEE				
LEGAL				
BUDGET/FLOAT/PER DIEMS				
TOUR SUPPORT				
PUBLIC LIABILITY INSURANCE				
PERFORMANCE INSURANCE				
EMPLOYERS/EQUIPMENT INSURANCE				

An example of a typical tour checklist

live performances

VENUE CHECKLIST

BAND		**PERIOD**	
VENUE		SHOW DATE	
ADDRESS		CAPACITY	
		LOAD-IN	
		DOORS	
TELEPHONE		SOUND CHECK	
FAX		SUPPORT	
PRODUCTION TELEPHONE		MAIN	
PRODUCTION FAX		CURFEW	
CONTACT			
PROMOTER		TELEPHONE	
PROMOTER'S REP		FAX	
		MOBILE	
DRESSING ROOMS		PRODUCTION OFFICE	
ITEM		**ITEM**	
STAGE SIZE	W: D: H:	CLEARANCE	
STAGE TYPE		PROSCENIUM ARCH	
PA WINGS		SIGHT LINES	
FOH POSITION		CRASH BARRIER	
LOAD-IN ACCESS		MASKING	
POWER LIGHTS		POWER SOUND	
FORK-LIFT		CHERRY PICKER	
SET		RISERS/MARLEY	
FOLLOW SPOTS		HOUSE LIGHTS	
PYROS/SMOKE		LICENCE/BY-LAWS	
DRY ICE/LASERS		SPECIAL EFFECT	
PARKING TRUCKS		PARKING BUSES	
LANDLINE POWER		PARKING PERMITS	
FERRIES		TOLLS	
CATERING AREA		CATERING POWER	
TOWELS		LAUNDRY/DRY CLEANING	
LOCAL CREW		FOLLOW SPOT OPS	
RUNNER		ELECTRICIAN	
FORK-LIFT DRIVER		RIGGER	
SECURITY		RED CROSS	
WARDROBE PERSON		WARDROBE CASES	
VISAS/WORK PERMITS		PASSPORT PHOTOS	
FIRE CURTAIN		SAFETY CERTIFICATES	
TICKETS SOLD		TICKET PRICE	
EXPENDITURE		INCOME	
WITH HOLDING TAX		PRS	
BROADCAST FEE		AGENTS/PROMOTERS FEE	
GUARANTEE/ADVANCE		COLLECTION	
TOTAL EXPENDITURE		TOTAL INCOME	
SHEET NUMBER:			

An example of a typical venue checklist

the IMF handbook a guide to professional band management

insurance

It is of paramount importance that the risks involved in touring and performing shows are covered by insurance, and there are several specialist insurance brokers who deal with the touring industry and understand its idiosyncrasies. The insurance necessary to cover a tour can be covered by three categories:

- Public, products and employers liability cover. This covers liability for claims issued by the public or for those issued by people who are employed by the tour. This variety of insurance is essential for absolutely all levels of touring activity.

- Equipment and personal possessions insurance. This should normally be taken out by individual musicians in respect of their instruments, but it is normal for rental companies to insist that the hirer takes out insurance to cover damage or theft to the equipment.

- Contingency insurance. This is insurance against cancellation which can cover expenses incurred on the tour and, if required, assure payment of the artists fees (including percentage payments), depending on the level of cover taken out.

paperwork

carnet

This is a document that lists the goods transported in the trucks, such as instruments, amplifiers, sound, lighting and stage equipment, and specifies their monetary value and their countries of origin. It is an essential document for tours which span a number of countries, and is usually issued by a chamber of commerce in the town or city from which the tour production originates. A bond is deposited with this chamber of commerce to cover the value of the equipment, which in effect signifies the intention of the people transporting it to use it on the tour, but also affirms that they will return it to its original point of departure and not sell or dispose of any of it in any countries along the way. The possession of a carnet simplifies the acquiring of customs clearances at the borders of countries, and means in effect that all that is required is a customs officer's stamp on the carnet on entry and departure from their country to verify that the items of equipment have been checked in and out, therefore reassuring the individual customs authority that the touring company harbours no intent to import the equipment on a permanent basis with a view to selling it to a resident of that country, and that the importation is purely temporary for the purposes of presenting the shows and will be followed by immediate exportation on completion of the shows, ultimately by return to its country of origin. If you are in possession of this document it means that you will be able to avoid the charging of import taxes or duties on equipment and instruments, and it is absolutely essential for an international tour.

post-production

On completion of the tour, it is the responsibility of the tour manager to liaise with each member of the crew and to arrange that all of the items that have been carried on the tour are returned to their owners or stored in the artist's warehouse space, especially ensuring that rental equipment is returned promptly and not left running up unnecessary rental charges. If a carnet is being used, the stamped copies, together with the rest of the paperwork, should be returned to the relevant authority from which they were issued and the deposited bond released. The tour manager should then work through the paperwork and check all of the invoices and budgeted bills. For those that have not been budgeted, he should be able to explain to the artist and its management why such overages have occurred. The tour manager should be able to produce a complete set of show settlements which have been agreed with the promoters and should ideally produce a summary of the number of people attending each show relative to the capacity of the venue, the relevant paperwork recording the guest lists and the number of complimentary tickets issued, whether or not these tickets were picked up, press items such as the names and contact details of those journalists who have either interviewed the artist or reviewed the show, and signed waiver forms submitted by the photographers who have taken pictures of the shows. He should also produce a set of accounts and receipts justifying all cash payments made by him during the tour.

Touring is a vital element of any artist's career. If a team of experienced and skilful professionals are employed, the complex business of planning and executing a tour will run smoothly, will be visually appealing and will provide the artists with the best possible conditions to reproduce their music for the audience, allowing them a chance to present themselves to their fans in a first-hand capacity, and – through

the IMF handbook a guide to professional band management

a professionally- and creatively-presented live show – develop that all-important relationship with those fans that will help them achieve commercial success.

chapter 9
press and PR

by Bernard Doherty

The job of a band's publicist can appear to be among the easiest and most attractive in the music business because there seems to be so much scope for mixing work and having a good time, and the job does not require special academic achievements. But the ability to think on your feet, however, is essential.

The publicist has regular access to artists and therefore has ample opportunity to observe their work at close quarters. For some people this may be an appealing bonus, but an awe-struck star-gazing publicist who wants to hang with the band is more all-round liability rather than asset! Although it is true that many PR people in the industry have the opportunity to work directly and closely with the bands that they represent, the job is particularly demanding in a number of ways and also has a great deal of stress and tension attached to it.

the IMF handbook a guide to professional band management

THE PUBLICIST'S ROLE

the working day

The publicist's average working day may begin at home with an unexpected phone call about a breaking news story in which one of his clients plays some part, and he will then make the necessary calls to the management personnel. Instead of heading for the office, he must then change the day's timetable to accommodate the event, and meetings and other routine affairs are postponed to so that he has time to deal with the new emergency.

Otherwise, the day that gets under way without such surprises may start with a skim-read of the morning tabloids, in which most music stories break. The mix of the routine day's work might include phone calls to clients and journalists either to talk about specific plans or merely to stay in touch, a drink with a useful media contact, a session of press interviews for an artist who has something new to promote and an appointment at a photographer's studio to supervise the shooting of some new publicity pictures. There could also be a meeting to attend with the record company people to lay down the foundations of a new album, tour PR project. The variations on this theme are endless, and as a rule almost always mean a long and busy working day.

The publicist needs to have a nose for sniffing out a promising news story, a well-developed sense of loyalty and discretion, a genuine devotion to the job, a willingness to work very unsociable hours, and a broad spread of skills and capabilities, some of which need to be almost instinctive while others are far from easy to learn and cannot be acquired from any textbook or solely via a university or college course.

where to start

Extremely few independent music publicists set themselves up in business without previous PR experience, and the most usual place to acquire this experience is in the press office of a record company.

There are equal opportunities for women and men in the field of public relations. In fact, if there is an element of discrimination it may very well favour women, and indeed some employers and some clients insist that, all other things being equal, women tend to make more persuasive (and therefore more successful) publicists, whether they are dealing with either male or female journalists.

Broadly speaking, the role of the music business publicist is much the same whether the service is performed as an in-house employee or as an outside independent consultant. Part of the job's appeal is that it is comprised of so many individual activities, and the work is seldom repetitious. Each day's activities differ from those from previous days.

who employs publicists?

Artists in all sectors of the music business can benefit from press and publicity representation. The launch of an unknown newcomer needs the boost of added publicity to increase public awareness of a first-record release or any initial public performances. The well-established box-office success and chart-topping recording star with a limited amount of time to spend on interviews and photo sessions needs the expert advice of a publicist concerning which editorial opportunities to take and which to turn down with the minimum loss of goodwill. The greater the artist's celebrity the more the publicist's role includes an element of protection against unfavourable stories. It is naïve to believe that all publicity is good publicity, or to underestimate the damage which can be done to an artist's reputation when bad press is printed in the media.

In the music business, the largest employers of PR services are the record companies, many of which have their own in-house press offices run by a team of publicists and their assistants. Medium-sized and smaller record companies may not operate a full-blown department but instead simply employ one or two publicists. Others who hire full-time publicists or who retain the non-exclusive services of independent PR consultants include music publishers, artists' managers and agents, independent record producers and recording studios, music industry associations, concert tour promoters and music video production companies and their distributors. Out-of-house publicists, whether self-employed individuals or those who are part of a consultancy, may be retained on a year-round basis or periodically to draw on when a client wants a short burst of PR activity to assist in the promotion and marketing of a product, which could be an album, a tour or a video.

Whatever the specific line of business in which the music publicist's employer or a client is engaged, an artist or a roster of artists will be at the core of most PR campaigns. Without waiting for others to act on their behalfs, individual artists often feel that their careers might benefit from the attention of a publicity consultant and they will approach an independent publicist directly. Such deals can be on a short-term single-campaign basis or can run for an open-ended period of time. As a rule, if both parties are

the IMF handbook a guide to professional band management

getting along well, the publicist will hope to keep the account running indefinitely. The clout of the independent consultant is linked intrinsically to the strength of his client roster and to the attractiveness of the names of those represented in the eyes of reporters.

what skills are needed?

Previous journalistic experience is a great asset to anyone contemplating a career in PR, although it should be recognised that not all journalists have the vocational inclination or the right temperament to move into PR. In theory, at least, a journalist who has had regular dealings with publicists should be better equipped to move from one end of the process to the other.

The publicist must be articulate, he must have a fairly large vocabulary, and he must also be a willing and able communicator, with an instinctive flair for spotting the makings of an interesting news story or an eye-catching picture. From the ragged jumble of biographical data or a heap of photographer's contact sheets, the publicist should be capable of picking out the tiniest speck of information which might be turned into some sort of media opportunity.

a dedicated profession

Office hours? Forget them! Early in the morning, breakfast television and radio reporters and evening newspaper journalists working on first editions may have urgent need to reach a publicist. Similarly, people writing for final editions of morning papers often work through until midnight or even later. PR work is therefore not for the person looking for a nine-to-five job. The responsible publicist or delegated deputy has a duty to remain available to the media 24 hours a day. To be unobtainable during the breaking of a news story concerning a client or employer can be major disaster.

areas of responsibility

acting as a source of information

It is a basic function of the publicist to be thoroughly informed about the activities of the bands which he represents. Accurate, adequate and up-to-date written information should be available to the media on request, and journalists should be able to acquire answers to questions promptly.

putting out the news

The publicist needs to know how to construct an instantly attractive news release, sometimes creating a good story from less than attractive raw material, putting the vital facts at the top of the copy and the background information lower down. Brevity is as important as accuracy. News – real news – should be delivered by the fastest possible and most efficient method, preferably by fax or e-mail.

image building

Whether acting individually as head of a small independent PR consultancy or within a team of full-time marketing and promotional executives at a major record company, the publicist is directly concerned with image creation and revision. This can involve the design or improvement of a company's overall public image (with the introduction of fresh corporate livery and logo) or the professional image of an artist. It can be a fascinating challenge for the publicist to start from scratch on the creation, development and establishment of a new artist's image prior to a launch. The image of an artist is projected not only via a style of music but also by his appearance and personality.

Areas which a publicist is likely to cover include the definition of an artist's musical style, his visual image for photo sessions and public appearances and live performances (grooming, hair, clothing), and a choice of the most suitable media for the occasion (which publications or programmes to go for, and which to treat as a lower priority or even to simply avoid). A publicist may also become involved in redefining an established artist's image, particularly to coincide with a change of career direction.

promotion and protection

Positive promotion of the employer's or client's activities in the public marketplace is the top priority of the publicist. However, there are times in which a reverse strategy needs to be applied, and in these cases a different approach comes into play. Such occasions arise when there is a call for damage limitation over a story which threatens to spoil the image of an artist. A publicist's protective know-how can be employed in putting the best possible face on an unfavourable story, perhaps by countering quickly with something positive, and can also mean calling in favours from friendly media contacts. This is the area in which a publicist's diplomatic skills come into play, and the strength and level of his relationships with media people is very important.

the IMF handbook a guide to professional band management

stimulating media interest

Mutual trust between a journalist and a publicist is the best basis for successful business. Schmoozing with media contacts in order to develop or consolidate relationships is fine, but the wise publicist delays hard-sell discussion of specific stories until another occasion rather than pushing specific stories. Many prefer to avoid hard-sell tactics altogether, knowing that there are few people journalists dislike more intensely than the time-consuming ear-bending publicist who hopes that sheer brute force verbal assault will compensate for a weak case. The publicist's task is to present the facts in a persuasive way, but not to press a case too zealously or aggressively and therefore cause irritation.

setting up interviews

As a routine part of the job, a publicist arranges media interviews for clients and employers. The majority of these will involve artists, and a necessary part the publicists job is linking each interview with the most suitable journalists and offer potential interviewers a mutually appropriate (and sometimes exclusive) angle. Popular artists will be in such media demand that some interview requests will have to be turned down, although on the other hand some unknown newcomers or rising stars will need the publicist's extra push. Often the two extremes can meet at the middle when a little subtle leverage is brought into play by the publicist.

arranging photography

As with writers and broadcasting journalists, photographers fall into two categories: freelance and staff. Among the freelancers are those who specialise in specific areas, such as album-sleeve photography. When pictures of an artist are being taken to accompany a particular article, the publicist may be less able to select a photographer by name because the decision will be taken by the journalist or picture editor. Otherwise, it is up to the publicist to learn which photographers work best with which artists, and a good rapport between the two should produce substantially better pictures. Past experience helps the publicist to choose the best photographer for each different situation.

travelling

The frequency of a publicist's out-of-town trips will vary hugely according to the jobs in hand. A major artist on the road for a large series of concerts may require on-site PR services at each new leg of the tour to handle media interviews and set up press conferences. The publicist should be prepared to travel sometimes, often at short notice, in order to accompany an important journalist to a gig and occasionally to cope with an unexpected surge of media interest (negative or positive) somewhere on the road.

receptions and conferences

Media receptions are held to launch publicity campaigns and are used to introduce new artists, sometimes with a showcase performance. Few such events are expected to generate immediate media headlines, and are arranged more to create general goodwill and prepare the way for more specific media situations at a later time.

Press conferences are more formal and should involve the announcement of some sort of news. Typically they are based on the distribution of a press release and a live question-and-answer session, in which the concerned parties face rows of journalists and their photographer from behind a table. As a rule, the publicist acts as a moderator, controlling the flow of questioning.

ways into the business

academic tuition

At the time of writing, ten universities and colleges throughout England, Scotland and the Republic of Ireland offer courses in Public Relations or Communication, and whose degrees and diplomas are recognised by the London-based Institute Of Public Relation for purposes of membership. Such courses theoretically provide a sound fundamental knowledge of PR machinery, although not of its practical application within the music business. Students often gain mid-course hands-on experience by offering their (unpaid) services to a suitable company (in this case a record company press office or an independent publicist's consultancy) during long vacations.

journalistic experience

Working for a local hometown newspaper or broadcaster can be a useful starting point, particularly if the chance exists to review concerts or records. A journalist receives press releases from publicists and learns to separate the useful and informative material from the badly-written or badly-targeted stuff, which can be a very valuable experience. Would-be publicists unable to find a job on a newspaper or a radio station can still submit reviews and other articles on music topics to feature editors and programme producers on a freelance basis. Even if they fail to be published, the writing experience will still be worthwhile.

experience in the music industry

Juniors in the press office of a record company can pick up a lot of useful knowledge of the industry, and some are even lucky enough to fill in for more senior people from time to time. The would-be publicist learns from what goes on and is not afraid to put forward ideas.

Only after accumulating sufficient qualifications by way of academic achievement and/or useful work experience should anyone contemplate applying for a publicist's job, probably with a record company. Smaller independent companies will take much less in the way of academic achievement if aspects of a candidate's personality seem to be right for the job. At this stage, timidity, uncertainty, hesitation or an inability to communicate your own best features will go against you. Moderate self-confidence, self-salesmanship, a controlled sense of humour, some intelligently inquisitive questions about the work you might be doing and a show of interest in the label's artists will go down well. Most importantly of all, the would-be publicist should demonstrate his knowledge of the media to the interviewers, and it is essential that he should know his subject: knowledge of music in all its contemporary guises.

chapter 10

managing merchandising

by Andy Allen, Steve Brickle and Jef Hanlon

There are only two reasons to get involved in music merchandising: to maximise on the potential revenue involved, and to heighten public awareness of your band by ensuring that their logo or image image is prevalent in the marketplace on T-shirts, posters or chewing gum. The fact that you can persuade people to pay for the privilege of becoming a walking billboard or to pay to allow their walls to become a marketing tool featuring that same logo or image for your band is something that most managers will obviously find attractive. How one maximises the revenue and enhances the market impact will vary from band to band, depending on the type of the band and the size of its audience. Metal? Pop? Dance? Mainstream? Marketing for bands of each of these genres will require a different approach.

Sales of merchandise can be broken down into two main areas: sales at concerts and sales through retail, mail order and any licensing or sub-licensing. This latter category covers everything, including the sales of shirts in record stores, sales of posters, badges, patches, and in fact anything that will benefit from association with your client's logo, image or endorsement. Fan club direct sales also fall into this category.

the IMF handbook a guide to professional band management

tour merchandise

When first starting on a commercial career, one of the first things a band should consider is whether or not to it is a worthwhile exercise to print some shirts to sell at their gigs. It is probably wise that a manager should refrain from this temptation until the demand is there, as the initial euphoria from being supported by a following of a few friends can lead to disappointing sales and, worse, the incurring of a debt before the band has even reached the bottom rung of the commercial ladder. As time passes and the demand for merchandising increases, it will be necessary to make a decision on how best to arrange this. There are three options outlined here that you may wish to pursue.

supply-only deal

Strike up a relationship with a merchandiser and operate on a supply-only basis. This deal requires you to accept the merchandise and then admit responsibility for the sales, and involves the venue supplying personnel who will check in and then sell the merchandise. You may encounter concession-hall fees or site-rental fees, but these are usually only charged at larger venues. At the end of the sales staff will return whatever stock is left over along with the cash they have taken, minus their percentage, which is generally 25% of cash taken including VAT, although at some larger venues they can charge more. This figure is calculated on the retail price, and at the stage that concession fees are charged the artist is generally VAT registered. This means that the artist will actually be charged 29.38% of the net (plus VAT) or 25% of the gross (plus VAT). It has been a contentious issue in the industry for a long time, but it appears that this arrangement will remain the way it is for the foreseeable future.

royalty-rate deal

In a royalty-rate deal, the rate is calculated on gross sales. It is important to note, however, that gross sales are considered to be the retail price less taxes (ie VAT), and on some occasions the concession fee from a venue is also deducted before the royalty rate is calculated. The royalty rate is usually in the region of 25% to 35%, but – depending on how large an artist you manage – you may be able to negotiate a better rate, should the tour generate a higher income, or even have an increase written into the deal depending on performance of the tour. A merchandiser will generally offer a lower rate in foreign territories, which usually tends to be 80% of the domestic rate.

split-profit deal

This deal is organised by the merchandiser responsible for the supply and sale of products on tour and for then analysing the figures at the tour's conclusion. Once calculated, an agreed split of the profits can anywhere between 65/35 and, in extreme cases, 90/10. Generally, however, the average split is calculated between 75/25 and 80/20 in favour of the artist. It should be noted, however, that the merchandiser will take a 10% administration fee, based on net sales.

retail

All other forms of income generated by the band, outside touring, will be calculated on a retail basis. A merchandiser will generally sell your T-shirts, sweatshirts, caps and other merchandise to a specialist music merchandise wholesaler. (The royalty rates for merchandising span from 16%-22% of wholesale.) Furthermore, he will negotiate to procure licensing deals with other non-clothing merchandisers to merchandise other goods (posters and badges, for example). In consideration, they will take a percentage of roughly 20%. The agreed royalty rate will be generally 10%-15% of wholesale.

Merchandising the good on a mail-order basis will result in the receipt of approximately 25% of gross sales, but be careful not to forget to deduct taxes before calculating this figure. With foreign royalties, once again this will be 80% of the UK rates.

Whether you arrive at a separate tour and retail deal, or a combined one, there are a few points which are very important to remember:

- The artist should approve all designs and items of merchandise, and if the funds are available then the artwork should be copyrighted and trademarked.

- There should be a restriction of sell of rights, which is important when the term comes to an end and there is excess stock left over. The merchandiser should at some point (approximately three months) to sell this stock, but the stock must then be destroyed or bought back.

- All sub-licensing deals need to be approved by the manager.

- Should an advance be received, it must be determined whether or not there will be cross-collateralisation on the tour and retail agreements.

- Deals operate either under a time limit or until the advance is recouped. However, there must be some contract term or time period stated to this effect in the contract or it is not legal.

advances

An artist can attain an advance from merchandisers, but these agreements will require that the money is paid back should recoupment not occur. Merchandisers will build various contingency plans to safeguard their investment should the tour not take place or is unsuccessful, and there will be various other clauses included (for instance, that the tour must take place over a specified amount of time, or that a minimum number of paying clients will be attending the shows).

As you can see, there are a variety of ways in which to put a deal together, and the setup depends on the requirements of artist.

appendix 1
societies

ASCAP

The American Society of Composers, Authors and Publisher is the oldest performing rights organisation in the US, representing over four million copyrighted works and generating the highest annual revenue (1998 revenues totalled more than $500 million). The society was founded in 1914 by a small group of songwriters and publishers to protect the rights of its members by licensing and collecting royalties for the public performance of their copyrighted musical works. ASCAP today boasts more than 86,000 members, and represents the music of more than 200,000 foreign writers and publishers through agreements with over 60 performing rights organisations worldwide.

advantages

ASCAP is the only membership society among US performing rights organisations and is the only US society governed by a board of directors consisting solely of composers, lyricists and publishers, who are elected by the members. Members also have a strong voice in the operation of their society, and can participate in any of the annual open membership meetings held in each of the three major US music centres: Los Angeles, Nashville and New York.

Changes in payment must be approved by the board of directors, the Department Of Justice and, in some cases, a federal court after an open court hearing. No changes can be made without prior notice to the society's membership.

Fair and equal treatment is a hallmark of ASCAP membership. Writers and publishers sign identical contracts, with the right to resign every year of the contract It is also the only society which determines royalties objectively over the life of the copyright.

The ASCAP worldwide web site (http://www.ascap.com) is a convenient gateway to ASCAP, with news of events, workshops along with other

the IMF handbook a guide to professional band management

information. Also available for access on the web is ACE (ASCAP Clearance Express), which provides quick and easy and continuous access to ASCAP title, writer and publisher information.

> ASCAP Chicago
> 1608 West Belmont Avenue
> Suite 200
> Chicago
> IL 6065
> Tel: 312 481 1194
> Fax: 312 481 1195
>
> ASCAP Los Angeles
> 7920 Sunset Boulevard
> Suite 300
> Los Angeles
> CA 90046
> Tel: 213 883 1000
> Fax: 213 883 1049
>
> ASCAP Nashville
> Two Music Square West
> Nashville
> TN 37203
> Tel: 615 742 5000
> Fax: 615 742 5020
>
> ASCAP London
> 8 Cork Street
> London
> W1X 1PB
> Tel: 0171 439 0909
> Fax: 0171 434 0073

AURA

The Association of United Recording Artists was set up by the IMF to safeguard the interests of artists with regard to the new Public Performance Right. The EC Directive requires that all relevant parties receive an equitable share of income derived from public performance.

The PPL and its members are currently negotiating the split of performance income per track from the date the instrument was passed by the government. AURA has been involved with the PPL in negotiating the principles of the split between various categories of performers. These discussions are ongoing, and there are still many unresolved issues which will have a considerable impact on performers in terms of the future income they receive from their recordings. Of course, the degree of influence AURA will be able to exert will depend on the level of support which is available.

AURA is an association, not a union, primarily representing featured recording artists and producers, and it doesn't limit the terms on which you do business. The organisation can help its members in a variety of ways, by representing their point of view in discussions with both industry bodies within the UK and abroad and with local, national, European and international governments.

For further information, contact the general secretary, Peter Horrey, at the address below:

AURA
11 Stoney Common
Stansted
Essex
CM24 8NF
Tel: 01279 647201
Fax: 01279 647205

BMI

The BMI is an American performing rights organisation which represents more than 120,000 US and foreign songwriters and composers and 60,000 US publishers. The company collects licence fees on behalf of those American creators it represents as well as for the thousands of creators from around the world who have chosen to be represented by the BMI in the US. The fees exacted for the 'public performance' of its repertoire of more than three million compositions – including performances featured on radio airplay, TV broadcast and cable TV transmission, as well as live and recorded performances by all other users of music – are distributed in the form of royalties to the appropriate writers of the songs and owners of the copyright.

the IMF handbook a guide to professional band management

The BMI's list of affiliates is unsurpassed. Among the songwriters it represents are many classic songwriters in different musical genres. It was founded in 1940 as a non-profit-making corporation whose aim was to provide performing rights representation for those songwriters and composers who were ineligible for protection from the older American performing rights societies. BMI offered first-time representation to songwriters of blues, jazz, R&B, gospel, folk, country, Spanish-language music and other types of American music. As several of these musical trends converged to produce rock 'n' roll, the BMI became the pre-eminent performing rights organisation in the country to represent songwriters of this new genre. The organisation quickly made reciprocal agreements with its sister performing rights organisations around the world to license its repertoire.

The BMI's pop, rock, R&B, country and jazz repertoire is extensive. A listing of the top 100 singles of the rock era by *Rolling Stone* magazine showed that the BMI represents 75% of these works. More than 75% of the inductees into the Rock And Roll Hall Of Fame are represented by BMI, as are more than 80% of the inducteed into Country Music Hall Of Fame and more than 90% of those honoured with Pioneer Awards by the Rhythm And Blues Foundation. For further information, contact Phil Graham at the address below:

BMI
84 Harley House
Marylebone Road
London
NW1 5HN
Tel: 0171 486 2036
Fax: 0171 224 1046

BMR

British Music Rights Limited was established at the end of September 1996 to promote, protect and develop the interests of music creators and publishers and to demonstrate the value of the British musical heritage in today's society. The BMR seeks to influence the formulating of national and international policies and to initiate and respond to legislative measures and technological developments which may affect the creative and rights-owning interests it represents. The BMR seeks to underline the economic and artistic importance of the work of creators and publishers, with emphasis on the consequent commercial, cultural, educational and social benefits of their efforts.

membership of the BMR

Some members of the BMR include the Music Publishers' Association, the Alliance of Composers Organisations (including the Alliance of Professioanl Composers, The Compser's Guild Of Great Britain and The British Academy Of Songwriters, Composers And Authors), the Performing Right Society and the MCPS.

For more information contact the director general, Nanette Rigg, at the address below:

British Music House
26 Berners Street
London
W1P 3DB
Tel: (44) 171 306 4446
Fax: (44) 171 306 4449

BPI

The economic success of the British record industry is undeniable. Retail sale of CDs, cassettes and LPs in the UK now total more than £1.6 billion, while physical exports and invisible earnings exceed £1 billion each year. Equally important is the recognition of the vital role that music plays in everyday life and in reflecting Britain's contemporary culture.

The BPI is the trade association for record companies in the UK. It boasts over 200 members, including all of the major record companies as well as many small independents. Each member company, regardless of its size, has a single vote. Together, member companies account for over 90% of UK record sales.

The BPI exists to protect the interests of its members in all areas of activity. Much of the work is unseen, involving lobbying in Westminster and Brussels, working with government departments, and protecting the industry by negotiation and (if necessary) litigation. An important element of the BPI's work involves liaising with other media, providing press information and promoting the music industry in general. The BPI also recognises that the growth in multi-media applications provides exciting opportunities for the music industry, but it is keen to ensure that the rights of its members are protected. Whenever a recording is used in a multi-media product, a licence must first be obtained from the record company which owns its copyright.

As well as providing services for its members, the BPI also provides a forum and an environment in which members can actively participate in the industry's future development. Through their involvement in committees, the representatives of record companies can take part in discussions with the retail sector, and can also play an important role in negotiations to help ensure that future legislation takes account of their interests.

Through its charity, the Brit Trust, the BPI supports the Brit School for Performing Arts in Croydon and other educational institutions and charities.

benefits of membership

Membership of the BPI carries with it automatic entitlement to a number of benefits: the legal department provides advice for members and negotiates on their behalf with other music-industry bodies; members can obtain sponsorship for attendance at international trade fairs such as MIDEM, MIDEM Asia and PopKomm; and the anti-piracy unit takes action on behalf of members to protect their rights from counterfeiting and other abuses of copyright. The BPI maintains an extensive specialist library, and the research department also provides members with a wide range of statistical and other market data, and CIN chart information is available at a discounted price. Members receive priority bookings for events such as the Brit Awards, and they are also entitled to claim BPI-certified awards.

For further information contact:

BPI
25 Savile Row
London
W1X 1AA
Tel: 0171 287 4422
Fax: 0171 287 2252

IFPI

The International Federation of the Phonographic Industry represents some 1,100 record producers in over 70 countries around the world, including independent producers and the six major record companies (BMG, EMI Music, MCA, Polygram, Sony and Warner Brothers). National groups representing the local record companies are officially recognised by the federation in 41 countries, and the RIAA (Recording Industry Association of

America) and PLAPE (Federation Latinoamericana de Productores de Fonograms y Videogramas) are also counted among its affiliates.

The IFPI's Secretariat is located in London and is responsible for central co-ordination and research, while the federation's Brussels-based European office deals with issues concerning the EU and EFTA. The IFPI also has other regional offices in Warsaw, Moscow, Hong Kong, China, Seoul, Kuala Lumpar, Singapore, Bangkok and Jakarta.

the IFPI's role

The recording industry's commercial success depends upon its ability to invest time and money in nurturing new talent, and to make this practical artists must obviously receive remuneration for its works. One of the aims of the IFPI is to ensure that the recording industry is able to realise its full potential throughout the world, and in order to achieve this the federation governs a number of activities in several areas, including those listed below.

PROMOTING NATIONAL LEGISLATION AND INTERNATIONAL CONVENTIONS

To protect its members' rights, the IFPI campaigns for the introduction, improvement and enforcement of copyright and other rights legislation at the national, European and international levels, voicing its members' concerns and representing their interests in negotiations for new legislation.

NEW TECHNOLOGIES

The IFPI is involved in the development of technical solutions for combating piracy, such as the SID (Source Identification) codes, and also strives to discover solutions which will allow the industry to collect remuneration for its work in both the digital and analogue environment, such as the ISRC (International Standard Recording Code).

PROVIDING INFORMATION

The IFPI provides a wide range of information and statistical analyses on the recording industry, including statistics on legitimate and pirate sales, reports on emerging markets and technical issues, and updates on legislative issues. It is also the federation's role to inform the media, through press releases and press briefings, of any developments in the recording industry.

membership of the IFPI

Any company or firm which produces sound recordings which are then made available to the public in reasonable quantities is eligible for membership. Others closely connected with the production or distribution of sound recordings may also be admitted.

For further information contact:

> IFPI Secretariat
> 54 Regent Street
> London
> W1R 5PJ
> Tel: 0171 434 3521
> Fax: 0171 439 9166

MCPS

As an agent, the Mechanical Copyright Protection Society represents thousands of composers and music publishers. It exists to ensure that the recordings of its members' works are properly authorised and commercially rewarded. Incorporated in 1924, it has been a subsidiary of the MPA since 1976. Its board of directors consists of twelve music publishers and four composers, and these composers represent the various UK composers bodies. Acting on the behalf of its members, the MCPS negotiates agreements with those who wish to record music, ensuring that the owners of the copyrights are rewarded for the use of their music.

The 'mechanical' right is defined as the right to record a piece of music, and by law anyone who records a copyrighted musical work must obtain the copyright owner's permission, who is then entitled to receive a royalty. The MCPS collects royalties from record, video, broadcasting, multi-media and independent production companies, along with many other organisations, who are obliged to pay whenever they use a work controlled by an MCPS member.

membership of the MCPS

The MCPS has no formal membership criteria, but it does expect prospective members (publishers or composers) to have had, or expect to have, works commercially recorded in some form. It is only necessary to join if mechanical royalties are being generated. If you have a publishing deal which includes all of your compositions, membership is probably not necessary as it is likely that the publisher will be a member. However, if your musical works remain unpublished and are likely to be recorded and released by someone other than yourself, you should consider joining the society.

The MCPS does not charge a fee for membership but instead extracts a commission on any royalties distributed to its members. The commission rates vary, depending on the source of the income, and currently range from 4.75% to 12.5% (the average in 1995 was 6.68% of total distributions). The last few years have seen a consistent growth in the royalty income collected and distributed by the society: 1995 saw distributions rise to £137.4 million, with a budgeted distribution for 1996 in excess of £140 million. The MCPS also has reciprocal agreements with societies in other countries, thus enabling it to protect its members works in a worldwide capacity.

For further information contact the society's corporate communications department, who can give general information on the services provided by the society as well as advice on other matters relating to copyright. A wide range of literature is also available on request. Enquiries should be addressed to:

Elgar House
41 Streatham High Road
London
SW16 1ER
Website: http://www.mcps.co.uk
Tel: 0181 664 4400
Fax: 0181 769 8792

MPA

Established in 1881, the Music Publishers' Association has always encouraged greater professionalism within its membership. It publishes a wide range of recommendations, advice and information on legal, commercial and general matters for the music publishing industry, along with a wealth of material used in training courses and seminars.

principle objectives

The aims of the MPA for the foreseeable future include the following:

- To promote and protect the interests of music publishers.

- To provide a forum to discuss mutual problems.

- To support the MCPS as a wholly-owned subsidiary company of the MPA.

- To originate and promote improvements in the law regarding music copyright and other topics of concern to music publishers.

- To assist publishers and their composers in maximising their income.

- To help combat resistance to paying for the use of copyrighted music.

- To improve communication and encourage active participation.

- To obtain feedback on important issues.

- To educate the public concerning the role of the music publisher.

- To underline the importance and value of copyright

- To emphasise the illegality of copyright infringement and pursue offenders.

- To campaign for greater professionalism within the industry.

The MPA, a non-profit-making company limited by guarantee, is controlled by its articles of association and governed by an elected council of popular and classical (standard) publishers. Day-to-day business is administered by the association secretary, his assistant and other staff. There are also specialist sub-committees which deal with specific interests.

For further details, contact Sarah Faulder at the address below:

MPA
3rd Floor Strandgate
18-20 York Buildings
London
WC2N 6JU
Tel: 0171 839 7779
Fax: 0171 839 7776

the musicians' union

The MU represents musicians and protects their interests, and negotiates with the record companies and the BPI in terms of payments to musicians for various endeavours, including recording and promotional work. It also establishes rates of payment with broadcasters for the appearances of musicians on radio and television, and also offers legal advice for artist members and competitive equipment insurance. Its suggested rates for someone performing as a session musician, a live performer or in a number of other capacities are published in a book of guidelines.

The union also acts as a collecting agency, recouping funds payable to its members, and offers legal and business advice for contracts and disputes. It publishes a monthly members' magazine, the *Musician*, along with directories of its members and a wealth of material on issues concerning musicians.

For further information, contact:

> *The Musicians' Union*
> *60-62 Clapham Road*
> *London*
> *SW9 0JJ*
> *Tel: 0171 582 5566*
> *Fax: 0171 582 9805*

PPL

Founded in 1934, the PPL is a non-profit-making organisation, established by British record companies, whose aim is to control the broadcasting and public use of their recordings and to issue licences for those purposes. Members of the PPL include over 1,900 companies, ranging from multinationals to small specialist producers, who together control 5,000 record labels. All radio and TV broadcasters in the UK pay annual blanket license fees to the PPL. In addition, tens of thousands of licences are issued annually to such public performance venues as discos, clubs, dance halls and jukebox operators.

The newest forms of use for PPL material include Discline telephone services (previously run by British Telecom and now run by private enterprise service providers) and those background music services supplied by specialist satellite services. In addition, the PPL will also be licensing the new generation of post-deregulation broadcasters, including satellite and community radio companies.

Wherever possible, the PPL negotiates its conditions and fees with national bodies representing the various types of user. It negotiates on the basis that higher fees should be paid by those who derive most commercial benefit from recordings. Therefore, radio stations, discos and jukebox operators should expect to pay more than theatres, shops or cinemas.

the IMF handbook a guide to professional band management

PPL income is distributed to its member record companies, to individual recording artists and to session musicians, and this distribution takes place on a regular basis. The amount required to be paid to each company and each recording artist is calculated by examining a list of detailed returns provided by broadcasters and by a sample of public performance venues. The rate per unit of time is the same for every member, whether large or small.

In December 1997, the PRC (Performer Registration Centre) – a division within the PPL's distribution department – was set up to issue each performer with a PID (Performer Identification) number, which will assist in the administration of performers' new statutory rights under the recent changes to UK copyright legislation.

For further information contact:

PPL
1 Upper James Street
London
W1R 3HG
Tel: 0171 534 1000
Fax: 0171 534 1111

PRS

Collective administration of rights has long been the bedrock on which the careers of composers and authors have been built. This fact, which was first recognised in Europe around a century ago, continues to be recognised globally as new copyright laws are developed and enacted in emerging territories.

Until composers, authors and music publishers came together to join forces and exercise their rights, through societies such as the PRS, there was very little the individual creator could do to collect what he was rightfully due from performances of his copyrighted works. The words 'rightfully due' are important here, particularly in today's world, where increasingly easy access to music in a proliferating variety of forms reinforces the public's long-preferred misconception that musical performance belongs to everyone and no-one, and that it should therefore be free.

societies

The right of composers and authors (and the music publishers to whom they assign their creative output) to control and be rewarded for public performance was protected by the 1911 Copyright Act in the UK, and has continued to be protected by the 1956 and 1988 Acts. Set up in 1914, the PRS is the UK association of composers, lyricists and publishers. Membership currently totals approximately 30,000, including more than 27,500 composers and lyricists and around 2,500 music publishers. The society is a commercial but non-profit-making company, and is limited by guarantee.

The essential function of the PRS has always been to achieve collectively what creators cannot effectively do for themselves – that is, to administer the non-dramatic performing and broadcasting rights in their copyrighted musical works. In those cases in which the use of music can be more easily controlled by writers and their publishers or agents (in plays, opera and ballet, for example), the PRS has generally not been required to control and administer the performing right. For many composers, whose music may be broadcast or performed in public thousands of times daily throughout the world, it is still impossible or intolerably costly to give personal permission to each would-be music user and to then collect the appropriate fee.

The PRS's policies and administration are controlled by an elected board of non-executive directors, guided by a chairman and two deputy chairmen. The council is divided evenly between composers and publishers, and each half is then broadly divided between classical and non-classical interests. In line with recommendations suggested in the society's Corporate Governance report, the board now also includes as executive directors the chief executive officer of the MCPS/PRS music alliance and the director of membership, and has also appointed two external directors.

The PRS has always played an important international role, through its position as a greatly respected member of CISAC and also through its reciprocal links with other societies worldwide (including those societies which it has helped to found in emerging countries). Further information concerning the society can be obtained by contacting John Sweeney at the address below:

PRS
29-33 Berners Street
London
W1P 4AA
Tel: 0171 580 5544
Fax 0171 306 4050

the IMF handbook a guide to professional band management

SESAC

SESAC, the smallest of the US performing rights organisations, has garnered international recognition in recent years by broadening its focus from primarily European and gospel music copyrights to include every mainstream musical genre. With its list of affiliates, SESAC has transformed the way in which performing rights societies in the US conduct business by being the first US performing rights organisation to utilise state-of-the-art broadcast data systems technology for monitoring broadcasts and distributing royalties. In 1996, SESAC began using BDS (Broadcast Data System) technology to track more than 8.3 million hours of radio airplay. The tracking includes formats such as Top 40, adult contemporary, country, modern rock, rhythm and blues, AAA and album-orientated rock. SESAC affiliates, therefore, enjoy the advantage of receiving royalties based on the most airplay monitored in the US. SESAC affiliates are paid quickly, with a gap of only one calendar quarter between performance and payment. SESAC's rapid payment schedule means that SESAC songwriters and publishers are paid up to two calendar quarters faster than other US performing rights societies.

European writers and publishers interested in learning more about SESAC should contact Wayne Bickerton, director of international affairs, by phone on 01923 228870, or by fax on 01923 228872. Alternatively, he can be reached at the following addresses:

SESAC
Gresham House
53 Clarendon Road
Watford
Hertfordshire
WD1 1LA

SESAC International
55 Music Square
East Nashville
TN 37203
Tel: 615 320 0055
Fax: 615 329 9627

appendix 2
international directory of IMF managers

TORILL AAS
CONTINENTAL MANAGEMENT AS
PO Box 4353
Torshov
0402 Oslo
Norway
Tel: 47 228 710 00
Fax: 47 228 710 04
torill.aas@powertech.no
current roster
Secret Garden
Ole Edvard Antonsen

JULIAN ABLE
JAM X MANAGEMENT LTD
22a Lambolle Place
London
NW3 4PG
England
Tel: 0171 813 0833
Fax: 0171 209 0019
jamx@easynet.co.uk
current roster
The Bluetones
Geneva

Mover
Contempo
The Disorientee

PHILLIP ABRAHAM
DANGEROUS COMMUNICATIONS INTERNATIONAL
242-757 West Hastings
#619
Vancouver
British Columbia
V6C 3M6
Canada
Tel: 604 540 9581
Fax: 604 540 9581
dci@direct.ca
current roster
Philip Abraham
Bonnie Ste-Croix
Solus

CONLEY C ABRAMS III
CCA3 PRODUCTION MANAGEMENT
11225 Ruffner Avenue
Granada Hills
CA 91344

USA
Tel: 818 363 1521
Fax: 818 253 5797

IVAN DOTSE ACOLATSE
ESTALOCA MANAGEMENT CONSULTANCY
19 Stopford Road
Plaistow
London
E13 0LY
England
Tel: 0181 472 8232
Fax: 0181 257 3142
Estalo@aol.com
current roster
Chris Bossman
Kris Bediiako
Mike McCleary

TOM ACKLEY
THE POLYGON RECORDING COMPANY
6305 Walton Avenue
Pennsauken
NJ 08109
USA

the IMF handbook a guide to professional band management

SCOTT ADAM
SCOTT ADAM MANAGEMENT
PO Box 418
Northbridge
WA 6865
Australia
Tel: 09 379 8115
Fax: 09 379 8115
jethro@iinet.net.au
current roster
Muse
Lynn Hazelton
Desert Child

ADEBOYE ADEFOLALU
YAM ENTERTAINMENTS
3 The Orchards
28-30 Edgwarebury Lane
Edgware
Middlesex
HA8 8LW
England
Tel: 0181 958 6319
Fax: 0181 958 6319
taejan98@aol.co.uk
current roster
Kwabe Kwei Arnah

VIVIENNE AHMAD
VAA MANAGEMENT
73 Merriman Road
Blackheath
London
SE3 8SB
England
Tel: 0181 319 1590
Fax: 0181 316 4690
Marc@wufog.freeserve.co.uk
www.musiciansnet.co.uk

current roster
Way Point 5

TODD ALAN
ALAN ARTIST DEVELOPMENT
68 West 68th Street
Suite 5B
New York
NY 10023
USA

JILL ALBROW
SUSPECT MANAGEMENT
31 Avondale Road
South Croydon
Surrey
CR2 6JE
England
Tel: 0181 686 3902
Fax: 0181 686 3902
ja1suspect@aol.com

ELIZABETH ALEXANDER
110 West 90th Street
Suite 4F
New York
NY 10024
USA

ANDY ALLEN
OFFSIDE MANAGEMENT
Unit 9
Ground Floor
Blenheim Court
62 Brewery Road
London
N7 9NY
England
Tel: 0171 700 2662
Fax: 0171 700 2882

andy@backst.demon.co.uk
current roster
Swervedriver

CAROL ALLEN
MCJ
PO Box 142
Preston
Lancashire
PR2 8FL
England
Tel: 01772 464112
current roster
Foxxx

GARY ALLEN
JMS MANAGEMENT
Noke Lane Business Centre
St Albans
Hertfordshire
AL2 3NY
England
Tel: 01727 846 038
Fax: 01727 846 658
current roster
Stun

IAN ALLEN
CREATIVE MANAGEMENT LTD
PO Box 1060
Birmingham
B1 3PQ
England
Tel: 0121 236 1060
Fax: 0121 236 1070
Ian@Creativeltd.com
current roster
Next of Kin
North Star
Teenage Rampage
21st Century Girls

Colin Dunne
Jean Butler
Gary Stevenson
Dave West
Sean Maguire

MELISSA ALLEN
7 TWENTY MANAGEMENT
312 East 23rd Street
Suite 6C
New York
NY 10010
USA

RICHARD JC ALLEN
BIG BROTHER MANAGEMENT
PO Box 1288
Gerrards Cross
Buckinghamshire
SL9 9YB
England
Tel: 01753 890635
Fax: 01753 892879
richard@delirium.co.uk
current roster
Porcupine Tree

ROBERT ALLEN
MANAGEMENT 22
137 Legion Place
Hillsdale
NJ 07642
USA

ELISA AMSTERDAM
AMI AMSTERDAM MANAGEMENT INC
40 Alexander Street
Penthouse 6
Toronto
Ontario
M4Y 1B5
Canada
Tel: 416 967 1421
Fax: 416 967 1991
ami@the-wire.com
current roster
Steve Fox
Kyn
Jana Lee Reid
Andre Bernard

TORFINN N ANDERSEN
GROOVY MANAGEMENT
PO Box 1291
N-5001 Bergen
Norway
Tel: 47 553 234 10
Fax: 47 553 118 75
rec90@bbb.no
current roster
Poor Rich Ones
Savoy

DOMENIC ANDREONE
THE FIFTH SUN
PO Box 54
Austral
NSW 2171
Australia
Tel: 042 97 6577
current roster
The Fifth Sun

PAOLA ARAMINI
PERIPHERY
PO Box 24680
London
E2 8TN
England
Tel: 0171 733 1773
Fax: 0171 684 0619

MICHAEL ARDENNE
ARDENNE INTERNATIONAL INC
Ste 44
World Trade Centre
1800 Argyle Street
Halifax
Nova Scotia
B3J 3N8
Canada
Tel: 902 492 8000
Fax: 902 423 2143
Mardenne@Ardenne
 International.com
current roster
Kris Taylor
Annick Gagnon

SHARUL ARIFFIN
PO Box 451
Greenacres
SA 5086
Australia
Tel: 08 8266 7402
Fax: 08 8266 7402
current roster
Yakspit

SUE ARLIDGE
SUE ARLIDGE ARTIST MANAGEMENT
PO Box 88
Fullarton
SA 5063
Australia
Tel: 08 8354 1809
fruitgos@senet.com.au
fruit.on.net
current roster
Fruit Music

the IMF handbook a guide to professional band management

TERRY ARMSTRONG
ARMSTRONG ACADEMY LTD
GMC Studio
Hollingbourne
Kent
ME17 1UQ
England
Tel: 01622 880599
Fax: 01622 880020
terry@tiplea.uk.com
www.triplea.uk.com
current roster
Danny Litchfield
Helena
Ki

JOHN ARNISON
J MANAGEMENT
55 Loudoun Road
St Johns Wood
London
NW8 0DL
England
Tel: 0171 604 3633
Fax: 0171 604 3639
j@jamjah.co.uk
current roster
Aswad
Rozalla
Nicky Love
Roland Orzabal
Tears For Fears
Dada

ROBERTA ARNOLD
ARNOLD ARTISTS
885 West End Avenue
Suite 12C
New York
NY 10025-3512
USA
Tel: 212 678 0808
Fax: 212 663 2723

jazz-baritonesax@world.net.att.net

TIM ARTINSTALL
MUSIC FIRST
4ta Tierney Road
London
SW2 4QH
England
Tel: 0181 6744024
Fax: 0181 6742130
tim@musicmanagement.demon.co.uk
current roster
Stash
Landspeed Loungers
Isobel Morris

NICK ATKINS
NICK ATKINS MANAGEMENT
29 Londesborough Road
London
N16 8RN
England
Tel: 0171 503 9199
Fax: 0171 503 4749
nickatkins@aol.com
current roster
Hugh Masekela
Elliot Green
Blair Booth
Glen Nichols
Soul

DAMIEN BAETENS
GENERATION MANAGEMENT
PO Box 6328
London
N2 0UN
England
Tel: 0181 444 9841

Fax: 0181 442 1973
current roster
(see David Woolfson)

DE QUINCEY BAILEY
QUINTESSENTIAL MUSIC
PO Box 546
Bromley
Kent
BR2 0RS
England
Tel: 0181 402 1984
Fax: 0181 325 0708
urbanmusic@msn.com
current roster
Marvin Springer
Ricky Turner-Brown
Urban Clearaway
Ayoka

RALPH BAKER
EQUATOR MUSIC
17 Hereford Mansions
Hereford Road
London
W2 5BA
England
Tel: 0171 727 5858
Fax: 0171 229 5934
rbequatormusic@btinternet.com
current roster
Jeff Beck
Tony Iommi

CHAS BANKS
C & S MANAGEMENT LTD
PO Box 41
Manchester
M32 8AT
England

Tel: 0161 718 6977
Fax: 0161 864 2848
chas@cands.u-net.com
current roster
Teenage Fanclub

CAMILLE BARBONE
B3 MANAGEMENT
59 West 28th Street
New York
NY 10001
USA

CHRIS BARBOSA
LIGOSA ENTERTAINMENT
185 Ardsley Loop
Brooklyn
NY 11239
USA

PETER BARDON
AVALON RECORDS LTD
Glengeary Office Park
Glengeary
Co Dublin
Ireland
Tel: 353 1 285 8711
Fax: 353 1 285 8923
bardis@iol.ie
current roster
Ronan Hardiman

DANIELLE BARNETT
WANNABE MANAGEMENT
1a Links Avenue
Gidea Park
Romford
Essex
RM2 6NB
England
Tel: 01708 735 934

Fax: 01708 735 934
wannabemngmnt@hotmail.com
current roster
Point Break
Bubblegum
Double Up

MICHAEL BARNETT
FARGUARD LTD
21 Broughton Road
Banbury
Oxfordshire
OX16 9QB
England
Tel: 01295 264 436
Fax: 01295 266 411
current roster
Gypsey Road

ROBERT BARNHAM
ROBERT BARNHAM MANAGEMENT
PO Box 1638
Strawberry Hills
NSW 2012
Australia
Tel: 02 9517 9100
Fax: 02 9517 9177
current roster
Christine Anu
Paul Kelly
Alex Lloyd

LU BARREN
TANK MANAGEMENT
Benmax House
8 Westgate Street
London
E8 3RN
England
Tel: 0181 985 9458
Fax: 0181 985 9590

lu@designtank.demon.co.uk
current roster
Jimpy
Black Liquid
Perl & Dean

KATE BARTLETT
LIFELINE MANAGEMENT
PO Box 20149
London
W10 6FT
England
Tel: 0181 9603333
Fax: 0181 9693359
kate@lifeline.se
www.lifeline.se
current roster
Robyn
Jennifer Brown
Titiyo

MARK BARTON
SHOTGUN RECORDS
PO Box 244
Hindmarsh
SA 5087
Australia
Tel: 08 8369 0841
Fax: 08 8258 3008
current roster
The Barflys

ADRIAN BASSO
BASBO MUSIC MANAGEMENT
PO Box 214
North Melbourne
Victoria 3051
Australia
Tel: 03 9417 7702
Fax: 03 9417 7624
basbo@hotmail.com

the IMF handbook a guide to professional band management

current roster
Trout Fishing In Quebec
Befuddle

TONY BEARD
SANCTUARY MUSIC MANAGEMENT
Sanctuary House
45-53 Sinclair Road
London
W14 0NS
England
Tel: 0171 602 6351
Fax: 0171 603 5941
tony@smml-net.com
current roster
DJ Downfall
Slick Sixty
Hobotalk
The Memory Band
Mika Bomb
Sing Sing
The Cuban Boys

RALPH BEAUCHAMP
ROGUE MANAGEMENT
332 Naughton Avenue
Staten Island
NY 10305
USA

JULIE BEAUME
DUCHESS MANAGEMENT
Chestnut House
Market Street
Hambleton
Lancashire
FY6 9AS
England
Tel: 01253 700 474
Fax: 01253 700 474

current roster
Clearwater
Shie

SKIP BEAUMONT-EDMONDS
CRANIUM MANAGEMENT
PO Box 240
Annandale
NSW 2038
Australia
Tel: 02 9660 6444
Fax: 02 9660 2898
cranium@enternet.com.au
current roster
Mental As Anything
Dog Trumpet
Louis Tillett
Lisa Maxwell
Aunt Jennifer's Tigers

SUZETTE TOLEDANO BECKER
215-225 Decatur Street
Suite 300
New Orleans
LA
USA

JO BECKETT
TOXIC MANAGEMENT
23 Ladbroke Grove
London
W11 3AY
England
Tel: 0171 221 2503
Fax: 0171 792 5636
beckett@dircon.co.uk
current roster
Fini Dolo
A New Funky Generation

CARL BEDWARD
ANGER MANAGEMENT
PO Box 6105
Birmingham
B43 6NZ
England
Tel: 0121 357 3338
anger.1965@virgin.net
current roster
Shamefaced

DAVID BEGG
HOLIER THAN THOU RECORDS LTD
Norton Hall
Broadmarston Lane
Mickleton
Gloucestershire
GL55 6SQ
England
Tel: 01386 438 931
Fax: 01386 438 847
httrecords@aol.com
current roster
Violet Ultra
Asthyxiator
Solitary
Red Letter Day
Gasheed
Brides Just Died
Farfisa
House Of Alice
Jabba
Ran
ZedsDed

GIDEON BENAIM
LEAP MANAGEMENT
33 Green Walk
London
NW4 2AL
England
Tel: 0181 202 4120

Fax: 0181 202 4120
artists@leap.dircon.
   co.uk
current roster
Sideffect
Momy
The Bridge

PATTI BENINATI
SURFACE
MANAGEMENT
PO Box 2935
Church Street Station
New York
NY 10008
USA

ANNETTE BENNETT
SAPHRON
MANAGEMENT
36 Belgrave Rd
London
E17 8QE
England
Tel: 020 82792308
Saphron@msn.com
current roster
Dywayne Valentino
Joy Silver

JULIAN BENNETT
INVICTA
PROMOTIONS
Unit 206
Liverpool Palace
6-10 Slater Street
Liverpool
L1 4BT
England
Tel: 0151 7095264
Fax: 0151 7098439
invictahifi@flashmail.
   com
www.invictahifi.co.uk

current roster
Ladytron
Hayely's Cake
DisneyPorn
DHK
Vada

LINDY BENSON
SHAMROCK MUSIC
LTD
9 Thornton Place
London
W1H 1FG
England
Tel: 0171 935 9719
Fax: 0171 935 0241
lindy@celtus.demon.
   co.uk
current roster
Celtus

NICOLE BENSON
NMIT
7 Griffiths Road
Upwey
Victoria 3158
Australia
Tel: 03 9754 3877
n_benson@hotmail.com
current roster
NMIT

LESLEY BENTLEY
34 Greenfields Close
St. Leonards-On-Sea
East Sussex
TN37 7LP
England
Tel: 01424 755 910
Lesley@Bentley.dialnet.
   com
current roster
Skin Deep
Further

18th Emergency

MARTIN BERCOTT
BERCOTT MUSIC
CONSULTING
Foframe House
35-37 Brent Street
London
NW4 2EF
England
Tel: 020 8457 3506
Fax: 020 8457 3507
bercott@saqnet.co.uk

KERRY BERGH
BERGH & ASSOCIATES
31 Copas Drive
Klemzig
SA 5087
Australia
Tel: 08 8261 1059
Fax: 08 8266 7717
berg@camtech.net.au
www.adelaide.net.au/
   ~bergh
current roster
Chariot

BARRY BERGMAN
BARRY BERGMAN
MANAGEMENT
350 East 30th Street
Suite 4D
New York
NY 10016
USA
Tel: 212 213 8787
Fax: 212 213 9797

BRUCE BERMAN
BRUCE BERMAN
ENTERTAINMENT
888 8th Avenue
Suite 15W

New York
NY 10019
USA
Tel: 212 757 4313
Fax: 212 757 6817
bbe@visual.radio.com

MICHAELA BETTS
FWD MANAGEMENT
16 Rabbits Road
London
E12 5HZ
England
Tel: 0181 514 7806
Fax: 0181 514 7806
dismgmt@aol.com
current roster
Girls World

STEVEN BETTS
ALOHA MANAGEMENT PTY LTD
PO Box 898
Glebe
NSW 2037
Australia
Tel: 02 9550 6149
Fax: 02 9550 3283
rock@mpx.dom.au
current roster
Shihad
The Superjesus
Front End Loader

PAUL BEVAN
665 Lexington Avenue
Suite B
New York
NY 10022
USA

GRAHAM BIDSTRUP
PO Box 195
Epping

NSW 2121
Australia
Tel: 02 9869 3138
Fax: 02 9869 0126
current roster
Raw Sugar
GANGgajang
The Stetsons

ALF BILLINGHAM
ABSTRACT MANAGMENT
PO Box 777
Sheffield
S5 7YF
England
Tel: 0114 261 7613
Fax: 0114 261 9116
current roster
Myro

JEFFREY BIRNBAUM
RELENTLESS MANAGEMENT
140 Riverside Drive
Suite 14E
New York
NY 10024-2605
USA
Tel: 212 496 1813
Fax: 212 496 1813

ERICA BLITZ
THE KLEZMATICS
151 1st Avenue
Suite 59
New York
NY 10003
USA

DAVID BLUESTEIN
BLUESTEIN ENTERPRISES
205-372 Richmond St West

Toronto
Ontario
M5V 1X6
Canada
Tel: 416 598 3330
Fax: 416 598 5428
bluejay@ican.net

DAVID BONE
CAPTAIN COURAGEOUS MM LTD
Fiddlers Green
Gunnislake
Cornwall
PL18 9NS
England
Tel: 01822 833290
Fax: 01822 833 299
captains@courageous.
   demon.co.uk
www.electrasy.org
current roster
Electrasy
X'ELL
(see Harry Eves)

JACK BOOKBINDER
DE-EL ENTERTAINMENT
PO Box 20806
Columbus Circle Station
New York
NY 10023
USA
Tel: 212 489 2425
Fax: 212 333 7226
weg@walrus.com

MOUREEN BOOTH
STEREE ENTERPRISE
Suite 5

international directory of IMF managers

1st Floor Office
335-347 Sheffield Road
Chesterfield
S41 8LQ
England
Tel: 01246 229 200
Fax: 01246 229 201
sdmbjj@msn.com
current roster
D'lear
Chill
Stepin Razor

SANDEE BORGMAN
SB MANAGEMENT
533 East 5th Street
Suite 20
New York
NY 10009
USA

SAMUEL BORRETT
DUMBLE COTTAGE
Water Lane
Oxton
Southwell
Nottinghamshire
NG25 0SH
England
Tel: 0115 965 2356
sam@borrett.force9.co.uk
current roster
Drunk Juice Puppies

ANDRÉ BOURGEOIS
ABC ENTERTAINMENT INC
1436 Highway 202
Kennetcook
Hants County
Nova Scotia
B0N 1P0
Canada

Tel: 902 632 2575
Fax: 902 632 2576
abcent@istar.ca
current roster
Natalie MacMaster
Rawlings Cross

LOUISE BOWLIN
THE ROCK EMPIRE
RR #1
Malakwa
British Columbia
V0E 2J0
Canada
Tel: 250 836 2187
Fax: 250 836 2182
ibowolin@jetstream.net
current roster
Robin Brock

NANCY BOWMAN
JUNGLEFEET MANAGEMENT
110 Greene Street
Suite 506a
NY 10012
USA
Tel: 212 343 9788
Fax: 212 343 0245
Junglefeet@aol.com
current roster
Reggae Cowboys

SAM BOYD
BOYD MANAGEMENT & CONSULTING
190 Marycroft Avenue
Suite 11
Woodbridge
Ontario
L4L 5Y2
Canada
Tel: 905 456 3346

Fax: 905 455 2497
samtour@aracnet.net
current roster
Johnny Lee Black
Vagabond Groove
Two For The Show
Teenage Head

LYNNE BRABY-PAVITT
WAREHOUSE RECORDINGS LTD
Woodbine Cottage
18 Queen Street
Chelmsford
Essex
CM2 0JS
England
Tel: 01245 609 220
www.webalias.com/warehouse
current roster
Warehouse Blues Band

BARBARA BRACEGIRDLE
MODENA RECORDS
15 The Lagger
Chalfont St Giles
Buckinghamshire
HP8 4DG
England
Tel: 01494 872 372
Fax: 01494 872 372
current roster
Chicane
Disco Citizens
Tomski

HEATH BRADBY
NAKED APE
PO Box 6529
East Perth

the IMF handbook a guide to professional band management

WA 6892
Australia
Tel: 08 9226 3330
Fax: 08 9226 3330
nakedape@iinet.net.au
current roster
Jebediah
Sinope

CHRIS BRADFORD
CB PRODUCTION
118 Byron Road
North Wembley
Middlesex
HA0 3PE
England
Tel: 0181 904 5304
Fax: 01628 472 457
current roster
Clearway

SOHEILA BRAMWELL
NAKID MUSIC LTD
PO Box 16553
London
SE1 3ZR
England
Tel: 0171 403 6521
Fax: 0171 407 0677
current roster
Colin Thurston
Nocoda

VICTORIA BRAVERMAN
BRAVERMAN ENTERPRISES
Flat 8
45 Gloucester Square
London
W2 2TQ
England

Tel: 0171 402 6183
Fax: 0171 402 2649
vicbiz@aol.com
current roster
Lyndon J Connah
The Pollinators
Alex Grayson

PAUL BREGANDE
ELEPHANT MEMORY MANAGEMENT
312 Hampton Drive
Atlanta
GA 30350
USA

NATHAN BRENNER
IDEAL MANAGEMENT
PO Box 1037
Caufield North
Victoria 3161
Australia
Tel: 03 9509 7575
Fax: 03 9509 2206
nathan@ozonline.com.au
current roster
George Dreyfus
Rig

ROGER BREUER
RICOCHET
5 Old Garden House
The Lanterns
Bridge Lane
London
SW11 3AD
England
Tel: 0171 924 2255
Fax: 0171 738 1881
roger.breuer@dial.pipex.com

current roster
(see Stephen King)

COLIN BREWER
FOX RECORDS LTD
Construction House
Grenfell Avenue
Hornchurch
Essex
RM12 4EH
England
Tel: 01708 478 860
Fax: 01708 478 862
current roster
Redhouse

BRIAN BRINKERHOFF
PO Box 2297
Redondo Beach
CA 90278
USA

SHARON BROOKS
AMI
58 Southoak Road
Streatham
London
SW16 2UD
England
Tel: 0181 769 4222
Fax: 0171 509 3083
current roster
Ashley

JOHN R BROOKSHIRE
OUTLAND PRODUCTIONS
8511 Hurst Avenue
Savannah
GA 31406
USA

international directory of IMF managers

PAUL BROWN
PAUL BROWN MANAGEMENT

103 Devonshire Road
London
W4 2HU
England
Tel: 0181 994 8887
Fax: 0181 994 2221
pbmanagement@virgin.net

current roster
Bird & Bush
David Bottrill
John Fryer
Head
Jack Hues
Tony Lash
Machine
Clive Martin
Giles Martin
Mark Plati
Walter Samual
Paul Schoeder
Phil Vinall

STEPHEN BUDD
STEPHEN BUDD MANAGEMENT

109b Regents Park Road
London
NW1 8UR
England
Tel: 0171 916 3303
Fax: 0171 916 3302
sb@stephenbudd.demon.co.uk
www.stephenbudd.demon.co.uk

current roster
Heaven 17
Darren Allison
Mike Hedges
Arthur Baker
Mick Glossop
Jamie Lane
Robyn Smith
Andy Whitmore
Mark Wallis
Gus Dugeon
Ian Grimble
Martyn Ware
Steve Lyon
Rick Nowels
Dave Anderson
Ash Howes
Rob Playford
Ashley Beedle
Mike Vernon
Rafe McKenna
Paulette Sinclair
Sie Medway Smith
Billy Steinberg
Yoyo
Lewis Taylor
James Sanger
Greg Fitzgerlad
Charlie Mollozzi
Sherena Dugani

IRENE BULL
BULL-SHEET MUSIC LTD

18 The Bramblings
Chingford
London
E4 6LU
England
Tel: 0181 529 5807
Fax: 0181 529 5807

current roster
Simon Proctor

RICHARD BURGESS
BURGESS WORLD CO

PO Box 646
Mayo
MD 21106-0646
USA
Tel: 410 956 9116
Fax: 410 798 0099

PETER BURTON
DCT (MANAGEMENT) LTD

Unit 34
Rainbow Estate
W Drayton
Middlesex
UB7 7XT
England
Tel: 01895 438 566
Fax: 01895 438 566
peter@dct-management.com

current roster
Jason Carter
Coney Green

NICOLA CAIRNCROSS
SYSTEM OF SURVIVAL MANAGEMENT

32 St Michaels Road
Worthing
BN11 4RY
England
Tel: 01903 527018
Fax: 01903 522 712
ncairncross@mistral.co.uk
www3.mistral.co.uk/ncairncross/first.htm

current roster
Funkstone

BARRY CAMPBELL
7HZ MANAGEMENT

3 Harvard Road
Isleworth

Middlesex
TW7 4PA
England
Tel: 0181 847 3556
Fax: 0181 232 8717
seven.hz@which.net
www.house.of.fun.
   co.uk
current roster
Peter Bruntnell
Redwood
Neil Davidge
Suna
Gaelforce Dance

EVE CANTELMI
FORCE 9
MANAGEMENT
61 Station Road
London
N3 2SH
England
Tel: 0181 349 4078
Fax: 0181 349 0498
EveDawwg@aol.com
current roster
The Dip

CHARLIE CARNE
EMPORIUM
MANAGEMENT
49 Windmill Road
London
W4 1RN
England
Tel: 0181 742 2001
Fax: 0181 742 2100
charlie@emporium.org
current roster
Curtis

GARRY CARPENTER
RAW CONVICTION
68 Gondola Road North

Narrabeen
NSW 2101
Australia
Tel: 02 9944 7669
Fax: 02 9955 7670
current roster
Raw Conviction

DARRYL
CARRINGTON
THE CARRINGTON
AGENCY
64 Laurel Avenue
Suite 1
Bloomfield
NJ 07003
USA

DAVE CARTER
INTENSELY MELLOW
PO Box 721
Kalamunda
WA 6076
Australia
Tel: 09 490 4394
current roster
Intensely Mellow

GINA CARUSO
CARUSO &
ASSOCIATES
1765 North Sycamore
   Avenue 101
Los Angeles
CA 90028
USA
Tel: 323 462 5256

SUE CAVENDISH
ACTIVE
MANAGEMENT
54 Boileau Road
London
SW13 9BL

England
Tel: 0181 748 9951
Fax: 0181 741 7886
suecavendish@
   compuserve.com
current roster
David Hughes
Paul Millus

PHIL CEBERANO
20/61 Illawong Avenue
Bondi
NSW 2026
Australia
Tel: 03 9510 1077
Fax: 03 9510 1422
current roster
Phil Ceberano

CHERIE CEBERANO-
BALFOUR
31 Greville Street
Prahan
Victoria 3181
Australia
Tel: 03 9510 1722

RON CHAPMAN
POLESTAR (MUSIC)
Welton House
Ings Lane
Scamblesby
Louth
LN11 9XT
England
Tel: 01507 343 463
Fax: 01507 343 130
style@mernet.co.uk
current roster
Redhill

CHARLIE CHARLTON
INTERCEPTOR
98 White Lion Street

international directory of IMF managers

London
N1 9PF
England
Tel: 0171 278 8001
Fax: 0171 713 6298
mccesq@aol.com
current roster
Suede
Mandalay
Echobelly

SUZANNE CHARNSTROM
LIMELITE MANAGEMENT
PO Box 255
Stepney
SA 5069
Australia
limelite@senet.com.au
current roster
Kaotic Lounge
Blacksheep

STEPHEN CHEERS
POWERPOINT PRODUCTIONS
PO Box W87
Wareemba
NSW 2046
Australia
Tel: 02 9713 6604
Fax: 02 9712 2708
powerpnt@zeta.org.au
current roster
Bhavani

GABRIELLA CHELMICKA
IE MUSIC LTD
59a Chesson Road
London
W14 9QS
England

Tel: 0171 386 9995
Fax: 0171 610 0762
current roster
(see David Enthoven)

YOTIN CHIJANLA
CONNECT MUSIC (THAILAND) LTD
8 The Grove
St Margarets Road
Twickenham
TW12 1RB
England
Tel: 0181 286 7067
Fax: 0181 286 7067
current roster
Cheryl Lin

HAYLEY CHILTON
WILDLIFE ENTERTAINMENT LTD
Unit F
21 Heathmans Road
Parsons Green
London
SW6 4TJ
England
Tel: 0171 371 7008
Fax: 0171 371 7708
wildlife@dircon.co.uk
current roster
(see Ian McAndrew)

ANITA CHINKES
7 Cornelia Street 2B
New York
NY 10014
USA

DERRICK CHUA
C DERRICK CHUA (BARRISTER & SOLICITOR)
2547 Eglinton Avenue East

Toronto
Ontario
M6M 1T2
Canada
Tel: 416 656 6500
   ext 311
Fax: 416 656 1420
c_derrick_chua@yahoo.com

AARON CHUGG
DILETTANTE P/L
PO Box 176
Potts Point
NSW 2011
Australia
Tel: 02 9371 0022
Fax: 02 9371 6886
aaron@erko.com

PETER CIACCIA
PC MANAGEMENT INC
140 West End Avenue
Suite 23F
New York
NY 10023
USA

KAREN CICCONE
FUNDAMENTAL MUSIC
103 London Road
Markyate
Hertfordshire
AL3 8JR
England
Tel: 01582 841914
Fax: 01582 842711
karen.ciccone@virgin.net
current roster
Alan Moulder
Markus Dravs

the IMF handbook a guide to professional band management

Andy Wilkinson
Nick Addison
Marco Pirroni

JAMES CITKOVIC
COUNTDOWN
ENTERTAINMENT
110 West 26th Street
3rd Floor
New York
NY 10001-6805
USA
Tel: 212 645 3068
Fax: 212 989 6459
citovic@aol.com

ALEX CLAPCOTT
CONSPIRACY
ILLUMINATI LTD
6 Poole Hill
Bournemouth
Dorset
BH2 5PS
England
Tel: 01202 318 585
Fax: 01202 293330

TIM CLARK
IE MUSIC LTD
111 Frithville Gardens
London
W12 7JG
England
Tel: 0181 600 3400
Fax: 0181 600 3401
tc@iemusic.co.uk
current roster
(see David Enthoven)

DARREN CLARK
INTERNATIONAL
PROFILE
MANAGEMENT
PO Box 1701

Fortitude Valley
Queensland 4006
Australia
Tel: 07 3256 0233
Fax: 07 3256 0377
ipm@odyssey.com.au
current roster
Jungle Boogie
The Ten Tenors
Ian Mourice

MADDY CLARKE
MAD FOR IT
MANAGEMENT
c/o Saffron Hill
London
EC1N 8PT
England
Tel: 0171 404 3333
Fax: 0171 404 2947
maddy@stardiamond.com
current roster
Ruby Barker

ALISON CLENTSMITH
4 Arden Street
Waverley
NSW 2024
Australia
Tel: 02 9665 8371
current roster
Rory Faithfield

DAVID COBBOLD
CATALYST VENTURES P/L
PO Box 476
Claremont
WA 6910
Australia
Tel: 08 9474 2262
Fax: 08 9474 2265

dysemin8@merriweb.com.au
current roster
Reykjarik
Bulimia
Taxi Cathedral
Jemima's Diner
Scott Arnold-Eyres

STEVE COHEN
ORIGINAL ARTISTS
826 Broadway
4th Floor
New York
NY 10003
USA

JANICE COLE
HEAD OFFICE/
HEAD INTREQUE
132 Hibbert Road
Walthamstow
London
E17 8HF
England
Tel: 0181 556 0422
wefld@wmin.ac.uk
current roster
Head
Janicis

JAC COLEMAN
KBC MANAGEMENT
720 Monroe Street E5-8
Hoboken
NJ 07030
USA

JUSTIN COLEMAN
PARTIAL CHIPMUNK
PROMOTIONS
60 William Smith Close
Cambridge
CB1 3QF

England
Tel: 01223 570 763
Fax: 01223 570 763
partialchipmunk@usa.
  net
current roster
Maker

CRAIG COLLANTINE
1000CC MANAGEMENT
Tropical House
2/3 Birdsall Row
Redcar
Cleveland
TS10 2AF
England
Tel: 01642 477 778
Fax: 01642 472 778
craig@1000cc.freeserve.
  co.uk
current roster
Sweet Sanity
Pica

SIMON COLLIER
TWO SISTERS MANAGEMENT
11 Chancery Walk
Chadderton
Oldham
OL9 6SQ
England
Tel: 0161 627 5860
Fax: 0161 627 5860
current roster
Dog Toffee
Pachinos
John The Raptist

TRACEY COLLIER
KICK MANAGEMENT
PO Box 34

Elanora Heights
NSW 2101
Australia
Tel: 02 9913 7786
Fax: 02 9970 8678
kickman@pzemail.com.
  au
current roster
Twenty Two
Christ Art Museum
Othermind

ROBERT COLLINGS
ROBERT COLLINGS MANAGEMENT
4/105 Regent Street
Regent
Victoria 3072
Australia
Tel: 03 9471 9842
amada@bigpond.
  com
current roster
Andrew Taylor

TIM COLLINS
MISSION IMPOSSIBLE MANAGEMENT
#2 2nd Floor
Enterprise Point
Melbourne St
Brighton
BN2 3LH
England
Tel: 01273 677 476
Fax: 01273 677 071
tim_mim@pavilion.
  co.uk
current roster
The Jellys
Chimera
Tim Benjamin

Steven Severin

TIM COLLINS
COLLINS MANAGEMENT
5 Bigelow Street
Cambridge
MA 02139
USA

DENNIS COLLOPY
MENACE MANAGEMENT
2 Park Road
Radlett
Hertfordshire
WD7 8EQ
England
Tel: 01923 853789
Fax: 01923 853318
dennis@menacemusic.
  demon.co.uk
current roster
Mark Van Hoen
Matt Aitken
Gary Benson
Paul Moessl
Lisa Millett
Mark Scarborough
The Blue Easy
Locust
The All Seeing I
Mojave 3

JAC COLMAN
KBC MANAGEMENT
6381 Hollywood
Boulevard
Suite 610
Los Angeles
CA 90028
USA
Tel: 323 962 6789

the IMF handbook a guide to professional band management

GAIL COLSON
GAILFORCE MANAGEMENT LTD
24 Ives Street
London
SW3 2ND
England
Tel: 0171 584 5977
Fax: 0171 838 0351
gailforce@dircon.co.uk
current roster
Peter Hammill
Chrissie Hynde
Stephen Street
Mike Edwards

RICHARD MORSE CONDO
UNICORN ENTERTAINMENTS
21a Brookfield Cottages
Lymm
Cheshire
WA13 0DH
England
Tel: 01925 757 702
Fax: 01925 757 703
unicorn@mail.talk-101.com
current roster
Wolf
Glass Child
Zephyr
Strange Street
Underline

ANDY COOK
AEC MANAGEMENT
PO Box 903
Sutton
Surrey
SM2 6BY
England
Tel: 0181 6425619

Fax: 0181 6425203
current roster
Susy Thomas
Derek Luckhurst

JONATHAN COOKE
JONATHAN COOKE MANAGEMENT
65 Tremadoc Road
London
SW4 7NA
England
Tel: 0181 7317740
Fax: 0181 840 9422
current roster
Gel
Janjay

ANDREW COOPER
RIFFIND MUSIC
41 Trustcott Avenue
Seacombe Heights
SA 5047
Australia
Tel: 08 8296 0401
Fax: 08 8296 0401
riffind@senet.com.au
current roster
self-managed artists

RUSSELL CORR
CRANIUM MANAGEMENT
PO Box 240
Annandale
NSW 2038
Australia
Tel: 02 9660 6444
Fax: 02 9660 2898
cranium@enternet.com.au
current roster
Mental As Anything
Dog Trumpet

Louis Tillett
Lisa Maxwell
Aunt Jennifer's Tigers

ROBERT CORRIVEAU
PO Box 224
N Gros
Dale
CT 06255
USA

RAY CORTIS
TOT
Flat 2
1 Vermont Road
Upper Norwood
London
SE19 3SR
England
Tel: 0181 653 1289
Fax: 0181 240 7414
TOT@cablenet.co.uk
current roster
Rick Wayne
J Jem
Cat Von Trappe

CHARLES COSH
MOKSHA MANAGEMENT LTD
Unit 258
Stratford Workshops
Burford Road
London
E15 2SP
England
Tel: 0181 555 5423
Fax: 0181 519 6834
charles@moksha.demon.co.uk
current roster
The Shamen
Joi

international directory of IMF managers

JHQ
Supercharger
Ecologist

LLOYD COTTON
THE ENTERTAINMENT REVOLUTION
6 Downie Crescent
Hamlyn Heights
Victoria 3215
Australia
Tel: 03 5278 2696
Fax: 03 5278 2696
current roster
Smokin' Joker

JESS COX
NEAT PRODUCTIONS
71 High Street East
East Wallsend
Tyne & Wear
NE28 7RJ
England
Tel: 0191 262 4999
Fax: 0191 263 7082
mdwood33@aol.com
www.lyndon.org/neat
current roster
Holocaust
Tygers Of Pan Tang
Blitzkrieg
Sleepy People

ANDREW CROOT
SKANK'N ARTIST MANAGEMENT
PO Box 2209
Rose Bay North
NSW 2030
Australia
Fax: 02 9386 0663
skankman@sia.net.au

ELIZABETH CROWDER
LIZWRD MANAGEMENT
PO Box 2815
Chicago
IL 60690
USA

BILL CULLEN
BILL CULLEN MANAGEMENT
PO Box 176
Potts Points
NSW 2011
Australia
billcullen@cwcom.net
current roster
OMC
Garageland
Arnold

MARSHALL CULLEN
MARSHALL CULLEN MANAGEMENT
64 Wattle Street
Ultimo
NSW 2007
Australia
Tel: 02 9660 8776
Fax: 02 9692 9915
crow@world.net
www.ausnet.net.au/~crow
current roster
Elia Bel
Noogie

GUS CULLENWARD
GUS CULLENWARD MANAGEMENT
351 Brunswick Street
Fitzroy
Victoria 3065

Australia
Tel: 03 9419 5500
Fax: 03 9419 2370
current roster
Horsehead
Box

IAN CUNNINGHAM
DARK WIND PRODUCTIONS
91 Cochranes Road
Moorabbin
Victoria 3189
Australia
Tel: 03 9532 2288
Fax: 03 9532 1971
darkwind@brighton.
  starway.net.au
current roster
The Chosen Few
Nausea

BOB CURRIE
SOUND MANAGEMENT DIRECTION
152-18 Union Turnpike
Suite 85
Flushing
NY 11367
USA
Tel: 718 969 0166
Fax: 718 969 8914
muzic4all@aol.com

PAUL CURTIS
CONSUME MANAGEMENT
PO Box 12700
Elizabeth Street
Brisbane
Queensland 4001
Australia

the IMF handbook a guide to professional band management

Tel: 07 3844 8477
Fax: 07 3844 8490
consume1@ozemail.com.au
current roster
Regurgitator
Kiley Gaffney
Pangaea
Sixfinick
Elevation
Soma Rasa

DAVID CUTBUSH
c/o Grosvenor Hotel
339 Hay Street East
Perth
WA 6000
Australia
Tel: 08 9325 3799
Fax: 08 221 3813

STEPHANO DALBELLO
SHEEWOLF
131 Bloor Street West
Suite 200-216
Toronto
Ontario
M5S 1RB
Canada
Tel: 416 975 1258
Fax: 416 975 0360
email@dalbello.com
current roster
Dalbello

KATE DALE
FICTION RECORDS LTD
4 Tottenham Mews
London
W1P 9PL
England
Tel: 0171 323 5555

Fax: 0171 323 3523
current roster
The Cure
XFM
(see Chris Parry)

WALTER R DALE
LIZWRD MANAGEMENT
PO Box 2815
Chicago
IL 60690
USA

DOUG D'ARCY
SONGLINES LTD
PO Box 20206
London
NW1 7FF
England
Tel: 0171 284 3970
Fax: 0171 485 0511
doug@songline.demon.co.uk
current roster
Emily Phillips

ROBERT DAVID
RDM MANAGEMENT
PO Box 1081
Fitzroy North
Victoria 3068
Australia
Tel: 03 9489 5300
Fax: 03 9482 6735
current roster
Yard Vadals
Sammy Fowler

JACKIE DAVIDSON
HARDZONE/ FULL SERVICE LTD
245 Brixton Road

Brixton
SW9 6LJ
England
Tel: 0171 737 1344
Fax: 0171 737 0476
jackie@hardzone.sonnet.co.uk
current roster
Ali
Wayne Hector
Mafia Fluxy
Java

TITUS DAY
TRADING POST AGENCY
PO Box 124
Round Corner
NSW 2158
Australia
Tel: 02 9651 4522
Fax: 02 9652 3229
current roster
Phloem

SHAUNA DE CARTIER
WORLD LEADER PRETEND INC
8826 93 Street
Edmonton
Alberta
T6C 3T1
Canada
Tel: 403 488 9800
Fax: 403 482 7621
decartier@connect.ab.ca
current roster
Captain Tractor
The Plaid Tongued Devils
The Hobnail Boots
Oh Susanna

international directory of IMF managers

LEO DEMETRIOU
FIG TREE MANAGEMENT
32 Apex Street
Belmont
Victoria 3216
Australia
Tel: 03 5282 3403
current roster
Mr Bus
Sons Of Korah

NATALIE DE PACE
DIVINE MANAGEMENT
Top Floor
1 Cowcross Street
London
EC1M 6DR
England
Tel: 0171 490 7271
Fax: 0171 490 7273
divine@dial.pipex.com
current roster
The Divine Comedy

BERNARD DEPASQUALE
TEA ROSE DUO
PO Box 411
Brighton
SA 5048
Australia
Tel: 08 8377 1832
Fax: 08 8377 2355
tearose@onaustralia.com.au
www.tearosedue.com.au
current roster
Tea Rose Duo

JACKIE DERING
BULLETHEAD MANAGEMENT
PO Box 637
Cooper Station
New York
NY 10276-0637
USA

STEPHAN DE SANTIS
SDS MANAGEMENT
21 Elm Street
Bolton
Ontario
L7E 1C3
Canada
Tel: 905 951 7235
Fax: 905 951 7236
sdsmngmnt@aol.com
current roster
Honeymoon Suite
Von Groove
Moratti

LEANNE DE SOUZA
MFN MANAGEMENT
PO Box 393
Paddington
Queensland 4064
Australia
Tel: 07 3369 5158
Fax: 07 3369 5128
mfn@quux.net.au
www.milesfromnowhere.com
current roster
Miles From Nowhere

JULIAN DE TAKATS
CEC MANAGEMENT
4 Warren Mews
London
W1P 5DJ
England
Tel: 0171 388 6500
Fax: 0171 388 6522
Julian@cecmanagement.freeserve.co.uk
current roster
Ben Folds Five
Furslide
Mo Solid Gold
Regular Fries
The Montrose Avenue
Southern Fly
The Mighty Wah!

BROOKES DIAMOND
BROOKES DIAMOND PRODUCTIONS
5151 George Street
Ste 1201
Bank Of Montreal Tower
Halifax
Nova Scotia
B3J 1M5
Canada
Tel: 902 492 4444
Fax: 902 492 8383
bdp@istar.ca
current roster
Bruce Guthro
Sharon, Louis & Bram
Bette MacDonald

TIM DILTZ
COLFAX MANAGEMENT
Black Meadow Road
Chester
NY 10918
USA

MARIE DIMBERS
DD MANAGEMENT CONSULTING
Lilla Nygatan 19
Stockholm

SE 11128
Sweden
Tel: 46 8 440 4595
Fax: 46 8 440 4594
marie.dimberg@desert.se
current roster
Roxette
Peter Jøback

BIJAL DODHIA
BLACK & WHITE INDIANS
PO Box 706
Ilford
Essex
IG2 6ED
England
Tel: 0171 704 9945
Fax: 0171 704 9945
bwi.bij@btinternet.com
current roster
Done Lying Down
Lig
Simon Breed And The Birthmarks

TRINA DOLENZ
TRIAD MANAGEMENT
173 Hills Road
Cambridge
CB2 2RJ
England
Tel: 01223 503107
Fax: 01223 515 974
current roster
Richard Barraclough

JO DONNELLY
70 Cambridge Gardens
London
W10 6HR

England
Tel: 0181 960 8417
Fax: 0181 960 8417
Jo-d@dircon.co.uk
current roster
Wood

KEVIN DONNELLY
19 Alderhaus Drive
Kinsley
WA 6026
Australia
Tel: 08 9409 9759
current roster
Kevin Donnelly

AUSTIN AGGREY-O DOOM
NEWGEN MUSIC GROUP LTD
1 Cherry Lodge
101 Palace Road
London
SW2 3LB
England
Tel: 0181 671 6383
Fax: 0181 674 9232
austin@newgenmusic.com
current roster
Melanie Ephson
Ray Lewis
Sam West

JURGEN DRAMM
BMP
303 Riverbank House
1 Putney Bridge Approach
London
SW6 3JD
England
Tel: 0171 371 0022
Fax: 0171 371 0099

current roster
Bob Rose
Juliet Edwards
CJ Nelson

JOHN DRENCH
FRENCH MANAGEMENT ENTERTAINMENT
165 West 91st Street
Suite 6A
New York
NY 10024
USA

DAVID DRYSDALE
2/22 Ball Avenue
Eastwood
NSW 2122
Australia
Tel: 02 9801 3516
current roster
The Blackbirds

ARYN DUANCE
32 Holmwood Street
Newtown
NSW 2042
Australia
Tel: 02 9557 4578
Fax: 02 9565 2777
karyn@acon.com.au
current roster
Eleven Gauge

SARAH DUN
DUNNWRIGHT MANAGEMENT
1st Floor
44 Arley Hill
Bristol
BS6 5PR
England

international directory of IMF managers

Tel: 0117 942 7973
Fax: 0117 942 7973
current roster
DJ Milo
Long Lasting
Jimmy Galvin
Trudi
Taslim

FIONA DUNCAN
LOOG MANAGEMENT
1st Floor
377 Brunswick Street
Fitzroy
Victoria 3065
Australia
Tel: 03 9416 3996
Fax: 03 9416 2708
spiderbait@werple.net.au
current roster
Spiderbait
Hot Rollers
The Shits

STEPHEN DUFF
PO Box 376
Mt Barker
SA 5251
Australia
Tel: 08 8398 2965
Fax: 08 8398 2965
current roster
Pure Bristle

DEBORAH DU REITZ
DDR PUBLICITY
201 Govetts Leap Road
Blackheath
NSW 2785
Australia
Tel: 047 876 338

Fax: 047 876 348
current roster
Kavisha Mazella
Neil Murray

BRIAN DUTTON
INCONTROL MANAGEMENT
Failsworth House
4 Hedges Street
Manchester
M35 9JR
England
Tel: 0161 684 7061
Fax: 0161 688 6656
www.incm1765@aol.com
current roster
Flood
Laura Mercer
Jason Glover

SANDY DWORNIAK
THIS MUCH TALENT
5-7 Vernon Yard
Portobello Road
London
W11 2DX
England
Tel: 0171 243 4667
Fax: 0171 243 4668
tmt@btinternet.com
current roster
Darling
APE
Hannah Robinson
Adrian Bushby
Dave Eringa
Jim Abbiss
Joe Dworniak
Matt Dunkley
Adrian Corker & Paul Conboy

Tim Goldsworthy
Tommy D

ANDREW EAST
27 Church Drive
North Harrow
Middlesex
HA2 7NR
England
Tel: 0181 866 2454
Fax: 0181 866 2454
hiphopcow@aol.com
current roster
Alix Ewande
Fenzar

DOUGLAS EASTERBROOK
INFINITY & BEYOND PRODUCTIONS
19/199 Auburn Road
Yagoona
NSW 2199
Australia
Tel: 02 9709 4857
Fax: 02 9709 8218
current roster
The Fifth Sun

KERRY ECHOLS
TIGERS EAT THEIR YOUNG
1312 20th Street South
Birmingham
AL 35205
USA

STEPHEN EDNEY
EU MANAGEMENT
Unit 13
Impress House
Mansell Road
London
W3 7QH

England
Tel: 0181 740 6060
Fax: 0181 743 8427
eduniverse@mcmail.
   com
www.moodystudios.com
www.pmff.com
current roster
Nigel Butler
Pmff
*Studio Manager (Moody
   Recording Studios)*

THADD EDWARDS
4905 Gilray Drive
Baltimore
MD 21214
USA

TREVOR EDWARDS
*TCE ASSOCIATES
LTD*
26 Midway
Walton-On-Thames
Surrey
KT12 3HZ
England
Tel: 01932 248 794
Fax: 01932 228 820
current roster
Elliott Tuffin

ADAM ELFIN
*ARCHANGEL
MANAGEMENT
LTD*
174 Camden High Street
London
NW1 0NE
England
Tel: 0171 267 3939
Fax: 0171 482 1955
current roster
Nervosa

**VICTORIA
ELLIOTT**
*DAVIX
MANAGEMENT*
Suite D
67 Abbey Road
London
NW8 0AE
England
Tel: 0171 604 3080
Fax: 0181 296 8896
davix@btinternet.com
current roster
*Steve Bellgrade
McQueen
Peel*

FRED ELLIS JR
*ELLIS
PRODUCTIONS*
400 8th Street
Brooklyn
NY 11215
USA

JANINE EMERSON
JETS
36 Warrimoo Avenue
St Ives
NSW 2075
Australia
Tel: 02 9449 1877
Fax: 02 9449 1877
current roster
Janine Emerson

ROSEMARY EMODI
97 Fernside Road
Balham
London
SW12 8LH
England
Tel: 0171 587 3639
Fax: 0171 587 1854

emodi4law@hotmail.
   com
current roster
Farrba

JEREMY ENGLISH
*MULTI J
ENTERPRISES*
16c Seahorse Lane
Discovery Bay
Lantan Island
Hong Kong
Tel: 852 2914 2943
Fax: 852 2914 1720
multijhk@netvigator.
   com
current roster
Jon English

ENGLISH CATHY
*TRANSATLANTIC
MANAGEMENT*
PO Box 2831
Tucson
AZ 85702
USA
Tel: 520 881 5880
Fax: 520 881 8001
engcathy@euphoria.org
www.rivergraphics.com
   /transmgt

ERIC ENJEM
*BIOSPHERE
ENTERTAINMENT*
21-42 Steinway Street
Astoria
NY 11105
USA

DAVID ENTHOVEN
IE MUSIC LTD
111 Frithville Gardens
London

W12 7JG
England
Tel: 0181 600 3400
Fax: 0181 600 3401
de@iemusic.co.uk
current roster
Bryan Ferry
Horace Andy
Robbie Williams
Espiritu
Jamie Catto
Christine Levine

DEBORAH ERIKSEN
234 East 25th Street
Suite 3
New York
NY 10010
USA

LOENE Z ESTWICK
76 Cecil Road
Croydon
CR0 3BJ
England
Tel: 0181 6840576
current roster
Nailah

TIM EVANS
SHADES
INTERNATIONAL
ARTIST MANAGEMENT
14a Knights Court
Knights Park
Kingston
Surrey
KT1 2QL
England
Tel: 0181 549 5261
Fax: 0181 549 5261
shades.int.ent@tophole.
 globalnet.co.uk
current roster

Oliver Cheatham

HARRY EVES
CAPTAIN
COURAGEOUS MM
LTD
Fiddlers Green
Gunnislake
Cornwall
PL18 9NS
England
Tel: 01822 833290
Fax: 01822 833 299
captains@courageous.
 demon.co.uk
www.electrasy.org
current roster
Electrasy
X'ELL
(see David Bone)

ALLAN EWART
ARENA PROMOTIONS
122-126 High Road
London
NW6 4HY
England
Tel: 0171 692 0607
Fax: 0171 692 0707
a.ewart@easynet.co.uk
www.beatbase.co.uk
current roster
Louca
Sensual
Jo Kemp

LAUREN
FACCIDOMO
DAWN TO DUSK
PROMOTIONS
5 Merrie Mill Lane
Holmdel
NJ 07733
USA

MARGEE FAGELSON
198 Hillcrest Terrace
Brattleboro
VT 05301
USA

TREVOR FARRELL
SOUL CITY
15 Braidwood Road
London
SE6 1QU
England
Tel: 0181 333 2581
Fax: 0181 333 2581
current roster
Adisa

LEE FARROW
ROCK CLUB
MANAGEMENT
Unit 4
27a Spring Grove Road
Hounslow
TW3 4BE
England
Tel: 0181 572 8809
rockriot@compuserve.
 com
current roster
Karen Heigham
Drown
Gus

TONY FASKE
130 68th Street
Guttenberg
NJ 07093
USA
Tel: 201 869 2738

DARRELL
FAULKNER
FALL
2 Joyce Avenue

Frankston
Victoria 3199
Australia
Tel: 03 9770 2196
current roster
Warrick Spence
Jerry Papadakis

FRAZER FEARNHEAD
BLUE SILVER MANAGEMENT

Unit 51
Bus Space Studios
Conlan Street
London
W10 5AP
England
Tel: 0171 460 2612
Fax: 0171 460 3489
current roster
Trippa
Silverman
London's Most Wanted
Lisa Unique
Sylvia Powell
Mucho Macho

DAVID FELLERMAN
MUSICAL AGENCY & MANAGEMENT LTD

The Seedbed Centre
Langston Road
Loughton
Essex
IG10 3TQ
England
Tel: 0181 501 2469
Fax: 0181 502 6863
info@musicman.uk.com

STEVE FERNIE
EAST CENTRAL ONE LTD

57d Hatton Gardens

London
EC1N 8HP
England
Tel: 0171 831 3111
Fax: 0171 831 9991
steve@eastcentralone.com
current roster
The Messenger

ARMANDO AGOSTINO DARIO FERRARI

4 Dakota Way
Renfrew
PA4 0NP
Scotland
Tel: 0141 836 5306
current roster
Oversoul

JOHN FETTER
NOW HEAR THIS PRODUCTIONS

117-38 141 Street
South Ozone Park
New York
NY 11438
USA

CLARE FFRENCH BLAKE
PERIPHERY

PO Box 24680
London
E2 8TN
England
Tel: 0171 613 3124
Fax: 0171 684 0619

ROB FIELDS
RONIN MANAGEMENT

322 West 14th Street

Suite 3C
New York
NY 10014
USA
Tel: 212 340 8039
Fax: 212 633 0014
ronin@nyo.com

PETER FILLEUL
MUSICARE

16 Thorpewood Avenue
London
SE26 4BX
England
Tel: 0181 699 1245
Fax: 0181 291 5584
101460.1764@compuserve.com

BRUCE FINDLAY
SCHOOLHOUSE MANAGEMENT

104 Constitution Street
Leith
Edinburgh
EH6 6AW
Scotland
Tel: 0131 554 6656
Fax: 0131 554 4405
current roster
Annie Christian

ROBERT FINDLAY
WEDGE MUSIC

1674 Broadway
Suite 7D
New York
NY 10019
USA

ANTONY FINN
BLUE'S BROWN THE PARTNERSHIP

3 Horwood Close

Rickmansworth
Hertfordshire
WD3 2RS
England
Tel: 0181 385 6605
bigdayout@blues-brown.co.uk
current roster
Big Day Out

GARRY FISHER

33 Ypres Road
Kelmscott
WA 6111
Australia
Tel: 09 495 1965
current roster
Cochineal

MATTHEW FISHER
THE SURGERY COMPANY

116 Netherwood Road
London
W14 0BQ
England
Tel: 0171 602 2937
Fax: 0171 602 2937
mattfisher@orangenet.co.uk
current roster
The Egg
Urban DK
Dan Parry
Jim Eliot

JOHN FISHLOCK

16 Church Street
Eastern Creek
NSW 2766
Australia
Tel: 02 9625 6406
Fax: 02 9832 0696
current roster
Rain House

STEINAR FJELD
ABC MANAGEMENT ANS

PO Box 576
Sentrum
0105 Oslo
Norway
Tel: 47 224 244 05
Fax: 47 224 299 64
current roster
Torgeir & Kjendisane
Bløff
Stephen Ackles
Bittobeat

GARY FLEMING
GARY FLEMING MANAGEMENT

3 Boyle Street
Croydon Park
NSW 2133
Australia
Tel: 02 9716 5545
Fax: 02 9716 5815
wooky@bigpond.com

TOMMY FLOYD
OUTLAW ENTERTAINMENT CORPORATION

#101-1001 West Broadway
Department 400
Vancouver
British Columbia
V6H 4E4
Canada
Tel: 604 878 1494

Fax: 604 878 1495
outlaw@istar.ca
current roster
The Cartels
Bates Motel
Shuvelhead

MARK FLYNN
LOVECRAFT MANAGEMENT

PO Box 177
Erskineville
NSW 2043
Australia
Tel: 02 9352 9930
Fax: 02 9352 9966
current roster
Lovecraft

BARRY FOOT
REAL POTENTIAL SONGS

163 Old Church Road
Chingford
London
E4 6RD
England
Tel: 0181 529 5048
Fax: 0181 529 5048
current roster
Footsy

NICK FORD
MADRIGAL MUSIC

Guy Hall
Awre
Gloucestershire
GL14 1EL
England
Tel: 01594 510 512
Fax: 01594 510 512
current roster
Anastasia
Cindy Stratton

the IMF handbook a guide to professional band management

ANTOINETTE FOSTER
BIG STORM PRODUCTIONS
90 Morrison Road
Pakenham Upper
Victoria 3810
Australia
Tel: 03 5942 7787
Fax: 03 5942 7786
current roster
The Tenants

COLLEEN FOSTER
STAGECOACH THEATRE ARTS
53 Nagazine Road
Ashford
Kent
TN24 8NR
England
Tel: 01233 611 696
Fax: 01233 611 696
current roster
Penny Foster

TRAVIS FRANKLIN
5 Sweeting Street
Guildford
WA 6055
Australia
Tel: 09 377 0288
current roster
Buz

ROCKI FRASSETTO
ROCKINA'S MANAGEMENT & TALENT
353 Avenue W South
Saskatoon
Saskatchewan
S7M 3G4
Canada
Tel: 306 382 0810
Fax: 306 978 1009
touchtonegurus@
 cyancorp.com
current roster
Touchtone Gurus
Mishi Donovan
Patrick James
Bird

MANDY FREEDMAN
WHATEVER NEXT! MANAGEMENT
Unit 24
Buspace Studios
Conlan Street
London
W10 5AP
England
Tel: 0181 9640637
Fax: 0181 9640638
mandy@whatnext.
 freeserve.co.uk
current roster
Ivory Towers
Cheyenne Marie
Becky Waterhouse

PETER FREEDMAN
PETER FREEDMAN ENTERTAINMENT
1790 Broadway
Suite 1316
New York
NY 10019
USA
Tel: 212 265 1776
Fax: 212 265 3678
think007@aol.com

DUNCAN ANDREW GABRIEL
FREEWILL MANAGEMENT LTD
Unit M
Chesham House
Chesham Close
Romford
Essex
RM7 7JP
England
Tel: 01708 744 334
Fax: 01708 762 492
wgabriel@vossnet.
 co.uk
www.TheStudioComplex.
 co.uk
current roster
Clarie-Louise

DEBORAH GANN
RESERVOIR PROMOTIONS
3/192 Brunswick Street
Fortitude Valley
Queensland 4006
Australia
Tel: 07 3852 3535
Fax: 07 3852 3553
reservoi@bit.net.au
current roster
Gresh
Surya

ALEX GARDINER
BLUE CHIP STYLE P/L
PO Box 59
Ballan
Victoria 3342
Australia
Tel: 03 5368 1048
Fax: 03 5368 1048
current roster
Ben Lowry

Steve Lowry Band

BRUCE GARFIELD
40 West 86th Street
Apartment 16A
New York
NY 10024
USA
Tel: 212 541 8440
Fax: 212 451 8260
garfbru@aol.com

GABRIELLE GEISELMAN
HELL BENT MANAGEMENT
5959 Franklin Avenue 306
Los Angeles
CA 90028
USA
Tel: 323 871 1434
hellbentla@aol.com

ALICIA GELRENT
ALICIA GELRENT MANAGEMENT
320 East 65th Street
Suite 218
New York
NY 10021
USA

SUSAN GENTILE
STARFISH ENTERTAINMENT
135-67 Mowat Avenue
Toronto
Ontario
M6K 3E3
Canada
Tel: 416 588 3329
Fax: 416 588 2842

susan@bluerodeo.com
current roster
Blue Rodeo
Jim Cuddy

ADAM GERBER
ADAM GERBER MANAGEMENT
63 Fortis Green Road
Muswell Hill
London
N10 3HP
England
Tel: 0181 444 8088
Fax: 0181 444 1838
adamgerber@agmuk.demon.co.uk
www.agmuk.demon.co.uk
current roster
Lunatic
Charlie Smith
Martin Astle

ERIC GERBER
ROYAL ARTIST GROUP
12727 Mitchell Avenue
Suite 109
Los Angeles
CA 90066
USA
Tel: 310 313 7246
Fax: 310 313 5346
ragman@gte.net

GERALD GERMANY
GERALD GERMANY MANAGEMENT
106 Nassau Street
Princeton
NJ 08540
USA

DANIEL GETZ
145 Hicks Street
Suite B-66
Brooklyn
NY 11201
USA

CHRIS GIBBS
SLAM
404 Grand Promenade
Dianella
WA 6059
Australia
Tel: 08 9375 9405
Fax: 08 9375 9405
full@opera.iinet.net.au
www.geocities.com/BourbonStreet/9401/full.index.html
current roster
FULL, Murcott

DEBBI GIBBS
LOOPHOLE LIMITED
218 West 10th Street
Suite 3F
New York
NY 10014
USA

STEVE GILMOUR
BACKLASH MUSIC MANAGEMENT
54 Carlton Place
Glasgow
G5 9TW
Scotland
Tel: 0141 418 0053
Fax: 0141 418 0054
current roster
Planet Fuse
Mero
Jim McLaughlin
Gordon Goudie

the IMF handbook a guide to professional band management

Paul Masterson
Dave James
Carol Laula

RONNIE GLEESON
GB2
Merry Hay House
Ilton Business Park
Ilton
Ilminster
Somerset
TA19 9DU
England
Tel: 01460 554 50
Fax: 01460 554 50
gbsquare@demon.co.uk
current roster
Marshal Peanut
Vicious Circle

JOHN GLOVER
BLUEPRINT MANAGEMENT
134 Lots Road
London
SW10 0RJ
England
Tel: 0171 351 4333
Fax: 0171 352 4652
matt_glover@lineone.
 net
current roster
Beverley Craven
Go West
Richard Drummie
Alison Limerick
Lena Fiagbe
Tony Hadley

KIM GLOVER
REAL RED INTERNATIONAL
PO Box 468
Maidstone

Kent
ME17 2DY
England
Tel: 01622 75 47 48
Fax: 01622 75 47 49
current roster
B*witched
Stephanie
Lee Murray
Rob Jeffery
*Narada Michael
 Walden*

MATT GLOVER
BLUEPRINT MANAGEMENT
134 Lots Road
London
SW10 0RJ
England
Tel: 0171 351 4333
Fax: 0171 352 4652
matt_glover@lineone.
 net
current roster
(see John Glover)

JAKE GOLD
MANAGEMENT TRUST LTD
219 Dufferin Street
Suite 309-B
Toronto
Ontario
M6K 3JI
Canada
Tel: 416 532 7080
Fax: 416 532 8852
mgmtrust@total.net
current roster
The Tragically Hip
Big Wreck
The Watchmen
Flux

TONY GOLDRING
JEF HANLON MANAGEMENT
1 York Street
London
W1H 1PZ
England
Tel: 0171 487 2558
Fax: 0171 487 2584
jhanlon@agents-uk.com
current roster
(see Jef Hanlon)

DANUSIA GORBUN
GEM ORGANISATION
Unit 309
Canalot Production
 Studios
222 Kensal Road
London
W10 5BN
England
Tel: 0171 565 9001
Fax: 0171 565 9002
Danusia@originalgem.
 demon.co.uk
www.originalgem.com
current roster
Brandon Cooke
Milki

CARLENE GORDON
BRONZE STAR ENTERTAINMENT
4001 Indian Creek Drive
Suite 12
Miami Beach
FL 33140
USA

MIKE GORMLEY
LA PERSONAL DEVELOPMENT
950 North Kings Road

Suite 266
West Hollywood
CA 90069
USA
Tel: 323 848 9200

JAINE GOULD
CREW MANAGEMENT

65 Golborne Road
London
W10 5NP
England
Tel: 0181 964 8192
Fax: 0181 984 8212
current roster
Sande
(see Jaine Gould)

DIANE GOWMAN
ROCKING ENTERTAINMENT

163 3rd Avenue
Suite 192
New York
NY 10003
USA

PETER GRAHAM
BIONIC MANAGEMENT

10 Sanford Walk
London
SE14 6NB
England
Tel: 0181 305 6989
Fax: 0181 305 6989
fluid-uk@dircon.co.uk
current roster
Fantasmagroover

CHRISTOPHER GRANGER

25 Acorn Lane
Levittown
NY 11756
USA

ANDY GREENAWAY
FEAT MANAGEMENT

47 Henry Road
Oxford
OX2 0DG
England
Tel: 01865 201 553
Fax: 01865 201 553
current roster
Amanda Tatum
Jamie
Fur Circus

RJ GUHA
MATRIX ENTERTAINMENT GROUP LTD

55 MaCaul Street
Box 150
Toronto
Ontario
M5T 2W7
Canada
Tel: 416 463 3857
Fax: 416 463 3097
matrix@passport.ca
current roster
The New Meanies
King Cobb Steelie

PETER HAINES
PETER HAINES MANAGEMENT

37 Harvey Road
Ilford
Essex
IG1 2NJ
England
Tel: 0181 478 8177
haines@easynet.co.uk
current roster
Jeremy Bird
The London Girls

BARRY HALES
BARRY HALES MANAGEMENT

PO Box 181
Guilford
NSW 2161
Australia
Tel: 02 9632 8781
current roster
Barry Hales

BJÖRN HALL

35 Pilgrims Lane
London
NW3 1SS
England
Tel: 0171 431 2122
Fax: 0171 813 4649
bjorn-hall@hotmail.com
current roster
Carina Andersson

LORENZO HALL
PHOENIX PRODUCTIONS

The Gramarye
Waynhete Avenue
Croydon
CR0 4BS
England
Tel: 0181 404 7083
current roster
Shade
Bloom
Angel Wax
Circle

the IMF handbook a guide to professional band management

ANTON HAMER
APOSTROPHE THE ROCK BAND
15 Edward Street
Baulkham Hills
NSW 2153
Australia
Tel: 02 9852 3430
Fax: 02 9621 6758
hammer7@zip.com.au
www.geocities.com/
   sunsetstrip/palms/
   1255
current roster
Apostrophe

JOHN HAMILTON
JOHN HAMILTON MANAGEMENT
10 Stanley Road
Watford
Hertfordshire
WD1 2QU
England
Tel: 01923 247 879
Fax: 01923 210 917
eqstudios@mcmail.
   com
current roster
Lucie Kaz

DAVID HANDLEY
BATHTUB MANAGEMENT
PO Box 560
Potts Point
NSW 2011
Australia
Tel: 02 9357 1457
Fax: 02 9357 2335
current roster
Rebecca Rennie
Freyja

JEF HANLON
JEF HANLON MANAGEMENT
1 York Street
London
W1H 1PZ
England
Tel: 0171 487 2558
Fax: 0171 487 2584
jhanlon@agents-uk.
   com
current roster
Gary Glitter
Martin Jenkins
Matthew Van Kan

RUSTY HANNAN
MILESTONE MUSIC MANAGEMENT
The Blue Suite
Studio Complex
Chesham House
Chesham Close
Romford
Essex
RM7 7JP
England
Tel: 01708 733 343
Fax: 01708 720 072
current roster
Peter Kelly
Daniel Lucas
Hyperbreed

MARTIN HANSELL
DOUBLE HIT RECORDS
PO Box 3207
Wokingham
Berkshire
RG41 5YA
England
Tel: 01252 877 952

Fax: 01252 878 003
martinrh@double-hit-
   records.co.uk
www.double-hit-records.
   co.uk/
current roster
Rose
Fragile Hopes
Stark

JOHN L HANSEN
JOHN L HANSEN ORGANISATION
PO Box 1
Ramsgate
NSW 2217
Australia
Tel: 02 9529 4822
Fax: 02 9529 3764
current roster
The Four Kinsmen
Kamahl
Anna Rojas
JJ Horne

HERIC HARLE
DEUTSCH-ENGLISCHE FREUNDSCHAFT LTD
31-33 Ansleigh Place
off Stoneleigh Place
London
W11 4BW
England
Tel: 0171 221 2525
Fax: 0171 221 2529
def@mail.bogo.co.uk
current roster
Moby
Sparks
Westbam
Vietnam Inc
Hardknox
Staggman

international directory of IMF managers

PAUL HARLEY
FOOTLIGHT MANAGEMENT
24 Watermill Close
Ham
Richmond
TU10 7UH
England
Tel: 0181 3327900
current roster
Syndrome

COLIN HARRIS
THE STRATFIELD ENTERTAINMENT CO
PO Box 3784
Christchuch
Dorset
BH23 8YS
England
Tel: 01425 673097
Fax: 01202 780077
Colin_G_Harris@
  compuserve.com
current roster
In My Skin

JOHN HARRIS
SIRRAH MANAGEMENT
4 Buckby Tinkers Bridge
Milton Keynes
MK6 3DP
England
Tel: 01908 662 158
Fax: 01908 662 158
current roster
Signs of Life
Yvonne Newman
Nardo Bailey

KEITH HARRIS
KEITH HARRIS MUSIC LTD
204 Courthouse Road
Maidenhead
Berkshire
SL6 6HU
England
Tel: 01628 674422
Fax: 01628 631379
Keitharris1@computer.
  com
current roster
Stevie Wonder
Omar

DAVE HART
HART MANAGEMENT
201 Wyoming Avenue
Maplewood
NJ 07040
USA

PHIL HARVEY
ÜBERBITCH
20 Southmoor Road
Jericho
Oxford
OX2 6RD
England
Tel: 01865 558 481
current roster
The Coldplay

RAE HARVEY
SIDELINE MANAGEMENT
PO Box 2113
Fitzroy
Victoria 3065
Australia
Tel: 03 9419 4556
Fax: 03 9419 4516
mgt@sideline.com.au
www.sideline.com.au
current roster
Bodyjar
The Living End
Caustic Soda

LIZ HAWIE
INTERVENUE
39 Ranulf Road
London
NW2 2BS
England
Tel: 0171 431 5011
Fax: 0171 431 5099
xbd63@dial.pipex.
  com
current roster
Peel
Zaylie

PETER HAYES
WPA MANAGEMENT
PO Box 1238
North Fitzroy
Victoria 3068
Australia
Tel: 03 9416 0940
Fax: 03 9416 1290
wpa@werple.mira.net.
  au
www.mira.net.au/wpa/
current roster
Weddings Parties
Anything
Michael Thomas

AMY HEAP
RICOCHET
5 Old Garden House
The Lanterns
Bridge Lane
London
SW11 3AD
England
Tel: 0171 924 2255
Fax: 0171 738 1881
current roster
(see Stephen King)

REG HEATH
PINNACLE MANAGEMENT
22 Selker Drive
Amington Fields
Tamworth
B77 3QT
England
Tel: 01827 64113
reg@amington.IDPS.
    co.uk
current roster
The Lilac Groove

TONY HEDEMANN
MYTHICA
156 Hindes Street
Lota
Queensland 4179
Australia
Tel: 07 3893 2622
thedeman@bit.net.au
www.ozemail.com.au/
    ~mythica

DUNCAN HICKEY
BLUE WORLD ENTERTAINMENT
PO Box 1243
Baulkham Hills
NSW 2153
Australia
Tel: 02 9634 3471
Fax: 02 9894 9557
current roster
Blue World

ANNA HILDUR HILDIBRANDSDOTTIR
HILL MANAGEMENT
19 Lezayre Road
Orpington
Kent
BR6 6BP

England
Tel: 01689 855 895
Fax: 01689 601 329
annah@netmatters.co.uk
www.bellatrix.co.uk
current roster
Bellatrix

SUE HILL
THE WORKSHOP
93 King William Street
Kent Town
SA 5067
Australia
Tel: 08 8363 1022
Fax: 08 8363 1129
workshop@camtech.net.
    au
current roster
Outshine

GRANT HILTON
ROCKINGHORSE RECORDING COMPANY
PO Box 597
Byron Bay
NSW 2481
Australia
Tel: 066 884 131
Fax: 066 884 007
current roster
Carmella
Cartoon

DAVID HITCHCOCK
DELANCEY BUSINESS MANAGEMENT LTD
220a Blythe Road
London
W14 0HH
England
Tel: 0171 602 5424

Fax: 0171 602 3404

NICK HOBBS
CHARMENKO
46 Spenser Road
London
SE24 0NR
England
Tel: 0171 274 6618
Fax: 0171 737 4712
ho@charm.demon.
    co.uk
current roster
David Thomas
Pere Ubu
Spearmint
Sonexuno
Gagarin
Laibach
The Kidney Brothers
Spaceheads

LESLIE HOEFLICH
317 West 77th Street
Suite 4F
New York
NY 10024
USA

STEVE HOFFMAN
SRO MANAGEMENT INC
189 Carlton Street
Toronto
Ontario
M5A 2K7
Canada
Tel: 416 923 5855
Fax: 416 923 1041
sro@sromgt.com
current roster
The Tea Party
Lenni Jabour
Matthew Good Band

Todd Ryan/John Kerns

BJØRN HOLBÊK-HANSSEN
BAHAMA BOOKING & MANAGEMENT
Osterhausgate 27
0183 Oslo
Norway
Tel: 47 229 936 40
Fax: 47 229 936 41
current roster
Ton Mathisen & Herodes Falsk
Jon Schau
Solfaktor X

JAMES S HOLLIDAY
JSH ENTERTAINMENTS
87 Ardrossan Gardens
Worcester Park
Surrey
KT4 7AY
England
Tel: 0181 873 3843
Fax: 0181 873 3843
sub-groove@hotmail.com
current roster
Suburban Groove

JANE HOLLOWAY
STRONGROOM MANAGEMENT
120-124 Curtain Road
London
EC2A 3SQ
England
Tel: 0171 426 5100
Fax: 0171 426 5102
jane@strongroom.co.uk
www.strongroom.co.uk

current roster
Mike Nielsen
Neil McLellan
Oskar Paul
Luke Gifford
Dave Pemberton
Gaetan Schurrer
Aidan Love

SHANE HOMAN
5/29 Croydon Street
Petersham
NSW 2049
Australia
Tel: 02 9560 8548
shoman@laurel.ow.mq.edu.au
music researcher/teacher

DAX HOPWOOD
HOT AND BOTHERED
Bank Chambers
Market Place
Stockport
SK1 1UN
England
Tel: 0161 480 6617
Fax: 0161 480 0904
dax@century21.prestel.co.uk
current roster
The Loved Ones

PETER HORREY
11 Stoney Common
Stansted
Essex
CM24 8NF
England
Tel: 01279 647 201
Fax: 01279 647 205
horrey@aol.com
current roster

Boo Hewerdine
Jacobs Ladder
The Bible

DAVID HOWELLS
DARAH MUSIC
PO Box 10649
London
SW10 0ZU
England
Tel: 0171 352 8393
Fax: 0171 376 8412
current roster
Steve Mac

PETER HOYLAND
HIT MANAGEMENT
20-30 Bourke Street
Melbourne
Victoria 3000
Australia
Tel: 03 9663 8055
Fax: 03 9663 8401
peterh@c031.aone.net.au
current roster
David Hirschfelder
David Hobson
Phil Buckle
Suzie Ahern
Andrew Grant

PHILIP HUDSON
IMPAK ENTERTAINMENT
18 East 105th Street
Apartment 18
New York
NY 10029
USA

JANE HUGHES
LITTLE BLACK BOOK MANAGEMENT
8 Brent Close

the IMF handbook a guide to professional band management

Thatcham
Berkshire
RG19 3YP
England
Tel: 01635 34099
Fax: 01635 528 623
janeannhughes@hotmail.com
current roster
Hotel Lounge
Natia Blue
Polar

GILLIAN HULME
SHALIT ENTERTAINMENT
Cambridge Theatre
Covent Garden
London
WC2H 9HU
England
Tel: 0171 379 3282
Fax: 0171 379 3238
jonathan@shalit.co.uk
current roster
Charlotte Church
Larry Adler

SUZANNE HUNT
STRESS MANAGEMENT
Unit 6217
49 Greenwich High Road
London
SE10 8JL
England
Tel: 0181 691 0262
Fax: 0181 691 0268
current roster
Glenn Tilbrook
Squeeze
Quixotic Records
(UK only)
Nick Harper

Ben Jones

MARK HURWITZ
1530 Palisade Avenue
Suite 11J
Fort Lee
NJ 07024-5421
USA

CRAIG HUXLEY
CRAIG HUXLEY MANAGEMENT
13 Christchurch Road
Crouch End
London
N8 9QL
England
Tel: 0181 292 1205
chuxleychm@aol.com
current roster
Jane Harvey
Fibrehead
Genelab

JEFF IRELAND
SHAKIN' THE TREE
67 Mowat Avenue #238
Toronto
Ontario
M6K 3E3
Canada
Tel: 416 588 5858
Fax: 416 588 3353
shkntree@interlog.com

JANINE IRONS
CROSBY IRONS ASSOCIATES LTD
11 Tudor Road
Harrow
Middlesex
HA3 5PQ
England

Tel: 0181 424 2807/2243
Fax: 0181 424 2807
janine@crosbyironsassoc.demon.co.uk
current roster
Gary Crosby
Denys Baptiste
J-Life
Guava
Nu Troop
Jazz Jamaica

PAUL IRVINE
WHIRLWIND ARTIST MANAGEMENT
71 Homestead Road
West Hill
Ontario
M1E 3S1
Canada
Tel: 416 282 7178
Fax: 416 282 7178
paulirvine@sandersonassociates.com
current roster
Derivation

MIKE IRVING
MIKE IRVING PROMOTIONS
5 Stockens Green
Knebworth
Hertfordshire
SG3 6DG
England
Tel: 07071 881154
Fax: 01438 816 299
MikeIrving@aol.com
current roster
Tony Royden
Shine
Define
Cat

international directory of IMF managers

ANNA M JACKSON
ARC MANAGEMENT
855 Park Avenue
Huntington
NY 11743
USA

PETE JACKSON
RICOCHET
5 Old Garden House
The Lanterns
Bridge Lane
London
SW11 3AD
England
Tel: 0171 924 2255
Fax: 0171 738 1881
pete.jackson@dial.
  pipex.com
current roster
(see Stephen King)

STEVE JACKSON
CREATIVE
MANAGEMENT LTD
PO Box 1060
Birmingham
B1 3PQ
England
Tel: 0121 236 1060
Fax: 0121 236 1070
Steve@Creativeltd.
  com
current roster
Next Of Kin
North Star
Teenage Rampage
21st Century Girls
Colin Dunne
Jean Butler
Gary Stevenson
Dave West
Sean Maguire

SAFTA JAFFERY
SJP PRODUCTIONS
1 Prince Of Wales
Passage
117 Hampstead Road
London
NW1 3EF
England
Tel: 0171 388 8635
Fax: 0171 387 0233
sjpdodgy@easynet.co.uk
current roster
John Leckie
Craig Leon
Ron Saint Germain
Nick Griffiths
Robin Millar
Chris Kimsey
Pat Moran
Ian Caple
Tony Mansfield
John Cornfield
Michael Brauer
Muse
Aquiessence

ALAN JAMES
ALAN JAMES
MANAGEMENT
PO Box 2727
Darwin
NT 801
Australia
Tel: 08 8941 2900
Fax: 08 8941 1088
yothuyindi@aol.com
www.yothuyindi.com
current roster
Yothu Yindi

IMKE JANIESCH
DEUTSCH-ENGLISCHE
FREUNDSCHAFT LTD
31-33 Ansleigh Place

off Stoneleigh Place
London
W11 4BW
England
Tel: 0171 221 2525
Fax: 0171 221 2529
defimke@bogo.co.uk
current roster
(see Eric Harle)

KAI JARRE
KAI JARRE
Erlandstuvn 5
N-1178 Oslo
Norway
Tel: 47 227 160 00
Fax: 47 227 160 06
kjarre@online.no
current roster
Velvet Belly

DAVID JARRETT
TARDIS MUSIC
PO Box 2379
Kent Town
SA 5071
Australia
Tel: 08 8362 0402
Fax: 08 8362 0402
jarrett@adelaide.on.net
current roster
Tantra
Michael Mills
Kranntus

SAMUEL P JEAN
MANPOWER
MANAGEMENT
100 Eastern Parkway
Irvington
NJ 07111
USA
Tel: 201 371 9465
Fax: 201 371 9465

PETER JENNER
SINCERE MANAGEMENT
Flat B
6 Bravington Road
London
W9 3AH
England
Tel: 0181 960 4438
Fax: 0181 968 8458
sinman@compuserve.com
current roster
Billy Bragg
Jerry Burns
Andy Kershaw
John Parrish
Deborah Conway
Scarfo
Eddi Reader
Grant Showbiz

ERLING JOHANNESSEN
SIRKUS MANAGEMENT AS
Cort Aldersgate 2
0202 Oslo
Norway
Tel: 47 224 317 00
Fax: 47 224 466 40
current roster
DDE
PostGiro Bygget
Jørn Hoel
Elisabeth Andreasson
Grethe Svensen
Bjelleklang
Reidar Larsen
CC Cowboys

GLORIA JOHNSON
GB2 MANAGEMENT
Merry Hay House
Ilton Business Park
Ilton
Ilminster
Somerset
TA19 9DU
England
Tel: 01460 554 50
Fax: 01460 554 50
gb2@demon.co.uk
current roster
Marshal Peanut
Vicious Circle

KAT JOHNSTON
GREYMALKIN MANAGEMENT
6 Marianne Way
Doncaster
Victoria 3108
Australia
Tel: 03 9387 3987
Fax: 03 9819 2256
kjohnston@swin.edu.au
current roster
Nine Degrees Left
Andrew Day

SHERI JONES
Jones & Co
100-5212 Sackville Street
Halifax
Nova Scotia
B3J 1K6
Canada
Tel: 902 429 9005
Fax: 902 429 9071
SheriJones@compuserve.com
current roster
Lamond
Laura Smith
MacKeel Music Group
Gordie Sampson

GEOFF JUKES
JUKES PRODUCTIONS LTD
PO Box 13995
London
W9 2FL
England
Tel: 0171 286 9532
Fax: 0171 286 4739
jukes@easynet.co.uk
www.jukesproductions.co.uk
current roster
Underworld
Rupert Hine
Bob Geldof
Jeannette Obstoj

GRAHAM JULES
UNDERGROUND
10a Acton Street
London
WC1X 9NG
England
Tel: 0171 837 3353
Fax: 0171 837 0383
active@lineone.net
current roster
Kirstey Prudence

CAROL KAHIL
17 Irving Place
New York
NY 10003
USA

RICHARD KAMMERER
KBC MANAGEMENT
6381 Hollywood Boulevard
Suite 610
Los Angeles
CA 90028

international directory of IMF managers

USA
Tel: 323 962 6789

DAWN M KAPLAN
KAPLAN MUSIC
15 Gloria Lane
Suite 200
Fairfield
NJ 07004
USA

ANDY KARLIC
POPE MANAGEMENT
16-46 Bell Boulevard
Bayside
NY 11360
USA

CAROL KATE
KAYOS PRODUCTIONS INC
16 West 19th Street
5th Floor
New York
NY 10011
USA

JOHN KAUFMAN
RIGHT MANAGEMENT
177 High Street
Harlesden
London
NW10 4TE
England
Tel: 0181 961 3889
Fax: 0181 961 4620
current roster
The Paddies

CHRISTIAN KEESING
80 Blenheim Crescent
London
W11 1NZ

England
Tel: 0171 2433108
christian.keesing@virgin.net

PETER KEMELFIELD
PETER KEMELFIELD MANAGEMENT
11 Alice Street
Malvern
Victoria 3144
Australia
Tel: 03 9824 4445
Fax: 03 9824 4447
kemel@bigpond.com
www.ussers.bigpond.com/kemel
current roster
Babba
Doors
Makin' Whoopee!

GRAHAM KENNEDY
KENNEDY MANAGEMENT
PO Box 240
Annandale
NSW 2038
Australia
Tel: 02 9660 2888
Fax: 02 9660 2898
current roster
Monica Trapaga
The Nissan Cedrics (aka Dannielle Gaha & Louise Anton)

RICHARD MAXWELL KENYON
USE LTD
24c/26 Charing Cross Road
London
WC2H 0DG

England
Tel: 0171 240 2578
Fax: 0171 240 8280
current roster
Will B
United States Of Eden
Artlaws
Wack
Sons Of Merops

BAHIA KERRY
GALLANT
45 Page High
Lymington Avenue
Wood Green
London
N22 6JQ
England
current roster
Times Like These

CHRIS KING
CHRIS KING & ASSOCIATES PTY LTD
484 Barkers Road
Hawthorn East
Victoria 3123
Australia
Tel: 03 9816 8024
Fax: 03 9816 8024
current roster
Bhima's Gate
Awesome Wells Band
The Whipping Post

RON KITCHENER
RGK ENTERTAINMENT GROUP
PO Box 243
Station C
Toronto
Ontario
M6J 3P4
Canada

the IMF handbook a guide to professional band management

Tel: 416 345 8891
Fax: 416 345 8879
rgkent@netcom.ca
current roster
Jason McCoy
Lynch

DEBORAH KLEIN
LMI MANAGEMENT
7 Eastburn Street
Brighton
MA 02135
USA

TAD KORBUSZ
BRIGHT FUTURE MANAGEMENT
273 Wick Road
Brislington
Bristol
BS4 4HR
England
Tel: 0117 977 7085
Fax: 0117 977 7085
current roster
Angel Tech
Originator

ROB KOS
METROPOLITAN ENTERTAINMENT GROUP
2 Pennsylvania Plaza
25th Floor
New York
NY 10121
USA
Tel: 212 868 7370
Fax: 212 629 3605

BANJAMIN KOSMAN
PASSIONATE ENTERTAINMENT
304 East 20th Street

PH C
New York
NY 10003
USA

KALIOPI KROSS
PURE MUSES MANAGEMENT
3/29 Yarra Street
Hawthorn
Victoria 3122
Australia
Tel: 03 9484 5557
Fax: 03 9818 8998
current roster
Kaliopi

LIZA KUMJIAN-SMITH
Little Giant Management
14 Old Compton Street
London
W1V 5PE
England
Tel: 0171 494 0535
Fax: 0171 494 0535
liza@sugarfree.demon.co.uk
www.sugarfree.demon.co.uk
current roster
Sugarfree

TRYGVE KVANDAL
TALENT FARM AS
Skuteviksboder 11
N-5035 Bergen
Sandviken
Norway
Tel: 47 553 100 05
Fax: 47 553 200 96
talent.farm@hl.telia.no
current roster
Helen Eriksen

CHARMAINE LACKO
FRESH ENTERTAINMENT
PO Box 1723
Dee Why
NSW 2099
Australia
Tel: 02 9982 2780
Fax: 02 9972 2780
current roster
Native Fear

WENDY LAISTER
MEAGUS ENTERTAINMENT
584 Broadway
Suite 506
New York
NY 10012
USA

DAVID LANDAU
BONZORAMA
177 High Street
Harlesden
London
NW10 4TE
England
Tel: 0181 961 3889
Fax: 0181 961 4620
current roster
TC Curtis

WADE LANGHAM
LUPINS PRODUCTION
PO Box 183
Sydney
Nova Scotia
B1P 6H1
Canada
Tel: 902 539 8874
Fax: 902 562 7012
lupins@fox.nstn.ca

international directory of IMF managers

current roster
Rita McNeil

ROB LANNI
COALITION ENTERTAINMENT MANAGEMENT

202-10271 Yonge Street
Richmond Hill
Ontario
L4C 3B5
Canada
Tel: 905 508 0025
Fax: 905 508 0403
cem@istar.ca

current roster
Our Lady
Peace Finger Eleven
Colin James Miller
Stain Limit

CATHERINE R LAPORTE
CATZ MANAGEMENT LTD

PO Box 146
Centerport
NY 11721
USA

INGE LASS
INGE LASS MANAGEMENT

PO Box 595
Epping
NSW 2121
Australia
Tel: 02 9876 4745
Fax: 02 9876 4947
maas@5054.aone.net.au

current roster
Martin Lass
Grimace
Saskia

DENISE LAW

31 Valley Avenue
London
N12 9PG
England
Tel: 0181 445 0850
Fax: 0181 445 0850

current roster
Pool

ERIC LAWRENCE
COALITION ENTERTAINMENT MANAGEMENT

202-10271 Yonge Street
Richmond Hill
Ontario
L4C 3B5
Canada
Tel: 905 508 0025
Fax: 905 508 0403
cem@istar.ca

PETER LAY
LMP

PO Box 207
Gloucester
GL4 6YB
England
Tel: 01452 537731
lmp@clara.net
www.lmp.clara.net

current roster
Journey's End
Disrupt

CLIFF LAZENBY
SPLOOSH MANAGEMENT

23 Prince Street
Suite 2
New York
NY 10012
USA
Tel: 212 431 7325
Fax: 212 4431 5686
splooshy@aol.com

HELEN LEE

94-12 46 Avenue
Elmhurst
NY 11373
USA

TOMMY LEE
GOLD & PLATINUM HIT MUSIC PRODUCTIONS

17 Coventrey Lane
Central Islip
NY 11722
USA
Tel: 516 582 8392

PETER C LEEDS
LEEDS-DAVIS MANAGEMENT

15 West 75th Street
Suite 7B
New York
NY 10023
USA

ADRIAN LEIGH
LEY-LINE MANAGEMENT

77 Tavistock Road
London
W11 1AR
England
Tel: 0171 221 2563
Fax: 0171 792 3524
adrian@ley-line.freeserve.co.uk

current roster

Chris Bandy
Fifth Amendment

COLIN LESTER
WILDLIFE ENTERTAINMENT LTD
Unit F
21 Heathmans Road
London
SW6 4TJ
England
Tel: 0171 371 7008
Fax: 0171 371 7708
wildlife@dircon.co.uk
current roster
Tasmin Archer
The Brand New Heavies
Bomb The Bass
Martyn Joseph
Tim Simenon
Carleen Anderson
Connor Reeves
Travis
J-Ray Ruffin

ALEXIS LEVINE
SELECT MUSIC
66 Woodlawn Avenue
West
Toronto
Ontario
M4V 1G7
Canada
Tel: 416 923 6768
Fax: 416 923 9672
jalevine@interlog.com
current roster
Urban Legend
Jaby Hedspin

CINDY LEVINE
CINDY LEVINE MANAGEMENT
PO Box 590

Needham
MA 02192
USA

JULIE LEVINE
LEVIN MANAGEMENT
130 West 57th Street
Suite 10B
New York
NY 10019
USA

MAXINE LEWIS
MAXEENE PRODUCTIONS
215 East 164th Street
Suite 51
Bronx
NY 10456
USA

PETER LEWIT
PML MANAGEMENT
145 West 57th Street
19th Floor
New York
NY 10019
USA

FRANK LIGHTER
SPECTER ENTERTAINMENT
129-49 154th Street
Baisley Park
NY 11434
USA

MARKUS LINDE
FREIBANK MUSIKVERLAGE
DitmarKoelStrasse 26
Hamburg 20459

Germany
Tel: 49 40 310 090
Fax: 49 40 313 411
linde@freibank.com
www.freibank.com
current roster
Niels Frevert
Lemonbabies
Regy Clasen

JOYCE LINEHAN
JOYCE LINEHAN ARTIST MANAGEMENT
10A Burt Street
Dorchester
MA 02124
USA

ROBERT LINNEY
MBL
1 Cowcross Street
London
EC1M 6DL
England
Tel: 0171 253 7755
Fax: 0171 251 8096
current roster
The Chemical Brothers
David Holmes
Photek
Air

QUINCY LINTON
MAGNUM OPUS ENTERPRISES
PO Box 877
Turku 20 101
Finland
Tel: 358 24 697 636
Fax: 358 24 697 622
moefin@netscape.net
current roster

Winnie Williams
Niko Nyman
Anayin
Maria Nyman
Heads & Bodies
Phonorigin

PHILLIP LISBERG
HARVEY LISBERG ASSOCIATES
6 Highgate
St Margarets Road
Altrincham
Cheshire
WA14 2AP
England
Tel: 0161 941 4560
Fax: 0161 941 4199
hlisberg@aol.com
current roster
10cc
Eric Stewart
Graham Gouldman
Wax
Stiles & Drewe
George Stiles
Anthony Drewe
Neville Wilding

TODD LITTLEFIELD
DIESEL MANAGEMENT
25b Tavette Street
Glouster
Ontario
K1B 3A1
Canada
Tel: 613 824 5285
Fax: 613 824 3080
diesel@comnet.ca
current roster
The Tony D Band
Suzie Vinnick

MICHAEL LEWIS LLEWELLYN
NAKED SUNDAY MANAGEMENT
15 Lackford Road
Chipstead
Surrey
CR5 3TA
England
Tel: 01737 277 462
Fax: 01737 277 462
current roster
Fonda

ELIZABETH LLOYD
MICHAEL NYMAN LTD
83 Pulborough Road
London
SW18 5UL
England
Tel: 0181 870 8961
Fax: 0181 875 9377
106703.1172@
   compuserve.com
current roster
Michael Nyman
Michael Nyman Band

PAUL LOASBY
ONE FIFTEEN
The Gallery
28-30 Wood Wharf
Horseferry Place
London
SE10 9BT
England
Tel: 0181 293 0999
Fax: 0181 293 9525
mail@one15.demon.
   co.uk
current roster
Jools Holland
Cradle Of Filth

Cathedral
Anathema
<<<b>>>
The Multi

SARAH LONGHURST
LONGSHOT COMMUNICATIONS
PO Box 509
Surry Hills
NSW 2010
Australia
Tel: 02 9310 4268
Fax: 02 9310 4267
longshot@next.com.au
current roster
Custard
Pollyanna
Sloan

TISH LORD
GEEZERS
Wendy House
Ground Floor
Chelsea Reach
London
SW10 0RN
England
Tel: 0171 3763196
Fax: 0171 3763192
g_geezers@hotmail.
   com
current roster
Geezers Of Nazareth

LIBOR LORENC
ALD MANAGEMENT
5 Holliday Close
Crownhill
Milton Keynes
Buckinghamshire
MK8 0AZ
England

Tel: 01908 568 812
Fax: 01908 568 812
current roster
A Lovesick Dragon

RICK LOWE
MIND OVER MANAGEMENT
18 Eaton Court
Boxgrove Avenue
Guildford
Surrey
GU1 1XD
England
Tel: 0973 258 129
Fax: 01483 838 424
current roster
Allan Dawson

BOB LUHTALA
ROBERT LUHTALA MANAGEMENT
869 Broadview Avenue
Toronto
Ontario
M4K 2P9
Canada
Tel: 416 406 2825
Fax: 416 406 2945
liquid@liquidrecords.com
current roster
Glueleg
Tomorrow The World

ABIGAIL LULHAM
THE JELLYSET
40 Riverview Gardens
London
SW13 8QZ
England
Tel: 0181 563 0256
Fax: 0181 563 0356

mail@jellyset.demon.co.uk
current roster
Heavyweight Champion

MICHAEL LYNCH
SMART ARTISTS MANAGEMENT
PO Box 2033
St Kilda West
Victoria 3182
Australia
Tel: 03 9521 2205
Fax: 03 9510 1063
info@smartartists.com.au
current roster
The Fireballs
TISM
The Earthmen
Dave Graney 'n'
 The Coral Snakes
Rail

JAMES MACLEAN
ENTERCOM MANAGEMENT
205-372 Richmond St West
Toronto
Ontario
M5V 1X6
Canada
Tel: 416 979 2669
Fax: 416 598 5428
entercom@inforamp.net
current roster
All Systems Go
Ivan Made
Voivod

SARAH MACPHERSON
ARTS END MANAGEMENT
PO Box 624

Paddington
Queensland 4064
Australia
Tel: 07 3255 1134
Fax: 07 3844 2449
artsend@thehub.com.au
current roster
Taxi

MAD DOG MANAGEMENT
122 East 57th Street
5th Floor
New York
NY 10022
USA

DAVID J MAHON
THE HUNTER WARD PARTNERSHIP
55 Archdale Place
New Malden
Surrey
KT3 3RW
England
Tel: 0181 715 5888
Fax: 0181 715 3775
current roster
Kurl

PRIYA MAHTANI
HEARTBEAT MUSIC PRODUCTIONS
Wildacre
The Woods
Northwood
Middlesex
HA6 3EY
England
Tel: 01923 823 804
Fax: 01923 833 527
pm@lumen.u-net.com
current roster
Flo

T'Anthony
Pink Y Lou

SELINA MAISANO
12/5 Mosman Street
Mosman
NSW 2088
Australia
Tel: 02 9383 0383
Fax: 02 9969 3896
current roster
students

JEFF MAIZE
SKYDIGGERS PRODUCTIONS LIMITED
RR 1
3077 4th Concession
Sahnty Bay
Ontario
L0L 2L0
Canada
Tel: 705 835 5491
Fax: 705 835 5880
jamize@bconnex.net
current roster
Skydiggers

MAJOR MUSIC
424 West 33rd Street
New York
NY 10001
USA

NANCI MALEK
BENTERTAINMENT
523 Indian Road
Toronto
Ontario
M6P 2B9
Canada
Tel: 416 516 4496
Fax: 416 410 3288

MAX MALEV
1/112 Bruce Street
Cooks Hill
NSW 2300
Australia
Tel: 02 4929 5218
current roster
Max Schneider
Dr Green

PAXON MALLOY
HELL BENT MANAGEMENT
5959 Franklin Avenue
306
Los Angeles
CA 90028
USA
Tel: 323 871 1434
hellbentla@aol.com

MONTE A MALNICK
SEARCH AND RESCUE ARTIST MANAGEMENT
58-28 Van Cleef Street
Corona
NY 11368
USA

CARLO MANITTA
SMALL HAND ARTIST MANAGEMENT
12/715 Mt Alexander Road
Moonee Ponds
Victoria 3039
Australia
Tel: 03 9375 4834
Fax: 03 9905 4162
Carlo@monash.edu.au
current roster
The Spurres

PHIL MANNING
TEAMWORK PRODUCTIONS
PO Box 302
Dulwich Hill
NSW 2203
Australia
Tel: 02 9558 4361
Fax: 02 9559 2669
teamwork@magnet.com.au
current roster
Graeme Connors
John Paul Young
Rosemary Rae

LAUREN MARKOW
UP ALL NIGHT PRODUCTIONS
868 Plymouth Rock Drive
St Louis
MO 63131
USA

ITA MARTIN
FICTION
4 Tottenham Mews
London
W1P 9PJ
England
Tel: 0171 323 5555
Fax: 0171 323 5323
ita@fictionsongs.co.uk
current roster
(see Chris Parry)

PETER MARTIN
FIREBIRD MUSIC
Kyrle House Studios
Edde Cross Street
Ross On Wye
HR9 7BZ

England
Tel: 01989 762 269
Fax: 01989 566 337
pmartin@firebirdmusic.com
www.firebirdmusic.com
current roster
Joan Martin

SHERI MARTIN
POWER BITCH MANAGEMENT
182 The Esplanade
Brighton
Victoria 3186
Australia
Tel: 03 9553 8225
current roster
Nude

BARRY MATHESON
CONTINENTAL AS
PO Box 143
2051 Jessheim
Norway
Tel: 47 228 710 00
Fax: 47 228 710 04
barry.matheson@powertech.no
current roster
Secret Garden
ELG (Eivind Elgenes)
Dance With A Stranger
Ole Edvard Antonsen

TINA MATTHEWS
SMALL WORLD
4 Taylors Yard
67 Alderbrook Road
London
SW12 8AD
England
Tel: 0181 772 0600
Fax: 0181 772 0700

smworld@dircon.co.uk
current roster
Blair
Aron Freidman
Jinny
Neil Palmer
Phil Taylor
Laura Pallas
Manuka
John Ravenhall

ANDREW MAURICE
THE YUKON MANAGEMENT
191 Goldhurst Terrace
London
NW6 3ER
England
Tel: 0171 681 9209
theyukon@msn.com
theyukon@hotmail.com
current roster
Angie May
Clare Turrell-Clark
Littlehouse

NANCY MAYER
SILVER STAR MANAGEMENT
174 Spadina Avenue
Suite 610
Toronto
Ontario
M5T 2C2
Canada
Tel: 416 504 6644
Fax: 416 703 9090
sstar@passport.ca
current roster
David Deacon & The Word
Lost & Profound
Ken Dirschl

PAUL MAYNARD
IMPACT MUSIC LTD
1 Silverdale Drive
Broomfield
Kent
CT6 7BW
England
Tel: 01227 372 787
www.alt-brighton.com/impact.html
impact@pmaynard.globalnet.co.uk
current roster
Dionysus
Kitten

MICK MAZZONE
MIGHTY MANAGEMENT
21 Castle Street
Randwick
NSW 2031
Australia
Tel: 02 9398 3200
Fax: 02 9398 8216
mickmazz@s054.aone.net.au
current roster
Ian Moss
Flower Pot Gang

ANDREW MCALLISTER
BIG MANAGEMENT & PROMOTIONS
PO Box 5266
Newcastle West
NSW 2302
Australia
Tel: 0249 216 450
Fax: 0249 218 631
mawsh@cc.newcastle.edu.au
current roster

The Porkers
The Wash
Clockwork
Brown House
Rats
On
Bruce Clarke

IAN MCANDREW
WILDLIFE ENTERTAINMENT LTD
Unit F
21 Heathmans Road
London
SW6 4TJ
England
Tel: 0171 371 7008
Fax: 0171 371 7708
Wildlife@dircon.co.uk
current roster
Tasmin Archer
The Brand New Heavies
Bomb The Bass
Martyn Joseph
Tim Simenon
Carleen Anderson
Connor Reeves
Travis
J-Ray Ruffin

GARY MCCLARNAN
POTENTIAL DEVELOPMENT
18 Sparkle Street
Manchester
M1 2NA
England
Tel: 0161 273 3435
Fax: 0161 273 3695
potential.dev@mcr1.
    poptel.org.uk
current roster

Free Agents
Moneyshot
Mr Scruff
Muki
Nick Faber

TIM MCDANIEL
OVERBITE PRODUCTIONS
255 West Channel Road
Santa Monica
CA 90402-105
USA
Tel: 310 573 2050

MICHAEL MCDONAGH
MICHAEL MCDONAGH MUSIC MANAGMENT LTD
The Studio
3c Wilson Street,
Winchmore Hill
London
N21 1DP
England
Tel: 0181 447 8882
Fax: 0181 882 7679
caramusicltd@dial.
    pipex.com
current roster
James McNally
Sunbear
Steve Carroll
Cyan2
Sabina

AJALA MCDONALD
BLUE WORLD ENTERTAINMENT
PO Box 1243
Baulkham Hills
NSW 2153
Australia

Tel: 02 9634 3471
Fax: 02 9894 9557
current roster
Blue World

AMY MCFARLAND
ALL ACCESS ENTERTAINMENT
425 Madison Avenue
Suite 802
New York
NY10017
USA

DEBI MCGRATH
DAZED MANGEMENT
Onward House
11 Uxbridge Street
London
W8 7TQ
England
Tel: 0171 221 4275
Fax: 0171 229 6893
current roster
Floyd Dyce (Dice)
Claudio Galdez
Melodrama

RONALD MCKAY
91 Northchurch Road
London
N1 3NU
England
Tel: 0171 226 4850
current roster
Antonio

MELINDA MCKENNA
CREW MANAGEMENT
65 Golborne Road
London
W10 5NP
England

Tel: 0181 964 8192
Fax: 0181 984 8212
current roster
Sande
(see Jaine Gould)

KAREN MCMANUS
51 Victoria Street
Lewisham
NSW 2049
Australia
Tel: 02 9560 1438
Fax: 02 9560 1438
mcmanusk@ozemail.
 com.au
current roster
Garis
Galura Bandung

MICHAEL MCMARTIN
MELODY MANAGEMENT
PO Box 598
Coogee
NSW 2034
Australia
Tel: 02 9665 0246
Fax: 02 9664 1623
mmcm@magna.com.au
current roster
Hoodoo Gurus
FiniScad
Cubby House
Eric Weideman
Charles Fisher

LEONARD MEADE
CHOIR CONNEXION
9 Greenwood Drive
London
E4 9HL
England

Tel: 0181 531 5562
Fax: 0181 523 4159
GroovKing@aol.com
current roster
The London Community Gospel Choir

TONI MEDCALF
TONI MEDCALF MANAGEMENT
Garden Flat
83 Cambridge Gardens
London
W10 6JE
England
Tel: 0181 960 3596
Fax: 0181 960 4330
current roster
Thunder
Charlie Dore
Karren Ramirez
Daniel Bowes

JAMES MEEK
MEEK MUSIC MANAGEMENT
136b Northcote Road
London
SW11 6QZ
England
Tel: 0171 350 2201
jamesmeek@
 compuserve.com
current roster
Marshall

ANNETTE MENCKE
10 Thirlmere Road
Muswell Hill
London
N10 2DN
England
Tel: 0181 444 2561
current roster

Sign Of The Times

LAUREN MERCOVICH
16 Jenkinson Street
Monash
ACT 2904
Tel: 02 6291 0491
Fax: 02 6291 0491
lauren_mercovich@
 dpa.act.gov.au
current roster
student and self-
managed artists

LAUREN YVONNE MERCOVICH
39 Belton Road
Dollis Hill
London
NW2 5QE
England
Tel: 0181 830 3236
lmercovich@postmaster.
 co.uk
www.dspace.dial.pipex.
 com/town/road/
 xmc90/impage.htm
current roster
Jacqui Seczawa

MERCK MERCURIADIS
SANCTUARY MUSIC MANAGEMENT
Sanctuary House
45-53 Sinclair Road
London
W14 0NS
England
Tel: 0171 602 6351
Fax: 0171 603 5941
Mmerck@aol.com
www.sanctuary
 management.com

international directory of IMF managers

current roster
The Almighty
Catherine Wheel
Dark Star
Bob Ezrin
Flight 16
Tim Friese
Kula Shaker
Lowfinger
The Overseer
Pet Shop Boys
  (USA only)
Tribe Of Gypsies
Ultra Violet
Wilt

FRED MEYER
MGR ENTERTAINMENT

1234 3rd Street
Suite 18
Santa Monica
CA 90401
USA
Tel: 310 899 9306
Fax: 310 899 9326
fredrockm@
  mgrentertainment.
  com
www.mgrentertainment.
  com

CHRIS MIKHAEL
DIGI-SOUND

Suite 2
41 Rawson Street
Epping
NSW 2121
Australia
Tel: 02 9869 0200
Fax: 02 9869 0233
awesome@real.com.au
current roster
Malakye Grind

JENNY MILICH
ARYTHMIA MUSIC MANAGEMENT

PO Box 1315
Albury
NSW 2640
Australia
Tel: 02 6040 6915
arythmia@yahoo.com
current roster
Keth Miles

KEEGAN MILLER

36 Kenton Way
Rockingham
WA 6168
Australia
Tel: 08 9592 5313
Fax: 08 9439 1577
current roster
Beanbag

OWEN MILLER
LAM

18 Petworth Grove
South Yardley
Birmingham
B26 1JF
England
Tel: 0121 764 5809
Fax: 0121 707 0495
current roster
Ju-Ju
Brad
Angellina

STELLA MILLER
NEXT STEP MUSIC MANAGEMENT

RR 3
PO Box 209-A
Kerhonkson
NY 12446
USA

MILLIE MILLGATE
SOUND GALLERY

PO Box 160
Westgate
NSW 2048
Australia
Tel: 02 9564 2427
Fax: 02 9850 4901
current roster
Rumanastone
Lantern

ELEANORE MILLS

44-15 Colden Street 2F
Flushing
NY 11355
USA

PETER JOHN MILLS
GHOST MANAGEMENT

RHU Corner
Pursers Lane
Peaslake
Surrey
GU5 9RG
England
Tel: 01306 731 536
current roster
Franchesca
Shade

KEVIN MOLLOY
WALK THIS WAY

16 Dicket Mead
Welwyn
Hertfordshire
AL6 9NX
England
Tel: 01438 712 905
Fax: 01438 712 905
current roster
Mace

NICK MOORE
BLUE DOG/BARFLY
234 Royal College Street
London
NW1 9LT
England
Tel: 0171 482 1155
Fax: 0171 482 4809
nick@bluedogrecords.
   co.uk
www.bluedogrecords.
   co.uk
current roster
The Crocketts

MOREBARN MUSIC
30 Hillcrest Avenue
Morristown
NJ 07960
USA

MARCIA MORGAN-PAYNE
MORPAY MANAGEMENT
236 Dacre Park
London
SE13 5DD
England
Tel: 0181 852 0428
Fax: 0181 244 4231
current roster
Ricky Payne

ROBERT ADRIAN MORRIS
FATE ENTERPRISES
3e Crabtree Court
Clays Lane
Stratford
London
E15 2UG
England
Tel: 0181 555 0867

current roster
Teri (Terri) Lynch

CHRISTIAN MORRISON
CMO MANAGEMENT (INTERNATIONAL) LTD
Unit 32 Ransomes Dock
35-37 Parkgate Road
London
SW11 4NP
England
Tel: 0171 228 4000
Fax: 0171 924 1608
cmboss1@aol.com
current roster
Blur
Elastica
Midge Ure
Linoleum
The Beloved
Tiana
Morcheeba
Ooberman

MELIKA MORRISON
SIMONES INTERNATIONALE
PO Box 15154
London
W5 3FW
England
Tel: 0181 861 3900
Fax: 0181 381 1571
current roster
Lounge Lizard
Jayne Raydio

PHILIP MORTLOCK
CUE MANAGEMENT
GPO Box 3265
Sydney

NSW 2001
Australia
Tel: 02 9299 5966
Fax: 02 9299 3059
origin@magna.com.au
current roster
Ian McNamarra
Harrestone Records
The Calm Centre

SAM MORTNER
36 Shelfon Avenue
Highgate
London
N6 4JR
England
Tel: 0181 3406042
Fax: 0171 2634303

ALLEN MOY
GANGLAND ARTISTS/ DIVINE INDUSTRIES
Box 181
101-1001 West Broadway
Vancouver
British Columbia
V6H 4E4
Canada
Tel: 604 685 5317
Fax: 604 682 8572
divine@gangland.com
current roster
54-40 Junkhouse
Copyright

DENNIS MUIRHEAD
MUIRHEAD MANAGEMENT
202 Fulham Road
London
SW10 9PJ
England
Tel: 0171 351 5167
Fax: 0171 352 1514

dennismuirhead@
  worldnet.att.net
current roster
Hugh Padgham
Nick Patrick
Denis Woods
Stuart Colman
Richard Bennett
Paul Grabowsky
Billy Swan
Jon Jacobs
Simon Dawson
Dave Charles
Colin Richardson
RS Field
Fernando Kral
Sun Studio (Memphis)
James Lott
Hugely Music Publishing
Acoustic Design Group

JOANNE MULCAHY
MULCAHY MEDIA & ENTERTAINMENT
1 Sapphire Court
Narre Warren North
Victoria 3805
Australia
Tel: 03 9704 7729
Fax: 03 9704 7729
jom57@ozemail.com.
  au
current roster
Envy

FELLY MUNGA
RAPID MANAGEMENT
The Ground Floor
26 Rochester Mews
Camden
London
NW1 9JB
England

Tel: 0171 267 2249
Fax: 0171 267 4277
current roster
T Impact

ANN MUNRO
IMF TRAINING
First Floor
Fourways House
18 Tariff Street
Manchester
M1 2EP
England
Tel: 0161 228 3993

ROSE MURPHY
DOUBLE HIT RECORDS
PO Box 3207
Wokingham
Berkshire
RG41 5YA
England
Tel: 01252 877 952
Fax: 01252 878 003
RoseMurphy@
  compuserve.com
current roster
Fragile Hopes
Stark

RENEE MURTAGH
9 Tannock Street
North Balwyn
Victoria 3104
Australia
Tel: 03 9816 3404
current roster
Student

LYNN MUTCHLER
EASTER RECORDS
2021 West Dickens
Chicago
IL 60647
USA

SIMON NAPIER-BELL
STREETFEAT MANAGEMENT
220a Blythe Road
London
W14 0HH
England
Tel: 0181 846 9984
Fax: 0181 846 9345
current roster
Candi Staton
Cuba
Katapus

SEBASTIAN NASRA
AVALANCHE PRODUCTIONS
3481 De Laurimier
Montreal
Quebec
H2K 3X5
Canada
Tel: 514 523 7200
Fax: 514 523 6929
cyrus@lesite.com
current roster
Soul Attorneys
Eric Filto
Joanne Peltier

NIKKI NEAVE
COLLABORATION
23 Avenue Crescent
London
W3 8ET
England
Tel: 0181 8962203
Fax: 0181 8962204
nikki@collaborationuk.
  com

the IMF handbook a guide to professional band management

www.collaborationuk.com
current roster
Courtney Pine

CHRIS NEEHAUSE
AIRLOCK STUDIO
959 Stanley Street East
East Brisbane
Queensland 4169
Australia
Tel: 07 3391 8258
Fax: 07 3252 1018
current roster
Travis

KIRK NELSON JR
1462 Parkview Terrace
Hillside
NJ 07205
USA

PHIL NELSON
FIRST COLUMN MANAGEMENT
The Metway
55 Canning Street
Brighton
BN2 2EF
England
Tel: 01273 688 359
Fax: 01273 624 884
fcm@btinternet.com
current roster
The Levellers
Octopus
Victoria

CLARE NETTLEY
PROPHECY ARTIST MANAGEMENT
143 Sherwood Avenue
Streatham
London
SW16 5EE

England
Tel: 0181 679 2787
Fax: 0181 679 2787
cnettley@globalnet.co.uk
current roster
Revolva
Jauray

FREDERICK WARE NEWSOME
NEWSOME GOSPEL MINISTRIES
71 Sidney Street
Rochester
NY 14609
USA

KEVIN NEWTON
MPP MUSIC MANAGEMENT
Melbroune House
Chamberlin Street
Wells
Somerset
BA5 2PJ
England
Tel: 01749 679 042
knewton@dial.pipex.com
current roster
Ronnie G
One Intention

NIK NICHOLL
153 Etchingham Park Road
London
N3 2EE
England
Tel: 0181 346 1508
Fax: 0181 346 1315

TRUDI NICHOLLS
OZ-X-PRESS MUSIC
PO Box 549

Terrigal
NSW 2260
Australia
Tel: 02 4385 6755
Fax: 02 4385 6755
paleride@integritynet.com.au
www.paleriders.com.au
current roster
Pale Riders

CONSTANTINA NICOLAOU
CONSTANTINA NICOLAOU MANAGMENT
Millennium Studios
Elstree Way
Borehamwood
WD6 1SF
England
Tel: 0181 236 1220
Fax: 0181 236 1221
niclaw@compuserve.com
current roster
Shena

DAVID NORRIS
DAN MANAGEMENT
7 Courtsknap Court
Swindon
Wiltshire
SN1 5JL
England
Tel: 01793 611 965
norrisstfc@aol.com
current roster
Mary Stares

JACQUI NORTON
CONTRAST MANAGEMENT
c/o 308 Queens Road
New Cross

international directory of IMF managers

London
SE14 5JN
England
Tel: 0171 252 8152
current roster
Jumbo

RALF OBERGFELL
25b Witherington Road
London
N5 1TN
England
Tel: 0171 6906478

MATTHEW O'BRIEN
BLESSING/O'BRIEN
561 Hudson Street
PO Box 91
New York
NY 10014
USA

TERRY O'BRIEN
JEF HANLON MANAGEMENT
1 York Street
London
W1H 1PZ
England
Tel: 0171 487 2558
Fax: 0171 487 2584
jhanlon@agents-uk.com
current roster
(see Jef Hanlon)

WALTER O'BRIEN
CONCRETE MANAGEMENT
301 West 53rd Street
Suite 11D
New York
NY 10119
USA

RICK O'GRADY
ETI
PO Box 847
Station M
Halifax
Nova Scotia
B3J 2V2
Canada
Tel: 902 423 0266
Fax: 902 423 0735
etimusic@fox.nstn.ca
current roster
Seed

ANDREW OLDHAM
OLDHAM-FARFAN COMPANY
Calle 70a
7-18 Apto 902
Bogota
Colombia
Tel: 571 255 9206
Fax: 571 310 4937
old-pro@andinet.com
current roster
The Andrew Oldham Orchestra

KENNETH OMOYA
OMOYA ENTERTAINMENT LTD
1 Hertford Avenue
London
SW14 8EF
England
Tel: 0181 878 8713
Fax: 0181 876 3597
management@omoya.com
www.omoya.com
current roster
Nic Ojok
Judith Lorde

STUART ONGLEY
SGO MUSIC PUBLISHING LTD
PO Box 26022
London
SW10 0FY
England
Tel: 0207 565 3942
Fax: 0207 565 4785
sgomusic@aol.com
current roster
Chris Eaton

DAVID O'REILLY
DEE O'REILLY MANAGEMENT
112 Gunnersbury Avenue
London
W5 4HB
England
Tel: 0181 993 7441
Fax: 0181 992 9993
current roster
(see John O'Reilly)

JOHN O'REILLY
DEE O'REILLY MANGEMENT
112 Gunnersbury Avenue
London
W5 4HB
England
Tel: 0181 993 7441
Fax: 0181 992 9993
current roster
Lovatux

MARC OSSWALD
DTK MUSIC & MARKETING
Provence Weg 14/1
72072 Tubingen
Postfach 2546/72015
Tubingen

the IMF handbook a guide to professional band management

Germany
Tel: 07071 38834
Fax: 07071 38867
DTKMusik@compuserve.com
current roster
Dieter Thomas Kuhn & Band
Brunch
Sils Moria

JAIME OVEREND
8/348 Balaclava Road
North
Caulfield
Victoria 3161
Australia
Tel: 03 9500 2575

STUART OWEN
BACKLASH MUSIC MANAGEMENT
54 Carlton Place
Glasgow
G5 9TW
Scotland
Tel: 0141 418 0053
Fax: 0141 418 0054
stuart.owen@backlash.co.uk
current roster
Planet Fuse
Mero
John McLaughlin
Gordon Goudie
Paul Masterson
Dave James
Carol Laula

OLU OYENIGBA
PROSPECTS ASSOCIATES
28 Magpie Close
London
E7 9DE
England
Tel: 0181 257 6452
Fax: 0181 257 6452
current roster
Shahin Badar
Tania Evans
Da-Banned
Es-Pee-Dee
Mad Dog Crew

LISA PAGE
BIG SOUND MANAGEMENT
38 Warwards Lane
Sell Park
Birmingham
B29 7RB
England
Tel: 0121 246 3433
Fax: 0121 414 1768
current roster
Jonathan Nash

MARK PAISLEY
WOOLLY MAMMOTH STUDIO
176 Midson Road
Epping
NSW 2121
Australia
Tel: 02 9557 2721
Fax: 02 9519 5030
current roster
Mockingbird

ANDREW PALMER
LEISURERIDE
19 Staverton Road
London
NW2 5EY
England
Tel: 0181 357 1614
Fax: 0181 933 3041

current roster
Kathy Yoo

ANN PALUMBO
URBAN EXCENTRICS
2/16 Alan Street
Cammeray
NSW 2062
Australia
Tel: 02 9909 0042
Fax: 02 9909 0042
property@iinet.net.au
www.iinet.net.au/~property
current roster
Urban Excentrics

GILLES PAQUIN
PAQUIN ENTERTAINMENT GROUP
1067 Sherwin Road
Winnipeg
Manitoba
R3H 0T8
Canada
Tel: 204 694 3104 ext 226
Fax: 204 697 0903
gilles@paquinentertainment.com
current roster
Susan Aglukark
The Jonah Stone
Amy Sky
Marc Jordan

SARAH PARHAM
COALITION ENTERTAINMENT MANAGEMENT
202-10271 Yonge Street
Richmond Hill

Ontario
L4C 3B5
Canada
Tel: 905 508 0025
Fax: 905 508 0403
cem@istar.ca
current roster

KAREN PARKER
G 'N' P ENTERPRISES
211 West 22nd Street
New York
NY 10011
USA

NORMAN PARKHILL
MGM
63-79 Miller Street
Pyrmont
NSW 2009
Australia
Tel: 02 9552 3444
Fax: 02 9660 4142
normanp@mushroom.
    com.au
current roster
Leonardo's Bride
The Badloves
Michael Spiby
Jackie Bristow

CHRIS PARRY
FICTION
4 Tottenham Mews
London
W1P 9PJ
England
Tel: 0171 323 5555
Fax: 0171 323 5323
current roster
The Cure
XFM

JO PARTRIDGE
AIRFIELD PRODUCTIONS LTD
Airfield Studios
St Merryn
Cornwall
PL28 8PU
England
Tel: 01841 520 869
Fax: 01841 520 888
current roster
Rootjoose

STEPHEN PAUL
STEPHEN PAUL MANAGEMENT
PO Box 2000
Boston
MA 02130
USA
Tel: 617 524 9000
Fax: 617 425 2444
sp@stevepaul.com

PHILLIP PAYNE
KARM PRODUCTIONS
PO Box 388
Five Dock
NSW 2046
Australia
Tel: 02 9712 3300
Fax: 02 9712 3884
alliedar@ozemail.com.au

CHRISTINA PAZZANCSE
X-MIX PRODUCTIONS
630 9th Avenue
Suite 912
New York
NY 10036
USA

GILES PEPPERELL
SVENGALI MANAGEMENT
15a Ashley Rise
Walton-On-Thames
Surrey
KT12 1NE
England
Tel: 0410 294 691
Fax: 01932 228 445
giles@militia.demon.co.uk
current roster
Power Circle
The Auranaut
Richie Sullivan
Mighty Aphrodite
Lou Burton

DEARA M PERSON
PERSON-L MANAGEMENT
PO Box 23696
Philadelphia
PA 19143-5726
USA
Tel: 215 729 0684
Fax: 215 729 0553

MILLY PETRIELLA
PLAYWORKS ENTERTAIMENT
PO Box 448
Crows Nest
NSW 1585
Australia
Tel: 02 9566 4770
Fax: 02 9566 4770
rdbass@qd.com.au
current roster
Doug Williams

BILL PHIFER
BIG MANAGEMENT
915 Broadway

the IMF handbook a guide to professional band management

Suite 1607
New York
NY 10010
USA

KATE PHILIPPE
INTERFACE
18 East 17th Street
New York
NY 10003
USA

DONATELLA PICCINETTI
SILVERBIRD LTD
Amersham Common House
133 White Lion Road
Amersham
Buckinghamshire
HP7 9JY
England
Tel: 01494 766 754
Fax: 01494 766 745
donatella@silverbird.demon.co.uk
current roster
Leo Sayer

JENNIFER PILLING
FRAMING WATSON
3/389 Glynburn Road
Kensington Park
SA 5068
Australia
Tel: 08 8300 6848
Fax: 08 8332 3336
current roster
Framing Watson

SM PILTON
HALYON MANAGEMENT LTD
21 D'Arblay Street

London
W1V 3FN
England
Tel: 0171 437 4909
Fax: 0171 437 4979
Halyon@Halyon.co.uk
www.Halyon.co.uk
current roster
Sara Sara

PAUL PITICCO
VALHALLA ARTISTS
PO Box 105
Paddington
Queensland 4064
Australia
Tel: 07 3831 6033
Fax: 07 3831 1838
valhalla@the
hub.com.au
current roster
Big Heavy Stuff
Powderfinger
Webster

GALIA PLAKHOVA-FRESHVILLE
92 The Green
Morden
Surrey
SM4 4HL
England
Tel: 0181 542 3044
Fax: 0181 542 3044
current roster
Xcel

FRED PORTER
ENDANGERED SPECIES MANAGEMENT
4 Berachah Avenue
South Nyack
NY 10960-4202

USA
Tel: 914 353 4001
Fax: 914 353 4332
endangers@aol.com

JAMES PORTER
RAMJAM ARTIST MANAGEMENT
8-306 Sackville Street
Toronto
Ontario
M5A 3G2
Canada
Tel: 416 966 9404
Fax: 416 966 9274
porter@ramjam.com
current roster
Stephan Moccio
The Immigrants
Scott McLoughlin
David Hardman

JOHN PORTER
MOOD INDIGO
c/o Mike Robertson Management
PO Box 10073
Nashville
TN 37212-0073
USA

OLIVER POSCHMANN
KAROL ARTCON GMBH
Am Riedborn 18
Usingen
D-61250
Germany
Tel: 49 6081 15831
Fax: 49 6081 2065
Karol-artcom@t-online.de
current roster

Brian O'Dougherty
Johnson Hansen Bros
Martin Posnett
Melba Moore

PRESTON POWELL
JAZZATERIA

112 West 72nd Street
Suite 2F
New York
NY 10023
USA
Tel: 212 724 0592
Fax: 212 724 5896
jazzateria@aol.com

JEREMY PRICE
PRESS X LTD

50 Enterprise Centre
Cranborne Road
Potters Bar
Hertfordshire
EN6 3DQ
England
Tel: 01707 852 247
Fax: 01707 852 248
Jeremy@otc-records.com
www.otc-records.com

current roster
Kajue
Chriss Ball
Jonathan Price
Obai Kajue
Steam (Hand Of Petat)
Wrong

RIKKI PRICE
DEUTSCH-ENGLISCHE FREUNDSCHAFT LTD

31-33 Ansleigh Place
off Stoneleigh Place
London
W11 4BW
England
Tel: 0171 221 2525
Fax: 0171 221 2529
def@mail.bogo.co.uk
current roster
(see Eric Harle)

JODIE PRYOR
JODIE PRYOR ARTIST REP

1/57-61 Alice Street
Newtown
NSW 2042
Australia
Tel: 02 9557 8434
Fax: 02 9557 8434
current roster
Ben Nightingale

JOHN PURNELL-WEBB
GOONBAG RECORDS

67 Toombul Tce
Nundah
Queensland 4012
Australia
Tel: 07 3256 7753
Fax: 07 3856 5580
johnpw@4zzzfm.org.au
current roster
Pyre
Torch
Station Wagon

ROLAND RADAELLI
STAMPEDE PRODUCTIONS

68 Sutherland Grove
London
SW18 5QW
England
Tel: 0181 780 3837
roland909@compuserve.com
current roster
Stampede
Simon Roberts
Maya

GREG RAGONA

605 1/2 Fletcher Lake Avenue
Bradley Brach
NJ 07720
USA

BARBARA A ROBINSON RAMIREZ
RAM MANAGEMENT

240 Mount Vernon Place
Suite 3J
Newark
NJ 07106
USA

BARBARA RATHE
DEE O'REILLY MANAGEMENT

112 Gunnersbury Avenue
London
W5 4HB
England
Tel: 0181 993 7441
Fax: 0181 992 9993
dorm@compuserve.com
current roster
(see John O'Reilly)

JOHN RAVENHALL
SCANDALOUS MUSIC

46 Chalk Hill
Bushy
Hertfordshire
WD1 4BX

the IMF handbook a guide to professional band management

England
Tel: 01923 255 389
Fax: 01923 255 389
jravenhall@hotmail.com
current roster
Honeylust
Wired To The Moon

OTIS READ
OTIS READ MUSIC
339 East 22nd Street
New York
NY 10010
USA

CHARLES REGAN
1 Green Drift
Royston
Hertfordshire
SG8 5DB
England
Tel: 01763 242 729
Fax: 01763 242 729

REMO REHDER
MUSIC BROKERS SCANDINAVIA AS
PO Box 337
N1301 Sandvika
Norway
Tel: 47 675 40201
Fax: 47 675 655 31
remo.mbs@riksnett.no
current roster
Hanaumi
Tønes

SHARON REID
5 Anglesey Road
Enfield
EN3 4HY
England
Tel: 0181 245 8840
Fax: 0181 245 8840

current roster
Andrea

STEPHANIE REID
625 Broadway
Suite 6B
New York
NY 10012
USA

SCOTT REILLY
BULLETHEAD MANAGEMENT
PO Box 637
Cooper Station
NY 10276-0637
USA

PERRY RESNICK
421 Hudson Street
Suite 523
New York
NY 10014-3651
USA

ANDREW HAKIN REYNOLDS
RAM MANAGEMENT
175 Berkeley Avenue
Newark
NJ 07107
USA

KLAUS RHYS-JONES
BASEDUAL LTD
31 Compton Road
Islington
London
N1 ZAB
England
Tel: 0171 2125667
Fax: 0171 2131330
klaus.rhys.jones@uk.
 pwcglobal.com

current roster
Lisa Arcari

ANDREI RIAZANSKI
SOYUZ (UK) LTD
65a Warren Street
London
W1P 5PA
England
Tel: 0171 387 0562
Fax: 0171 387 48 77
106444.2634@
 compuserve.com
current roster
DJ Ivanov
DJ Motor
Hi-Fi

PAUL RICHARDSON
BRIGHT ORANGE BISCUIT
143 Silverhill Drive
Newcastle-Upon-Tyne
NE5 2JP
England
Tel: 0191 240 3750
Fax: 0191 240 2792
popgunsupreme@
 hotmail.com
www. members.tripod.
 com/~popgun
 supreme
current roster
Double Galaxy
Jumbo
Applecatcher

YVETTE RICHARDSON
RICHARDSON PRODUCTIONS
86 Maybourne Avenue
Scarborough
Ontario

M1L 2W2
Canada
Tel: 416 756 6072
Fax: 416 755 6072
rprod@shaw.wave.ca
current roster
OPM

TONI RIGGIO
FIREFLY PRODUCTIONS
399 East 72nd Street
Suite 17C
New York
NY 10021
USA
Tel: 212 249 7367

LUKE RINALDI
TEAM JEDI
7 Chenard Street
Carine
WA 6020
Australia
Tel: 09 246 4667
current roster
Team Jedi

PAULINE RIVE
21 Coppice Drive
Marus Bridge
Wigan
WN3 5QS
England
Tel: 01942 740 880
current roster
Mindhive

PETER RIX
PETER RIX MANAGEMENT
PO Box 957
Crows Nest
NSW 1585
Australia
Tel: 02 9966 5511
Fax: 02 9966 5444
rixman@ozemail.com.au
current roster
Marcia Hines
Deni Hines

KYA ROBINSON
REAL WORLD PRODUCTIONS
4000 Gypsy Lane
Suite 534
Philadelphia
PA 19144
USA

TRACI ROBOTTI
125 Sullivan Street 14
NY 10012
USA

FRANCIS ROCKLIFF
ROCKLIFF MUSIC MANAGEMENT
Travis Cottage
Whitebard
Sandy Lane
Boars Hill
Oxford
OX1 5HH
England
Tel: 01865 735457
Fax: 01865 735 457
frockliff@aol.com
current roster
Nick Bicat
David Gordan
Dominic Miller
Phil Pickett
Philip Ridley
Ric Sanders
Martin Allcock
Bob Heath
David Freeman

PIERRE RODRIGUE
Global Manager
3060a Lacombe
Montreal
Quebec
H3T 1L4
Canada
Tel: 514 345 0886
Fax: 514 341 9366
current roster
Bran Van 3000
Lhasa Daniel
Belanger
Lawrence Jalbert

JEFF ROGERS
SWELL MUSIC INC
181 Clinton Street
Toronto
Ontario
M6G 2Y4
Canada
Tel: 416 531 3333
Fax: 416 530 0877
swell@passport.ca
current roster
Crash Test Dummies
Rusty Ashely MacIsaac

KATE ROGERS
8/61 Fletcher Street
Tamarama
NSW 2026
Australia
Tel: 03 9510 1077
Fax: 03 9510 1422
current roster
Kate Ceberano

RICHARD ROGERS
42a Northway

the IMF handbook a guide to professional band management

Burgess Hill
West Sussex
RH15 0PN
England
Tel: 01444 239 486
Fax: 01444 239 486
rich@ncompass-imn.
    demon.co.uk
www.ncompass-imn.
    demon.co.uk

CIRO ROMANO
PUMKIN MUSIC LTD

43a Gloucester Square
London
England
Tel: 0171 7061478
Fax: 0171 7061478
ciro.romano@umusic.
    com
current roster
Milo

ŸYSTEIN RONANDER
SR-71

Niels Juelsgate 39A
0257 Oslo
Norway
Tel: 47 225 600 70
Fax: 47 225 600 71
oronander@online.no
current roster
Seigmen
Subgud
Real Thing

BRIAN ROSS
ROSS MANAGEMENT

409 Washington Street
Suite 353
Hoboken
NJ 07030
USA

DAVID ROSS
DAVIX MANAGEMENT

Suite D
67 Abbey Road
London
NW8 0AE
England
Tel: 0171 625 8949
Fax: 0181 296 8896
davix@btinternet.com
current roster
Steve Bellgrade
McQueen
Peel

MARLENE ROSS
MARLENE ROSS MANAGEMENT

1-2 York Street
Aberdeen
AB11 5DL
Scotland
Tel: 01224 573 100
Fax: 01224 572 598
current roster
Runrig

CHRISTOPHER ROSSI
GUITAR SOURCE CENTRAL

350 Maywood Avenue
Maywood
NJ 07607
USA

KEITH ROWE
SLAP BACK MANAGEMENT

4 Beeching Stoke
Marlow
Buckinghamshire
SL7 1JH
England

Tel: 01628 635 414
slapback1@compuserve.
    com

PHIL ROWLEY
DRAGNET MANAGEMENT

40 Burton Bank Lane
Moss Pit
Stafford
ST17 9JW
England
phil-
rowley@hotmail.com

NICK RUBENSTEIN
DANGEROUS MANAGEMENT

Norton House
Dorchester Road
Poole
BH16 6JE
England
Tel: 01202 632 558
Fax: 01202 632 263
nick@ruby.co.uk
www.dangerous
    management.com/
current roster
The Hanging Tree
Sons Of Geronimo
Michelle Law
Kiosk
Andrew Heath

ANNE MARIE RUDD
GORDON & RUDD P/L

10/49 Ben Boyd Road
Neutral Bay
NSW 2089
Australia
Tel: 02 9959 5029

mgar@bigpond.com
current roster
Anne Marie Rudd

CLAUDIA RUFFIN
2301-402 Pentland Drive
Baltimore
MD 21234
USA

KEVIN RUSSETH
TREADMILL
PO Box 32
Scarborough
WA 6019
Australia
Tel: 08 9445 7852
Fax: 08 9445 7852
tmill@iinet.net.au
current roster
Knievel
Flanders
Bucket
Avid Grey

JOE RYALL
TRAPPED ATOM
PO Box 1275
Balmain
NSW 2041
Australia
Tel: 02 9810 0343
Fax: 02 9810 0776
current roster
Glide

JEAN SAGENDORPH
REDHEAD MUSIC MANAGEMENT
PO Box 2476
New York
NY 10163
USA

JULIE SAMUEL
DIAMOND SOUNDS MUSIC MANAGEMENT
The Fox & Punchbowl
Burfield Road
Old Windsor
Berkshire
SL4 2RD
England
Tel: 01753 855 420
Fax: 01753 831 194
samuel.dsm@aol.com
current roster
Sarah Cracknell
Janey Lee Grace
Jayni Hoy
Fondle

CHERYL NORRIS SANDERS
BABY LEAP ENTERTAINMENT
PO Box 49018
Philadelphia
PA 19141
USA

NEDA SARMAST
241 West 36th Street
Suite 2F
New York
NY 10018
USA

MICHAEL SAURI
MICHAEL MASON MANAGEMENT
2748 Loch Haven Drive
Ijamsville
MD 21754
USA

SEVEN SCHARF
STEVEN SCHARF ENTERTAINMENT
126 East 38th Street
New York
NY 10016
USA
Tel: 212 779 7977
     ext 308
Fax: 212 779 7920
sscharf@carlinamerica.com
current roster

COLIN SCHAVERIEN
STREETFEAT MANAGEMENT LTD
220a Blythe Road
London
W14 0HH
England
Tel: 0171 371 3313
Fax: 0171 371 3339
current roster
Candi Staton
Cuba
Dubstar
Katapus
Mississippi Fly

LISA SCHMIDT
CRISIS MANAGEMENT
1288 West Laurelton
Teaneck
NJ 07666
USA
Tel: 201 837 9440
Fax: 201 837 1775
crisismgt@aol.com

JAMES SCHOENFELD
ACHORD MANAGEMENT
207 West 106th Street

Suite 4A
New York
NY 10025
USA

MARTINA SCHOLDERLE
NOISE 'N' MUSIC MANAGEMENT
10 Glenhill Close
London
N3 2JS
England
Tel: 0181 349 3330
Fax: 0181 349 3330
current roster
Mark Abada
The Exploding Dragonflies
Spycatcher

MARK SCHULZ
DARKMARK MANAGEMENT
129 Fayette Street
Conshohocken
PA 19428
USA

VANESSA SCIPIO
313 Putnam Avenue
Brooklyn
NY 11216
USA

HELEN SEBER
HELEN SEBER MANAGEMENT
12 Fordham Close
New Barnet
Hertfordshire
EN4 9AJ
England
Tel: 0181 441 4681

Fax: 0181 441 4681
current roster
Jonny Bridgwood

JONATHAN SHALIT
SHALIT ENTERTAINMENT
Cambridge Theatre
Seven Dials
London
WC2H 9HU
England
Tel: 0171 379 3282
Fax: 0171 379 3238
current roster
Leo Sayer
Larry Adler
Charlotte Church
Joanne May

NOLA SHANEL
SPHINX MANAGEMENT
66 Swallowfield
Werrington
Peterborough
Cambridgeshire
PE4 5BN
England
Tel: 01733 770 381
nola@solar1.freeserve.co.uk
current roster
The Promise

FRANK SHAPIRO
BACKLASH MUSIC MANAGEMENT
54 Carlton Place
Glasgow
G5 9TW
Scotland
Tel: 0141 418 0053

Fax: 0141 418 0054
frank.shapiro@backlash.co.uk
current roster
Planet Fuse
Mero
John Mclaughlin
Gordon Goudie
Paul Masterson
Dave James
Carol Laula

ADAM SHARP
CA MANAGEMENT
Air Studios
Lyndhurst Road
London
NW3 5NQ
England
Tel: 0171 794 0660
Fax: 0171 916 2784
cam@zarucci.demon.co.uk
current roster
Velvet Jones
Giles Martin
George Martin
Autopilot

NORMAN SHARPE
WIDE MOUTH MANAGEMENT
11519-72 Avenue
Edmonton
Alberta
T6G 0B7
Canada
Tel: 403 438 6214
Fax: 403 436 8705
nsharpe@powersurfr.com
current roster
Mouth Mason Nelcome
Hyper Psyche

GAYNOR SHAW
HOBSONS

62 Chiswick High Road
London
W4 1SY
England
Tel: 0181 747 8326
Fax: 0181 742 1511
current roster
Sophie Morrish

GLADSTONE SHAW
A & G CONNECTIONS/ MANAGEMENT

PO Box 435
Huddersfield
HD4 5YD
England
Tel: 01484 559 099
Fax: 01484 559 099
current roster
Zxtreme
Steve Simpson
PC Choir
Jimmy Edwards

MARK SHAW
FLICK PRODUCTIONS

PO Box 888
Penzance
TR20 8ZP
England
Tel: 01736 788 798
Fax: 01736 787 898
info@flickpro.demon.
   co.uk
current roster
Pasha
Catacoustics

RICHARD SHAW
R & S PROMOTIONS LTD

615a London Road
Westcliff-On-Sea
Essex
SS0 9PE
England
Tel: 01702 306 758
dj.rs@virgin.net
www.soundmanagement.
   com/djrs.htm
current roster
The Nice Ones
Lunch

ANDREW SHEEHAN
CUCKOO HALL MUSIC MANAGEMENT

The Basement
15 Delancey Street
London
NW1 7NP
England
Tel: 0171 209 5984
Fax: 0171 209 5985
current roster
Alchemicals

ELVIRA SHEFFIELD
ETHAN JAMES & ASSOCIATES

PO Box 172
Hunters Hill
NSW 2110
Australia
Tel: 02 9870 7255
Fax: 02 9870 7355
current roster
Grace
Island Groove
Phin
Igelese

MARK SHELLEY
MASTERCLASS MUSIC

PO Box 240
Glenbrook
NSW 2773
Australia
Tel: 02 4739 4536
Fax: 02 4739 4536
current roster
The Roberston Brothers
Mark Travers

JIM SHERIDAN
JW SHERIDAN MANAGEMENT

1f Swan Road Altadale
WA 6156
Australia
Tel: 08 9336 5930
Fax: 08 9336 5931
current roster
Joob

DREW SHERMAN
FINE TUNE MANAGEMENT

322 West 57th Street
Suite 44E
New York
NY 10019
USA

STEVEN SHIP
MAINLINE MANAGEMENT

18 East 53rd Street
New York
NY 10022
USA

BEN SHIPLEY

61 Racton Road
Fulham
London
SW6 1LW
England
Tel: 0171 386 0170

the IMF handbook a guide to professional band management

Fax: 0171 386 0170
current roster
The Envy

SUSAN SIDEL
SUSAN SIDEL
MANAGEMENT
80 Varick Street
Suite 3D
New York
NY 10013
USA

MARC SILAG
RIGHT SIDE
MANAGEMENT
1619 Broadway
Suite 540
New York
NY 10019
USA

DAN SILVER
VALUE ADDED
TALENT
MANAGEMENT LTD
1-2 Purley Place
London
N1 1QA
England
Tel: 0171 704 9720
Fax: 0171 226 6135
vatlondon@aol.com
current roster
Ruff 'n' Tumble

ANDREW SIMMONS
76b Ballards Lane
London
N3 2BU
England
Tel: 0181 922 3046
Fax: 0181 964 4445

ANDREW@ADI2.
freeserve.co.uk
current roster
Guidance

KEVIN SIMMS
RAPID
MANAGEMENT
Ground Floor
26 Rochester Mews
Camden
London
NW1 9JB
England
Tel: 0171 267 2249
Fax: 0171 267 4277
current roster
T Impact

ROBERT SIMS
BOB JAMES
CONSULTANTS
2 Roselle Court
7 Park View Road
Ealing
London
W5 2JX
England
Tel: 0181 567 2020
Fax: 0181 567 2244
current roster
Jane Hurni

SHARON KAY SITAHALL
SW9 RECORDS
14 Crawshay Court
Eythorne Road
Myatt Field Estate
London
SW9 7RJ
England
Tel: 0171 582 0546
current roster

Troublesome

DERRICK SIU
EMPOWER
MANAGEMENT
PO Box 1080
Spring Hill
SA 4004
Australia
Tel: 08 3263 3150
empower@mailbox.oq.
edu.au
current roster
Nayyer
Firefly
Master

TEDDY SLATUS
SLATUS
MANAGEMENT
208 East 51st Street
Suite 151
New York
NY 10022
USA

ROD SMALLWOOD
SANCTUARY MUSIC
MANAGEMENT
Sanctuary House
45-53 Sinclair Road
London
W14 0NS
England
Tel: 0171 602 6351
Fax: 0171 603 5941
management@smml-net.
com
current roster
Apollyon Sun
Bruce Dickinson
Helloween
Iron Maiden
Marillion

Psycho Motel

MICHAEL SMILGIES
HIDDEN FORCE MUSIC
Lichtstrasse 38
Köln 50825
Germany
Tel: 49 221 546 5100
Fax: 49 221 546 5105
hfmusic@netcologue.de
current roster
Spacechild
Vivid
Bandaloop
Maedchen
Lungbutter

SIMON SMITH
MAG MUSIC
PO Box 1042
Brighton Road
LPO Elwood
Victoria 3184
Australia
Tel: 03 9934 5567
Fax: 03 9934 5578
ssenter@alphalink.com.au
current roster
The Brown Hornet
Jimi Hocking

TIM SMITH
ZOMBA MANAGEMENT
Zomba House
165-167 High Road
London
NW10 2SG
England
Tel: 0181 459 8899
Fax: 0181 459 9809
tim.smith@zomba.co.uk
current roster
Stephen Lipson
Harding & Curnow
Steve Power
Mutt Lange
Cheiron Productions
Souled Out! Productions

TONY SMITH
HRM
30 Ives Street
London
SW3 2ND
England
Tel: 0171 590 2600
Fax: 0171 584 5774
current roster
Genesis
Phil Collins
Mike & The Mechanics

WILLIAM SMITH
WS MANAGEMENT LTD
1 St Edmunds Avenue
Ruislip
Middlesex
HA4 7XW
England
Tel: 01895 639 701
Fax: 01895 678 766
bill@wsmgt.demon.co.uk
www.wsmgt.demon.co.uk

MIKE SOLOMON
BREAKTHROUGH ARTISTS LTD
207 East 27th Street
Suite 3E
New York
NY 10016
USA

CYNTHIS SOROKA
ARIEL STARR PRODUCTIONS
PO Box 767
Closter
NJ 07624-0767
USA

ATITI SOSIMI
GBEDU LTD
c/o 58 Mayo Road
Neasden
London
NW10 9HP
England
Tel: 0181 357 0663
Fax: 0181 357 0663
current roster
GBEDU Resurrection
Jigida
Dele Sosimi

DOUGIE SOUNESS
NO HALF MEASURES MANAGEMENT
9 Kelvin Crescent
Bearsden
Glasgow
G61 1BT
Scotland
Tel: 0141 563 9989
Fax: 0141 563 9979
Dougie@nohalfmeasures.com
current roster
Yvonne Tipping

PAMELA SOUTH
43 Mousehold Lane
Norwich
Norfolk
NR7 8HL

the IMF handbook a guide to professional band management

England
Tel: 01603 424 574
Fax: 01603 424 574
charley@passion.u-net.com
www.passion.u-net.com
current roster
Pure Passion

COLIN SPENCER
11 Oaklea Park
Liverton
Devon
TQ12 6YU
England
Tel: 01626 821 978
current roster
Endorphin

AVALON SPERRING
FAT CITY KITTY
PO Box 8153
Station Arcade
SA 5000
Australia
Tel: 08 8293 3756
Fax: 08 8351 4490
avalon@senet.com.au
current roster
Temporal Lobe
Dogboat
Stonehouse
Circle Clan

JANINE SPIKINGS
Top Flat
12 Avington Grove
London
SE20 8RY
England
Tel: 0171 5905119
Fax: 0171 5905103
Janine.spikings@scout.org.uk

current roster
Grand Central

PATRICK SPINKS
SUBLIME MANAGEMENT
65 Overdale Road
London
W5 4TU
England
Tel: 0181 840 2042
Fax: 0181 840 5001
patrick@sublimemusic.demon.co.uk
current roster
Elizabeth Gray
Manitou
Alphawave

VANESSA SPOCK
WINTERSWEET
9/27 Merlin Street
Neutral Bay
NSW 2089
Australia
Tel: 02 9904 4600
Fax: 02 9904 4956
vspock@hotmail.com
www.wintersweet.com.au
current roster
WinterSweet

GRAHAM STAIRS
POP GURU SOUND & VISION
64 Tanbark Crescent
Toronto
Ontario
M3B 1N6
Canada
Tel: 416 444 4859
Fax: 416 444 2814
popguru@ibm.net

current roster
Damhnait Doyle
Red Autumn Fall
Chris Tait
Ken Myhr

CRAIG STANLEY
NATIVE FEAR
c/o 7/38 The Crescent
Dee Why
NSW 2099
Australia
Tel: 02 9972 2780
current roster
Self
Native Fear

GILES STANLEY
MUIRHEAD MANAGEMENT
202 Fulham Road
London
SW10 9PJ
England
Tel: 0171 351 5167
Fax: 0171 352 1514
current roster
(see Dennis Muirhead)

STEVE STAVRINOU
ART:X MANAGEMENT
25 Berkshire Gardens
London
N13 6AA
England
Tel: 0181 372 2698
stav@netcomuk.co.uk

GEORGE STEIN
ZISSU, STEIN & MOSHER
270 Madison Avenue

international directory of IMF managers

Suite 1410
New York
NY 10016
USA
Tel: 212 683 5320
Fax: 212 686 2142

GEOFFREY STEINREICH
ROYAL ARTIST MANAGEMENT
12727 Mitchell Avenue
Suite 109
Los Angeles
CA 90066
USA
Tel: 310 313 7246
Fax: 310 313 5346
ragman@gte.net

PAUL STEPANEK
PO Box 343
Willoughby
NSW 2068
Australia
Tel: 02 9415 4390
Fax: 02 9415 4009
stepane@ibm.net
current roster
Simoriah

SANDY STERN
STROBE MUSIC
Wakehurst
13 Highland Road
Bromley
Kent
BR1 4AA
England
Tel: 0181 464 2535
Fax: 0181 698 0596
current roster
Danny, Ben &
 Gordon Hannah

ROSS STEWART
ROCKET RECORDS & DISTRIBUTION
PO Box 863
Mirrabooka
WA 6001
Australia
Tel: 09 249 3721
Fax: 09 249 5712
current roster
Martian Radio
Greenroom
Crawlspace
Hifalutin
Full
Stoneface
Elysium

TONY STIMPSON
BABY LEAP ENTERTAINMENT
PO Box 49018
Philadelphia
PA 19141
USA

JOHNNY STIRLING
GANG FORWARD/ HIT & RUN
25 Ives Street
London
SW3 2ND
England
Tel: 0171 590 2600
Fax: 0171 584 5774
current roster
Frank Musker
Richard Darbyshire
Jo Cang
Scott English

DAVID STOPPS
FRIARS MANAGEMENT LTD
33 Alexander Road
Aylesbury
Buckinghamshire
HP20 2NR
England
Tel: 01296 434 731
Fax: 01296 422 530
davidayles@aol.com
current roster
Howard Jones
Bad Hair Day

DAVID STRONG
TWO UP MANAGEMENT
1a Highett Place
Fitzroy
Victoria 3065
Australia
Tel: 03 9419 4520
icewookie@hotmail.com
current roster
Ruby Fruit Jungle
Treehouse

FALCON STUART
FALCON STUART LTD
59 Moore Park Road
London
SW6 2HH
England
Tel: 0171 731 0022
Fax: 0171 731 1715
current roster
Stephanie Johnston
Pin-Ups

CAROL STUBLEY
HEAD MILES MANAGEMENT
6 Wolseley Road

the IMF handbook a guide to professional band management

Point Piper
NSW 2027
Australia
Tel: 02 9328 6095
Fax: 02 9328 0749
headmiles@acay.com.au
current roster
The Funeral Clowns
The Panadolls

DOUGLAS STURROCK
SE MANAGEMENT

Unit 103
49 Greenwich High Road
Greenwich
London
SE10 8JL
England
Tel: 0181 469 3940
Fax: 0181 4693940
doug@serecords.freeserve.co.uk
current roster
Orange Can

JACKIE SUBECK
JACKIE SUBECK MANAGEMENT

1240 North Flores Street 6
West Hollywood
CA 90069
USA
Tel: 323 650 4850
management@jennamusic.com
www.jennamusic.com/site/home.htm

SCOTT SUTCLIFFE
STRATEGY MATTERS

Suite D

304 King Street
Newtown
NSW 2042
Australia
Tel: 02 9519 7580
Fax: 02 519 7429
strategy@amaze.net.au
current roster
Fruit
1st Degree

DAVID SUTHERLAND

39 Abbey Barm Road
High Wycombe
Buckinghamshire
HP11 1RR
England
Tel: 01494 452 028
Fax: 01494 452 028
current roster
Flo
T Anthony

PAUL TAGE
AMBER

PO Box 1
Chipping Ongar
CM5 9HZ
England
Tel: 01277 362 916
Fax: 01277 366 736
current roster
Bridget Metcalfe

ERDINCH TAHIR

26 Harlech Road
Southgate
N14 7BX
England
Tel: 0181 886 6098
current roster
Dakini

STEPHEN TAVERNER
OUT THERE MANAGEMENT

37 York Rise
Dartmouth Park
London
NW5 1SP
England
Tel: 0171 267 1333
Fax: 0171 267 1313
tav@outthere.co.uk
current roster
Ash
Carrie

CHRIS TAYLOR
CHRIS TAYLOR MANAGEMENT

c/o 179 John Street
Suite 404
Toronto
Ontario
M5T 1X4
Canada
Tel: 416 971 6616
Fax: 416 971 4144
ctaylor@sandersonassociates.com
current roster
Benjamin

MICHELLE TAYLOR
NIA ENTERTAINMENT

1 Clifton Terrace
Suite 3
Weehawken
NJ 07087
USA

RACHEL TAYLOR
WEAVE

PO Box 5618
West End
Queensland 4101

Australia
Tel: 07 3255 0116
Fax: 07 3215 1467
racheltaylor@dtir.qld.gov.au
candlerecords.com.au
current roster
Weave

ROB TAYLOR
BLUE HIPPO MANAGEMENT
188 Shenley Fields Road
Selly Oak
Birmingham
B29 5BP
England
Tel: 0121 604 9067
Fax: 0121 357 0179
Rob@bluehippomanagement.freeserve.co.uk
current roster
Lemonte
Ben Okafor
Mowglee
Mustard

STEVE TAYLOR
11 Daisy Street
North Balgowlah
NSW 2093
Australia
Tel: 02 9948 3601
Fax: 02 9948 2348
current roster
Raw Sugar

STEPHEN TEMPLETON
HIGH RISE MGMT
52 Tompion House
Percival Street
London
EC1V 0HX
England
Tel: 0171 490 0928
Fax: 0171 490 0928
current roster
Claudia Agius

WILLIAM 'SKINNY' TENN
PANDYAMONIUM/ WILLIAM TENN ARTIST MANAGEMENT
67 Mowat Avenue
Toronto
Ontario
M6K 3E3
Canada
Tel: 416 534 7763
Fax: 416 534 9726
pmwtm@ican.net
current roster
The Waltons
Hayden
Merlin
By Divine Right

KIM THOMAS
BLACK YAK MANAGEMENT
PO Box 512
Surry Hills
NSW 2010
Australia
Tel: 02 9282 6970
Fax: 02 9281 2546
current roster
The Whitlams
Tim Freedman
The Olive Branch

LOUIS THOMAS
QUAY ENTERTAINMENT SERVICES LTD
1208-5151 George Street
Halifax
Nova Scotia
B3J 1M5
Canada
Tel: 902 491 1991
Fax: 902 491 1839
louist@ns.sympatico.ca
current roster
Great Big Sea
Sandbox

WAYNE THOMAS
DARWAY MANAGEMENT
708 South Randolph Street
Suite 200
Philadelphia
PA 19147
USA

ANDY THOMPSON
PA COMMUNICATIONS
1st Floor Offices
12a Bourbon Street
Aylesbury
Buckinghamshire
HP20 2RR
England
Tel: 01296 398 071
Fax: 01296 398 089
current roster
Martin Grech
Toyman

DEBRA THOMPSON
DNA MANAGEMENT
24b Alexandra Road
London
N8 0PP
England
Tel: 0181 881 3532
Fax: 0181 808 9885
debra@roundway.com

the IMF handbook a guide to professional band management

current roster
Fuze
Hoodlum Priest

ROGER TICHBORNE
TEXMAIN LTD
29 Millway
London
NW7 3QS
England
Tel: 0181 959 3987
Fax: 0181 906 8164
current roster
Andy Marshall
Doc Watson
The Falsedots

ANDERS TIDEMANN
WORD OF MOUTH PROMOTION
265 Lafayette Street
Suite C22
New York
NY 10012
USA

TERRI TILTON
TERRI TILTON MANAGEMENT
7135 Hollywood Boulevard
Suite 910
Los Angeles
CA 90028
USA
Tel: 323 851 8552
Fax: 323 850 1467
ttmanagement@
    earthlink.net

JON TOPPER
TOP ARTIST PRODUCTIONS
64 Fulton Street

1st Floor
Weekawken
NJ 07087
USA

KJELL-OVE TORKILDSEN
DUCK MANAGMENT ANS
Havnabakken 2c
N-0874 Oslo
Norway
Tel: 47 220 250 16
Fax: 47 220 250 17
current roster
Divin' Ducks

GREG TORRINGTON
GREG TORRINGTON MANAGEMENT
146-2255B Queen Street East
Toronto
Ontario
M4E 1G3
Canada
Tel: 416 698 1648
Fax: 416 698 6929
gregtorr@ican.net
current roster
Laury Schedler
Kiva

JUDY TOTTON
JUDY TOTTON MANAGEMENT
EBC House
Ranelagh Gardens
London
SW6 3PA
England
Tel: 0171 371 8158
Fax: 0171 371 7862

judy@judytotton.com
current roster
Lawrence Gowan

ANTHONY TOUPIUSSANT
MANPOWER MANAGEMENT
100 Eastern Parkway
Irvington
NJ 07111
USA
Tel: 201 371 9465
Fax: 201 371 9465

DMITRI TOURKOV
SOYUZ MUSIK MARKETING GMBH
Schillingstrasse 26-28
Köln
D-50670
Germany
Tel: 49 221 276 0110
Fax: 49 221 733 599
soyuz@t-online.dk
current roster
D Jam

GEOFF TRAVIS
ROUGH TRADE MANAGEMENT
66 Golborne Road
London
W10 5PS
England
Tel: 0181 960 9888
Fax: 0181 968 6715
geoff@rough-trade.
    demon.co.uk
current roster
Pulp
Mazzy Star
Beth Orton

Ultrasound
Marie Therere
Chicks

CARL TROIA
CLIK MANAGEMENT
19 Mercia Grove
Lewisham
London
SE13 6BJ
England
current roster
Emanuela

LESLIE J UHREN
BLUE JEAN MANAGEMENT
PO Box 587
Perryopolis
PA 15473
USA
Tel: 412 736 8001
Fax: 412 736 8004

WILLIAM URSELL
BANDWAGON MANAGEMENT
5 West Laitue
Heptonstall
Hebdon Bridge
West Yorkshire
HX7 7LX
England
Tel: 01422 846 438
current roster
Cane
Sunflowers
Swear

LIAN VAGG
METAL PROMOTIONS
135 Meares Avenue
Parmelia

WA 6167
Australia
Tel: 09 336 4577
Fax: 09 336 4577
metpromo@ois.net.au
current roster
Pathogen

SABINA VAN DE WATTYNE
OPL MANAGEMENT
4 The Limes
North End Way
London
NW3 7HG
England
Tel: 0181 209 0025
Fax: 0181 458 6148
current roster
Taf

JAM VAN KEULEN
METAGLOBE MANAGEMENT LTD
PO Box 133
Woking
Surrey
England
Tel: 01483 761880
Fax: 01483 761880
jos.van_keulen@virgin.net
current roster
Milena-eum Music
Milena Dezelioca

RUSSELL VAUGHT
LUNA PARK MANAGEMENT
Suffolk House
1-8 Whitfield Place
London
W1P 5SF
England

Tel: 0171 813 5555
Fax: 0171 813 4567
mail@lunapark.co.uk
current roster
Biosphere
Grantby

MAURICE VELENOSI
MCM ENTERTAINMENT MANAGEMENT
2860 Boulevard De La Concorde East
Suite 201
Montreal
Quebec
H7E 2B4
Canada
Tel: 514 669 4088
Fax: 514 669 5838
velenosi@mamartists.com
current roster
Natalie Choquette
Laplante-Duval
Ouliana Tchaikowski
Bernard Levasseur

MARK VERNON
FIREBRAND MANAGEMENT
12 Rickett Street
London
SW6 1RU
England
Tel: 0171 381 2375
Fax: 0171 386 5528
firebran@globalnet.co.uk
current roster
John Cale
BJ Cole
Kate St John

Patrice Chevalier

STEINAR VIKAN
RAMALAMA MANAGEMENT
Bispegata 12
N-0191 Oslo
Norway
Tel: 47 221 709 40
Fax: 47 221 709 33
ramalama@online.no
current roster
DumDum Boys
Einmal Kommt Die Liebe
Sugarpops
Ivar Eidem

DAVID VODICKA
RUBBER RECORDS
PO Box 32
Hawksburn
Victoria 3142
Australia
Tel: 03 9699 2018
Fax: 03 9696 0027
rubber@ozonline.com.au
current roster
Even
Underground Lovers

HOLGER VOGT
HYPERNORM MUSIC/MEDIA MANAGEMENT
Grafingerstrasse 6
München
D-81671
Germany
Tel: 49 89 49 00 1561
Fax: 49 89 4900 1562
holger.vogt@
   muenchen.roses.de

current roster
Bananafishbones
Ringsgwandl
FM-Einheit
GRY

OLE WAAGE
NAMA ENTERTAINMENT AS
Karl Johansgate 2
0154 Oslo
Norway
Tel: 47 224 200 00
Fax: 47 224 179 52
ole@nama.no
www.nama.no
current roster
Jon Eikemo
Harald Heide-Steen Jr
Arve Opsahl
Brit Elisabeth
   Haagensli

DIANE WAGG
RISE MANAGEMENT
First Floor
8 Wendell Road
London
W12 9RT
England
Tel: 0181 740 8444
Fax: 0181 749 1877
rise@dial.pipex.com
current roster
Republica
Rialto
John Reynolds
Miles Hunt
Planet Claire
Sunhouse
Ghostland
Underwolves

RICHARD WAITHE
X-CALIBRE MANAGEMENT
34 Willett House
Queens Road West
London
E13 0RX
England
Tel: 0181 472 8792
Fax: 0181 472 8792
current roster
Trillars
Susan Abidakun
Neelam

PAUL WALKER
IDLE HANDS
PO Box 129
Stevanage
SG1 2DN
England
Tel: 01438 311 633
Fax: 01438 724 777
pwa1734347@aol.com
current roster
The Real Abba Gold
The Star Association
Blackfoot Sue
Son Of A Bitch/Saxon
Abba 2000
Sweet Home Chicago
The Bohemians
Viva
Little Willy (Sweet Tribute)
The British Blues
   Brothers Inc.

SCOTT WALKER
SOUL STRIPPER
65 Lienster Grove
Northcote
Victoria 3070
Australia

international directory of IMF managers

Tel: 03 9482 5191
Fax: 03 9639 1220
current roster
Soul Stripper

JO WARD
BUTLER PRODUCTIONS
62 Brand Road
High Wycombe
WA 6057
Australia
Tel: 08 9380 2291
Fax: 08 9454 2240
jo@gu.uwa.edu.au
current roster
John Butler

JAMES WARE
AWARE MANAGEMENT SERVICES LIMITED
144 Camden High Street
London
NW1 0NE
England
Tel: 0171 468 2637
Fax: 0171 287 5731
jware@davenportlyons.com
current roster
Penguin Cafe Orchestra

NEIL WARNOCK
PHANTOM MUSIC LTD
c/o The Agency
370 City Road
London
EC1V 2QA
England
Tel: 0171 278 3331
Fax: 0171 278 5406
neil@the-agency.co.uk

current roster
Right Said Fred

JOHN WATSON
JOHN WATSON PROMOTIONS P/L
PO Box 281
Surry Hills
NSW 2010
Australia
Tel: 02 9310 1000
Fax: 02 9310 1923
current roster
Silverchair
Paul Mar

SIMON D WATSON
SIDEWINDER MANAGEMENT LTD
43 Hove Park Road
Brighton & Hove
East Sussex
BN3 6LH
England
Tel: 01273 249700
Fax: 01273 249701
WATSONSD@aol.com
current roster
Made In London
Naimee Coleman
Human League
Radiator
Moa
Paul Carrack

ANDREW WATT
RAVEN'S NEST MANAGEMENT
Suite 6N
85 East 10th Street
NY 10003
USA
Tel: 212 387 9926
Fax: 212 387 0958

andwatt@earthlink.net
current roster
Julia Darling

KATHRINE WAWATAI
2/53 Sir Thomas Mitchell Road
Bondi Beach
NSW 2026
Australia
Tel: 02 9365 1705
current roster
Reuben Fry

GEOFFREY WEBB
WEBB MUSIC MANAGEMENT
72 Trentham Street
London
SW18 5AR
England
Tel: 0181 870 1023
current roster
Omniac

SCOOTER WEINTRAUB
W MANAGEMENT
225 Lafayette Street
New York
NY 10013
USA

WOLFRAM WEISS
RECHTSANWALTE HEIMANN & WEISS
Richard Wagner Strasse 37
Köln
D 50674
Germany
Tel: 49 221 233 240
Fax: 49 221 233 241
raweiss@netcologne.de

current roster
The Sons Of Cuchulainn

STEPHEN WELLS
STEPHEN WELLS MANAGEMENT
9 Woodchurch Road
London
NW6 3PL
England
Tel: 0171 372 5488
Fax: 0171 372 5488
current roster
Tom Kimball

DJ WENDT
CLONE MANAGEMENT
PO Box 604
Paddington
Queensland 4064
Australia
Tel: 07 3217 5341
Fax: 07 3271 4100
current roster
Lyngren
Denvar

CHARLES D WESTMORELAND
C & R MANAGEMENT CONSULTANTS
PO Box 1585
Lorton
VA 22199-1585
USA

GLENN WHEATLEY
TALENTWORKS PTY LTD
Suite 1A
663 Victoria Street
Abbotsford
Victoria 3067
Australia
Tel: 03 9429 6933
Fax: 03 9428 7433
mail@talentworks.com.au
current roster
John Farnham
Glenn Shorrock
Eva Trout
Jon Stevens
Tommy Emmanuel

DEREK WHITE
AXIS PRODUCTIONS
46 Brook Street
Aston Clinton
Aylesbury
Buckinghamshire
HP22 5ES
England
Tel: 01296 631 898
Fax: 01296 630 321
current roster
The Kynd

RUSSELL J WHITE
RUSSELL J WHITE MANAGEMENT
PO Box 325
South Melbourne
Victoria 3205
Australia
Tel: 03 9696 5661
Fax: 03 9696 6026
rjwman@mira.net
www.rjwman.com.au
current roster
Greg Arnold
Bigger Than Jesus
Brett Kingman
Tracy Kingman
Tina Kopa

YVONNE WHITE
CHOIR CONNEXION
9 Greenwood Drive
London
E4 9HL
England
Tel: 0181 531 5562
Fax: 0181 523 4159
GroovKing@aol.com
current roster
The London Community Gospel Choir

PETER WHITEHEAD
THE BAND REGISTER
65 George Street
Oxford
OX1 2BE
England
Tel: 01865 201 174
Fax: 01865 798 796
nbr@bandreg.co.uk
www.bandreg.com
current roster
Eb & The System

ALLISON WHYTE
WHYTEWING ENTERTAINMENT
1769 North Sycamore Ave 4
Los Angeles
CA 90028-8615
USA
Tel: 323 850 7463
Fax: 323 850 7463
whytewing@distantshore.com

ALF WIGEN
WIGEN PARTNERS AS
Skippergata 8-10
N-0152 Oslo

Norway
Tel: 47 22 414 650
Fax: 47 22 414 654
wigpart@online.no
current roster
TNT
De Lillos
Young Neils
SD Crew

DESMOND WILDER
DIAMOND MANAGEMENT CO
284 Atlantic Avenue
Brooklyn
NY 11201
USA

SIL WILLCOX
CRUISIN' MUSIC
21 Gay Street
Bath
BA1 2PH
England
Tel: 01225 336653
Fax: 01225 333224
Cruisin_Sil@msn.com
current roster
The Stranglers
Neil Taylor
Headbound
World Gut Barging Association
Alamo
Rachel Stamp

DEBRA WILLIAMS
DEBRA WILLIAMS MANAGEMENT
45 Roxeth Hill
Harrow
Middlesex
HA2 0JP
England
Tel: 0181 423 1078
Fax: 0181 423 1078
current roster
Monkeybutt

EVAN WILLIAMS
WILLIAMS/KAPUR MANAGEMENT
Unit 2/127 9th Avenue
Inglewood
WA 6052
Australia
Tel: 08 271 8574
current roster
Blind

PATRICK WILLIAMS
BIG HOUSE ENTERTAINMENT
1261 East 52nd Street
Brooklyn
NY 11234
USA

MATT WILLIS
CEC MANAGEMENT
4 Warren Mews
London
W1P 5DJ
England
Tel: 0171 388 6500
Fax: 0171 388 6522
matt@cecmanagement.freeserve.co.uk
current roster
Ben Folds Five
Furslide
Mo Solid Gold
Regular Fries
The Montrose Avenue
Southern Fly
The Mighty Wah!

ROD WILLIS
ROD WILLIS MANAGEMENT
PO Box 464
Avalon
NSW 2107
Australia
Tel: 02 9979 6833
Fax: 02 9997 8914
rodw@wr.com.au
current roster
Don Walker
Gumption
Cold Chisel
Sixty One Silver

ALEX KERR WILSON
O-MIX
Unit 1Y
Cooper House
2 Michael Road
London
SW6 2AD
England
Tel: 0171 371 8754
Fax: 0171 371 8754
current roster
Sarjant D
Oxman
Sweet Pea

ANDREW WINTERMAN
WINTERMAN & GOLDSTEIN
PO Box 156
Newtown
NSW 2042
Australia
Tel: 02 9517 9285
Fax: 02 9417 9285

wintermn@ozemail.
   com.au
current roster
John Reed Club
Hoolahan
78 Saab
Youth Group

ANDREW R WINTERS
TARGO ENTERTAINMENT CORPORATION
271 Royal College Street
London
NW1 9LU
England
Tel: 0171 482 0115
Fax: 0171 267 1169
manager@targo.co.uk
current roster
Bird Man Ray
The Mediaeval Baebes
Dodgy
Moses
It's Jo & Danny

ADAM WITHFORD
22 Horsell Road
Islington
London
N5 1XP
England
Tel: 0171 607 5075
current roster
Self

JANA WOLFF
JANA WOLFF MANAGEMENT/ WOLFFSONGS
Waldemarstrasse 33
Berlin 10999
Germany
Tel: 49 30 616 787 0
Fax: 49 30 616 787 15
jana.wolff@wolffsongs.de
current roster
Plexiq
Aleksey
Broon
The Mix Mob
Acacia
The Walkabouts

ALAN WOLMARK
CEC MANAGEMENT
107 West 25th Street
Suite 3C
New York
NY 10001
USA
Tel: 212 206 6765
Fax: 212 807 9288
cecus@aol.com

ANDREW WOOD
FIFTY FIRST RECORDINGS LTD
Alaska Works
61 Grange Road
London
SE1 3BH
England
Tel: 0870 729 4955
Fax: 0171 237 9444
woody@fiftyfirst.co.uk
www.fiftyfirst.co.uk
current roster
Tuff Jam
Mark Yardley
London Connections

DAVID WOOD
ONE WAY MANAGEMENT T/A NEAT PRODUCTIONS
71 High Street East
Wallsend
Tyne & Wear
N28 7RJ
England
Tel: 0191 262 4999
Fax: 0191 263 7082
mdwood33@aol.
   com
www.lyndon.org/neat
current roster
Alan B Evans
Debbie

HADYN WOOD
THE SOUND FOUNDATION
PO Box 3001
Wokingham
RG41 3YQ
England
Tel: 0118 962 9100
Fax: 0118 962 9100
hadyn@soundfoundation.
   co.uk
current roster
Matt Tanner
Beehive

MARK WOOD
MODERN WOOD MANAGEMENT
50a Waldron Road
London
SW18 3TD
England
Tel: 0181 947 2224
Fax: 0181 946 6545
mark_modernwood@
   compuserve.com
current roster
Imogen Heep
Kelia Philipsz
Nik Kershaw
Mick Lister

Gina Burrows
Ian Siegal
Horn
Jethro East
Darren Hatch
The Dum Dums

JOHN WOODRUFF
JWM PTY LTD
PO Box 250
Kings Cross
NSW 2011
Australia
Tel: 02 9357 4966
Fax: 02 9358 6853
current roster
Insurge

DAVID WOOLFSON
PARLIAMENT MANAGEMENT
PO Box 6328
London
N2 0UN
England
Tel: 0181 444 9841
Fax: 0181 442 1973
woolfman@compuserve.com
current roster
Gary Jackson
Sel Balamir
Rico

FAY WOOLVEN
ONE FIFTEEN
28-30 Wood Wharf
Horseferry Place
London
SE10 9BT
England
Tel: 0181 293 0999
Fax: 0181 293 9525
fwoolven@hotmail.com
current roster
Jools Holland
Cradle Of Filth
Cathedral
Multi
<<<b>>>
Anathema

KRISTINA WRECH
FIRST LANDING LTD
101 East 16th Street
Suite 1F
New York
NY 10003
USA
Tel: 212 477 4910
Fax: 212 477 4910
wreckage.ny@aol.com

RON YOUNG
V8 ENTERTAINMENT
11835 1/2 Victory Boulevard
North Hollywood
CA 91606
USA
Tel: 818 760 2424

LARRY YOUNGER
MANPOWER MANAGEMENT
100 Eastern Parkway
Irvington
NJ 07111
USA
Tel: 201 371 9465
Fax: 201 371 9465

DAVID ZAOUI
PENNYWISE ENTERTAINMENT P/L
PO Box 647
Edgecliff
NSW 2027
Australia
Tel: 02 9361 6456
Fax: 02 9331 4086
emerald@compassnet.com.au
current roster
Vinyl

COLLEEN ZULIAN
THE AUSTRALIAN SONGWRITERS' ASSOCIATION
PO Box 882
Werribee
Victoria 3030
Australia
Tel: 03 9216 7713
Fax: 03 9974 0137
asa@one.net.com.au
avoca.vicnet.net.au/~aussong

also available from sanctuary publishing

THE BAND'S GUIDE TO GETTING A RECORD DEAL
Will Ashurst
£11.95 ● 1-86074-243-2

MUSIC TECHNOLOGY – A SURVIVOR'S GUIDE
Paul White
£14.95 ● 1-86074-209-2

RECORDING AND PRODUCTION TECHNIQUES
Paul White
£12.99 ● 1-86074-188-6

HOME RECORDING MADE EASY
Paul White
£11.95 ● 1-86074-199-1

MIDI FOR THE TECHNOPHOBE
Paul White
£11.95 ● 1-86074-193-2

CREATIVE RECORDING PART I – EFFECTS & PROCESSORS
Paul White
£11.95 ● 1-86074-229-7

CREATIVE RECORDING PART II – MICROPHONES, ACOUSTICS, SOUNDPROOFING & MONITORING
Paul White
£11.95 ● 1-86074-231-9

LEGENDS – PLAY AND COMPOSE LIKE THE WORLD'S GREATEST GUITARISTS
Adrian Clark
£19.99 ● 1-86074-220-3

GUITAR WORKOUT FOR THE INTERMINABLY BUSY
David Mead
£19.99 ● 1-86074-239-4

GIANTS OF BLUES
Neville Marten
£19.99 ● 1-86074-211-4

FOR MORE INFORMATION on titles from Sanctuary Publishing Limited visit our website at www.sanctuarypublishing.com or contact Sanctuary Publishing Limited, 32-36 Telford Way, London W3 7XS. Tel: +44 (0)181 749 9171 Fax: +44 (0)181 749 9685.

To order a title direct please ring our credit card hotline on 0800 731 0284 (UK only) or write to Sanctuary Direct, PO Box 2616, Great Dunmow, Essex CM6 1DH. International callers please ring +44 (0)181 749 9171 or fax +44 (0)181 749 9685. To order via e-mail contact spub@mail.easynet.co.uk